THE NITTANY LIONS

A Story of Penn State Football

THE
NITTANY LIONS

A Story of Penn State Football

by
Ken Rappoport

THE STRODE PUBLISHERS

To My Wife
Bernice
With Love

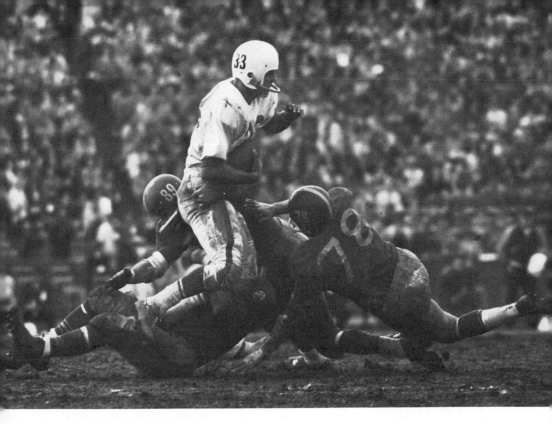

Contents

Foreword

We are proud of the football tradition at Penn State—but, more importantly, we are proud of the people who have made this tradition. People, not touchdowns, have made us winners. In this first book on the history of Penn State football, author Ken Rappoport takes us on an illuminating odyssey back in time. We started playing football way back in the 1880s. So there's a lot of history—and a lot of people—covered within these pages. It's a story of nobility, dedication, loyalty and winning. I have a feeling that you'll stand up and cheer after reading *The Nittany Lions.*

Edward M. Czekaj
Director of Athletics
The Pennsylvania State University

Introduction

The main campus comprises 14,775 acres, but only one hundred yards of that real estate magnetizes large crowds on Saturday afternoons in fall. Beaver Stadium is the place, and football is the only game in town when Penn State's Nittany Lions entertain.

The steel superstructure is a house of worship for thousands of adoring fans. Cold figures confirm that. In the 1972-73 season, the Nittany Lions broke previous attendance records by drawing 320,122 people to their six home appearances. That is an average per game of 53,354 in the 57,538-seat stadium.

Considering the geographical location, it is a modern miracle. The campus is situated in little State College on a plateau at the base of Mt. Nittany, smack in the center of Pennsylvania and just about in the middle of nowhere. Harrisburg lies to the south, about 90 miles away; Pittsburgh is 140 miles off in the west; and Philadelphia is some 200 miles distant to the east.

"Normally we're sold out for the season by August 1," says Athletic Director Ed Czekaj. "And if I can read the mood of the public, we're going to have to enlarge that stadium again."

The quiet town begins to bulge with people on Friday nights, creating a festive climate. A lot of the visitors stay through Sunday and make a weekend of it. Some even pitch tents when rooms fill up.

Not all of the fans are intruders from the outlands, of course. The Nittany Lions also draw heavily from their campus population of 27,000 and townspeople. It is traditional for farmers to wake up especially early on Saturday and finish their chores in time to attend the kickoff.

"When you see 60,000 people at some games you say to yourself, 'Where do they come from?'" Czekaj reflects.

It is apparent that classy football will draw fans, no matter the awkwardness of the location. At Penn State, people have been spoiled for some time now. The Nittany Lions have not had a losing season since 1938. And in recent years under Coach Joe Paterno they have enjoyed their greatest national prominence.

When the crowds come, Penn State is ready.

"I don't think anyone can touch us on football parking," Czekaj insists. "We can park 14,000 cars and get everyone out within an hour."

This seemingly magical act that makes traffic jams disappear almost instantaneously is done with the cooperation of the state and local police. Cops are installed at key intersections, at the university's expense, to keep traffic flowing. All lanes are one-way into town the morning of the game, and one-way going out after the contest is over.

"They know they can get in, get out, and see good football," says Czekaj. "We give the fans everything they want. And they keep coming back."

The stadium, once hard by the athletic offices on the original Center Campus location, was relocated in 1960 on its present East Campus site. Once known as Beaver Field, when it seated 30,000, the structure was dismantled after the 1959 season and reassembled a mile away beneath sparkling, new ribs of steel.

The original capacity of the new arena was 46,284. An additional 2,060 seats were added in 1959 and 9,194 more in 1972 to bring Beaver Stadium to its present capacity. With three sides closed, and most of the seats between the goal lines, the park has a horseshoe effect. The seats rise at a pleasant pitch 80 rows on one side and 90 on the other while the end zone is 40 rows high. Some 3,000 temporary bleacher seats can also be squeezed into the open end of the horseshoe, if needed.

On an autumn afternoon, it is football heaven. This is the story of how it got that way.

Old Timer's Day

There is sometimes a disparity between recollection and fact, but you can believe an oldtimer when he tells you that football was no fun for the quarterback before the turn of the century.

"He'd have these large loops on his belt, see, and a teammate on each side of him would hoist him up and throw him over the line," recalls Dutch Herman. "They gained ground, but lost a lot of quarterbacks that way."

Luckily for Herman this barbaric nonsense had been abolished by the time he played quarterback for Penn State in 1909 and 1911. Someone apparently wised up and said: "Hey, don't you think it would be a better idea if we threw the ball instead of the quarterback?"

That, according to Herman, was the start of the forward pass.

On a spring evening, Herman and two Penn State associates—Joe Bedenk and Dutch Ricker—tell similarly wonderful football stories over a piece of applesauce cake and cup of coffee.

And when an enraptured listener leaves the long talk session late at night, he has been filled as well with a generous serving of Penn State football lore.

By sheer power of longevity, the 84-year-old Herman is able to reach farther back into history. But the other two stately gentlemen are no less proficient at weaving stories.

Bedenk has seen a lot of football in his day, as an

all-America guard on the 1923 team, and later as an assistant to longtime Penn State Coach Bob Higgins. Ricker was a guard on Nittany Lion teams in the late 1920s and, like Herman, a historian of the first order.

With these three reminiscing, it is inevitable that the subject of Hugo Bezdek should come up. They had all been touched at one time or other by the legendary figure who ruled Penn State's athletic fortunes from 1918 until 1936 as coach and athletic director.

The three oldtimers settle back in their easy chairs and exchange stories about Bezdek, a man respected but wholly feared by his players.

One tells the story of the time Bezdek was driving some of his players to a game. While making a turn in the road, his car edged uncomfortably close to a ditch. But the players were all afraid to speak to their tough coach to warn him of a possible accident. "You tell him," said one. "No, you," said another. By the time anyone got up the courage to speak it was too late, and the car slipped into the ditch. They all walked to the game that day.

Another of the story-tellers recalls that Bezdek often cruelly responded to a player's injured leg with the sarcastic suggestion that he "cut it off." Once, when Bezdek was involved in a foot race with one of his charges, the volatile coach hurt his leg and had to be escorted off the field. At this point a voice, protected by darkness, hollered to Bezdek: "Cut if off." No one, naturally, would admit they said it. They were scared to death of him.

Football in the "good, old days" was certainly old, but not all that good, the oldtimers agree. A fellow was lucky to get through practice uninjured, no less a game. They recall an exercise called "Bloody Tuesday" during which "we'd scrimmage every defense in the world until everybody couldn't stand up anymore."

Bezdek's fiber was further illuminated in his militant approach to coaching. Bedenk broke his collarbone while tackling dummies one practice session and, despite the serious injury, suited up three days later. Bezdek ordered him to take "21 laps around the track," reasoning that there was nothing

12

wrong with his legs even if his collarbone was broken.

"I ran 21 laps around that damn track," Bedenk recalls.

An authentic museum piece was soon produced by Bedenk—an old-fashioned nose guard. He had discovered it in his garage and offered a free demonstration to his curious audience. It had an elastic band on top, so it could fit snugly on the head. The hard, gray material contained breathing holes near the bottom and a mouthpiece to grip it securely between the teeth. It looked awfully uncomfortable.

"We protected our noses, but it was rough," says Bedenk. "Everytime someone knocked it off your face, your front teeth came with it."

Along with the bothersome nose guard, players in the "good, old days" also wore torturously long wooden cleats at times on their shoes. That was a Bezdek specialty to counteract a watered-down field. It was suspected, but never proven, that the University of Pittsburgh usually made its field wet to slow Penn State runners. The special cleats, several inches long, were theoretically supposed to give Nittany Lion runners better footing, but one of the oldtimers recounted "you could run better barefooted."

When it rained, Bezdek also made his players wear rubber pants over the regular uniform, but they were so stiff that the players could hardly run in them. It was no fun, as well, to maneuver with bamboo poles that players had planted in their upper pant leg for "protection." After a game, there were always black and blue marks on each leg from the poles.

The rules-makers of the early 1900s might have recognized the practicality of the forward pass, but it was not the same kind of play you observe today in football stadiums across the land. Herman reflects:

"You didn't have to catch the ball. If it hit you, it belonged to you. I remember watching a game in 1907 against Pitt. A Penn State guy threw a pass and hit a big Pitt tackle. He didn't know where the ball was, it hit him right in the head. Another Pitt guy grabbed the ball, went in for a touchdown and they beat us 6-0."

Herman is reminded of other such absurdities of early football life such as the hidden-ball trick, where a player stuffed the ball inside his jersey and blithely ran for a

13

touchdown before anyone knew what had happened.

Herman also produces another vignette which he calls "partially legend." Lafayette was playing Penn State and a center for Lafayette, Morton Jones, left the field to get a new headgear. He was not missed, and the action continued. A Penn State halfback ran with the ball to the 10-yard line. There Jones suddenly stepped out of the crowd and tackled the runner, who dropped the ball. Jones ran it back to the 40-yard line, and Lafayette took over. The play was accepted. There was no rule against it at the time.

Some teams cheated in subtle ways. Bedenk recalls a game with Syracuse in 1923 where the Orangemen made their field five yards wider than regulation size so their swift halfback, Ray Barbutti, could have more room on end runs. Syracuse won, 10-0. No one ever caught on, and the Syracuse coach never told anyone until he changed jobs several years after.

Herman spellbinds his audience with another story of ancient history, this one about the worst defeat ever suffered by a Penn State team:

"We were down to play Lehigh, I think it was about 1897 (actually, 1889). There was no telegraph, no wire service, nothing of that type to find out how the game came out. In those days the students would meet the players at the train station when they came back. The students were very enthusiastic and several thousand went down to meet the returning players.

"Some called for the captain to come out and tell them what happened. Meanwhile, the score had leaked to the crowd somehow—Penn State lost badly and all this time, the captain was telling them: 'Oh, it was a tough game. It was a good game, though. We played well. We did all right.'

"Then someone in the crowd said: 'If you did all right, how did you manage to get beat 70-0? (actually the score was 109-0). The captain said: 'Well, we couldn't get at the son-of-a-gun who had the ball!' "

The structure of the game at that time was so unorderly, explains Herman, "you just ganged up on anybody. You pushed and shoved and just knocked people down all the time. It was a bloody mess."

14

During the birth of football at Penn State, it was no less primitive than anywhere else. The beginning was 1881, or 1887, depending on how you look at it.

1881 Or 1887?

"Dear Classmate: I have late been in touch with several of the old boys..."

Thus began a letter from I. P. McCreary of Erie, Pennsylvania, to J. G. White of New York on December 9, 1922, that provoked an investigation into the beginnings of Penn State football.

Until this letter it had long been accepted that the first team at Penn State was organized in 1887.

"I have recently received letters from (C. C.) Chesney, (Robert) Tait, and (Mark) Baldwin, and they feel as I do that the 1887 team has accepted honors that rightfully belong to the *real pioneer* team of '81," McCreary's letter continued.

The letter was prompted by a reunion of the '87 squad at the 1922 Syracuse-Penn State game in New York. McCreary's annoyance was evident in his note to White, who was manager of the 1881 team. McCreary refereed the 1881 game.

"I, for one, am not at all content to remain silent and let the claim of the '87 team go undisputed and unchallenged and I am in favor of concerted action on the part of the survivors of the team of '81 to have Penn State records written right," said McCreary in the letter. "You, of course, recall the trip to Lewistown for the game with Bucknell..."

After McCreary's opening salvo, the first public protest appeared in a Pittsburgh newspaper as an interview with the aforementioned Dr. Mark E. Baldwin, who played tackle on the '81 team. McCreary then fired off a provocative letter to a Mr.

16

Sullivan, who was secretary of Penn State's Alumni Association. He explained fully the background of the first game:

"Prior to '77 there had been some desultory football kicking by the students on the old front campus for several years with no organization and practically according to no rules other than such as might be agreed upon by those taking part in the sport. But in the fall of 1880, as football was becoming quite a feature in the other colleges of the country, we at Penn State caught the fever and an organization was perfected.

"A book of rules was gotten (Peck & Snyders) and certain players were assigned to positions—backs, tackles, etc.,—under the leadership of a captain. Rules were studied and observed, with the opening of the college year '81-'82. The game began anew and with vigor. Early in October '81, or late in September, it was suggested by someone that it would be a good idea to play a game with some other college.

"As I had an acquaintance attending Bucknell at that time, I wrote him asking if they had an organized team at that institution and if so, would they entertain a proposition to play a match. He promptly replied that they would be very glad to entertain such a proposal and at the same time, gave me the name of the manager. I laid the matter before our Penn State team and so soon as the sanction of the faculty was gotten, a challenge was mailed to the manager of the Bucknell team; an early acceptance was returned and we got down to business.

"I thought at the time and still think yet that the faculty were quite as enthusiastic over the coming match as we were for they at once accorded us everything we asked. A uniform was decided upon, and old Billy Hoover of Shingletown Gap was secured to make the 'togs.' Strenuous practice was instituted and as I recall it, we left State College on Friday afternoon, November 11th, in two conveyances for Spring Mills at which point we left our rigs at a livery and took a train for Lewisburg where we were met by the Bucknell boys and I can say that we were royally entertained by them.

"The game was played the next forenoon on a muddy field in a drizzling rain and but little short of sleet. The result was in favor of Penn State, 9-0. Immediately after the game I went to the Western Union Telegraph Office and sent this message to John W. Stewart at Bellefonte: 'We have met the enemy and

17

they are ours; nine to nothing!'" (A vignette later surfaced about McCreary's telegram. The operator at Lewisburg was at first reluctant to send the message. But McCreary argued: "You send it or I'll come over the counter and send it myself." The operator sent it.)

McCreary's letter continued:

"Before leaving State College I myself had arranged with Mr. Stewart, then postmaster there, to send someone to Bellefonte for the message I proposed sending him, there being no wire of any kind to State College at that time. The message was delivered at State College late Saturday afternoon and Mr. Stewart broadcast the news by writing it big on a sheet of pasteboard and tacking it up over the delivery window of the post office.

"We left Lewisburg in the afternoon of Saturday, November 12th, by train, changed to horse-o-biles at Spring Mills, stopped at Myers Hotel Old Fort for supper and arrived at State College not much before midnight, only to find everybody up, waiting our coming to give us an enthusiastic and appreciative reception, and that epoch-making event in State College history belonged to the ages.

"I might say in passing that in connection with that historic game the present college colors were adopted and the first college yell of Penn State was composed. One thing more, upon our return from that Bucknell game the ball used in the match was delivered to Professor W. A. Buckhout, secretary of the faculty and also of the Alumni Association, to be placed by him with the other souvenirs of the college of which he was ex-officio custodian. Accompanying this letter you will find the roster of all those who took part in the real first game played by Penn State with another college."

Enclosed with the letter was a piece of paper headed: "Roster of Penn State Football Game in Penn State-Bucknell Game at Lewisburg, Penna., November 12th, 1881."

It contained the following names: J. G. White, umpire; I. P. McCreary, referee; G. C. Bute, scorer; Wm. Bruner; G. S. Chadman; J. M. Dale; Robert Tait; J. H. Hollis; C. C. Chesney; R. F. Whitmer; R. D. Foster; W. R. Foster; J. D. McKee; M. E. Baldwin.

McCreary was the gadfly who started the ball rolling, and many others picked it up along the way. The controversy lin-

18

gered for several years after his letter.

There was immediate reaction, especially from members of the 1887 team. In one letter between teammates on that squad, Watson L. Barclay wrote to George H. Lins:

"I am of the opinion that the statement that they played football some time early in the eighties is undoubtedly true, but I am also of the opinion that this was a rather pick-up aggregation that went into this game and football was not continuous at Penn State from that date. In other words, 1887 was the date of the first organized football team and it has been played continuously there since."

Lins disputed McCreary's claim as a football pioneer at Penn State.

"When I arrived at Penn State in the fall of 1886, there was absolutely no evidence of any football having been played previously. The only college activities of that period that I can recall were baseball, the Y M C A , the Cresson and Washington Literary Societies and military drill. And, if I remember correctly, there was even no class organization. The year 1887 marks the beginning at Penn State of all student activities than those mentioned above. In addition to football, the Athletic Association was organized and our first athletic records established in that year.

"It is quite certain that football was instrumental in putting Penn State on the map, but surely not through any team that played one game in 1881 and then dropped completely out of existence. It was the 1887 team that started the ball rolling in this direction. This team did not go any further away than Bucknell, but the 1888 team, which included SIX members of the 1887 team, traveled as far as Dickinson and Lehigh, where we were entirely unknown at that time.

"The 1889 team, which included FOUR members of the 1887 team, went a little further, taking in Lehigh and Lafayette. The 1890 team, which included TWO members of the 1887 team, made Penn State still better known to the outside world by getting as far as Franklin and Marshall and the University of Pennsylvania. From the above you can realize how the influence of the 1887 team must naturally have extended to the teams of 1888 and 1889, and even further, since the fine qualities and spirit of this old team have been very apparent in

19

all of our later teams."

Penn State's Alumni Association, with noted historian Ridge Riley playing detective, got involved in the mystery. In the investigatory work, the *Alumni News* uncovered an editorial about the game printed in the Bucknell University *Mirror* (it was known then as the University at Lewisburg).

The editorial in the *Mirror's* issue of February, 1882, reported:

"The first football match which has been played for some time on our campus came off near the close of last term, between the University team and the State College boys. The University team was defeated; but were willing to accept the defeat with the lesson. The State College team was well uniformed and disciplined, whereas our boys, although having considerable practice, were not up to all their dodges.

"It was apparent in this game that our team was a match for, if not superior to the antagonists, in all but practice and knowledge of their arts. These can be acquired. Having met them once, and having gained experience by practice, they may reasonably expect victory in the coming game."

Two other newspapers, the *State College Times* and *Democratic Watchman* of Bellefonte both verified the report of the Bucknell editorial. Said the *Watchman* in no uncertain terms: "The *Watchman* can settle the squabble as to when football was first played at Penn State. From our issue of November 24, 1881 we note that a 'match game' was played with Bucknell University at Lewisburg 'one day last week' and State won."

Despite this dramatic evidence, Bucknell steadfastly refused to recognize the 1881 game. And as late as April, 1940, the affair was still alive with this statement from W. A. Toland, a Bucknell representative:

"The first intercollegiate football game in which Bucknell competed occurred in 1883. Lafayette, the Bucknell opponent, won the game 59-0. Bucknell, despite the Penn State records, did not play Penn State until 1887. Penn State won that game, 54-0.

"I checked through all our publicity office files (complete) and interviewed Dr. William Bartol, president emeritus, who is 93-years-old and has a remarkable memory. He bears me out that I am right."

"There's no doubt that the game had an unofficial flavor, but it was most certainly played and is on our record book as the first football game," countered Riley.

The famed "Phantom Game" of Penn State history actually took place, if you believe I. P. McCreary and what you read in the newspapers. But even today, an air of mystery still surrounds the situation. Penn State itself has added to the confusion. The school's football guide for the press neglects to mention 1881 at all, but starts its seasonal breakdown from 1887 when Penn State had a 2-0 record.

Ironically, both of those games were against Bucknell.

"Lucy" And The Boys

George Lins always carried two things with him—his nickname "Lucy" and his football. It was a well-worn football, to be sure, but one could still knock it around.

Of course there was a time at Penn State when playing football was taboo. In 1870, for instance, students used to kick a ball around on campus, but this practice was frowned on by the faculty. The teachers eventually passed a resolution to ban football participation within a specific distance of Old Main, the administration building and the only building on campus at the time.

But 1887 was an "enlightened age" since it was at this time that sports was given a proper place in university life. The year marked the beginning of earnest development of athletic facilities at Penn State for an appreciative student body of 170.

Lins and his battered football were inseparable. He had played the sport at Episcopal Academy of Philadelphia and brought the ball with him when he entered as a freshman at Penn State in the fall of 1887. He soon found an accomplice, Charles C. Hildebrand, and they decided that two literary societies were not enough extra-curricular activity for Penn State students.

"We can use some football here," one said while they kicked the ball around before some of the admiring, athletic-minded students.

"There was plenty enthusiasm at the outset," said James C. Mock, one of the members of the 1887 team. "I recall no opposition to the idea among the faculty and I know that at least two faculty members were helpful.

"I think our first move was to organize the Penn State Athletic Association, with a student as president, and out of this recognition came a student manager and also two games with Bucknell."

Although an athletic association had been formed in 1886, it apparently did not function well. A reorganization occurred in 1887, with students comprising the entire membership. Within this new association was a Football Department, whose members were in complete charge of intercollegiate football at Penn State. The football committee, made up of five students including two players, managed the affairs of the team and selected the players for the games.

Penn State's 1887 team had no official coach, but English Professor Nelson E. Cleaver, who had played the game at Dickinson, volunteered to help.

"There were plenty of student volunteers," Mock explained, "and Cleaver helped the older boys select the best of them for the team."

Along with Lins, the captain, Hildebrand and Mock, Penn State's 1887 team included: Watson Barclay; Harvey McLean; John Weller; Charles Kessler; James Rose; Harry Leyden; John Jackson; John Mitchell; and John Morris.

Using Lins' ball—the only one the team had—these Nittany Lions made a successful debut with a 54-0 victory over Bucknell at Lewisburg on November 5, 1887. Obviously dissatisfied with their showing in the first game, Bucknell's players asked for a rematch at State College. It was played two weeks later, and Penn State won that one, too, this time by a 24-0 score. The season would have been extended for one more game, but a match with Dickinson was cancelled because Dickinson could not meet a guarantee of $40 to play at Carlisle and refused a guarantee of $50 to play at State College.

"Cancellation of games was common," wrote Earle L. Edwards in a thesis about Penn State football. "Guarantees were small and in some cases lightly honored."

Edwards, a player at Penn State in the late 1920s and later a coach at North Carolina State, described football in the 1880s as tenuous at best.

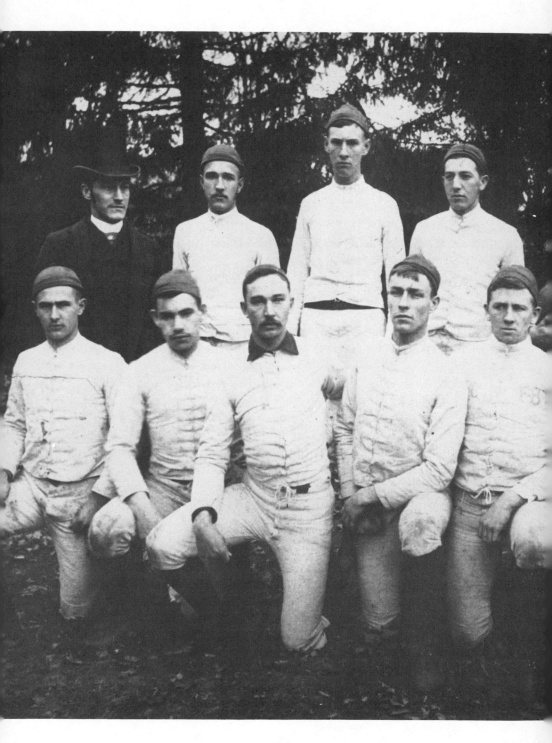

Penn State's First Official Football Team 1887
Front row, left to right: Watson Levret Barclay, Harvey B. McLean, John S. Weller, Charles Milton Kessler, Charles C. Hildebrand, James Reuben Rose, Harry R. Leyden. Back row: Advisory Coach Nelson E. Cleaver, John Price Jackson, John G. Mitchell, James C. Mock, George H. Lins, John Fletcher L. Morris.

"The rules of the game itself were constantly and rapidly changing," Edwards wrote in his 1939 master's thesis entitled: "A History of A College Program of Football, An Historical Analysis of Intercollegiate Football at the Pennsylvania State College."

Edwards noted that "officiating was very poorly done, in comparison to present-day technique, and many games ended in squabbles and disputes.

"There were practically no eligibility rules and it was not uncommon for a man to play five years or more on the same college team, or to transfer from one school to another.

"Also, coaches of the teams often participated in games. In some games, the halves were of ten minutes duration, and in other games the halves might be forty-five minutes long. Transportation offered a major problem and schedule-making was a difficult task. A team might play three games in five days and not play again for several weeks."

At least Penn State had uniformity in one thing—its uniforms. In both games with Bucknell, the Nittany Lions were attired in swashbuckling, tight-fitting, canvas jackets and knee-length pants. There was virtually no padding and the initials "PSC-FB" (Penn State College Football) brightened the front of the jackets. Snug "beanies" were also the Penn State football dress of the day.

The original school colors were not "Penn State Blue" and white, as they are today. Blue and white was a second-choice color scheme back in those days, as a matter of fact.

"We wanted something bright and attractive," said George Meek, class of 1890, "but we could not use red or orange as these colors were already in use by other colleges. So we had a very deep pink—really cerise—which with black made a very pretty combination."

Meek had striped pink-and-black blazers made up, and the gaudy combination was accepted by enthusiastic students. But after two or three weeks of exposure to the sun, the cerise faded so badly that the once-dazzling colors turned to plain black and white.

"So the colors were quickly changed to blue and white," said Meek.

Another version of the color change came from F. J. Pond,

class of 1892. He maintained that the switch to blue and white came about because of a parody of the Penn State yell by Dickinson College students.

The Penn State students cheered their players on with:

"Yah! Yah! Yah! Yah! Yah! Yah!

"Wish-whack! Pink, black!

"P! S! C!"

But, Pond said, Dickinson came to town one day for a baseball game, and the visiting students made fun of the Nittany Lions' chant with this version:

"Yah, yah, hay. Yah, yah, yeh.

"Bees wax. Bees wax.

"A. B. C."

"This so disgusted the boys," Pond said, "that soon after, they not only changed the college yell but also the colors from pink and black to blue and white."

After a "perfect" season in 1887, another one followed—only this one was perfectly awful. The Nittany Lions not only did not win any games in 1888, but also lost an argument with Bucknell that resulted in a game without a decision. The first contest of the season on October 27 at Lewisburg ended in a dispute, and no score was recorded. The financial arrangements for the game were a $20 guarantee and meals for Penn State players, and they almost choked on the food.

In a home-and-home series with Dickinson, Penn State tied the first game 6-6 and lost the second, 16-0. A 30-0 loss to Lehigh closed out Penn State's second season with an 0-2-1 record.

The season of 1889 was a record year for the Nittany Lions—but, unfortunately, it is a record they would like to forget. The team won two games and lost two, but one of those losses was the worst suffered in Penn State history, a 109-0 defeat by Lehigh at Bethlehem on November 13. There was a legitimate excuse, though. They were outnumbered. Because of injuries suffered in a 26-0 loss to Lafayette four days earlier, Penn State only played with nine men instead of the regulation eleven. The game was stopped five minutes early, or the score might have been even worse.

Bucknell and Penn State continued their hostility in 1890. Their opener was cancelled at the field in Lewisburg because

The 1891 Penn State squad became the university's first title-winning team when it won the championship of the Pennsylvania Inter-Collegiate Football Association.

28

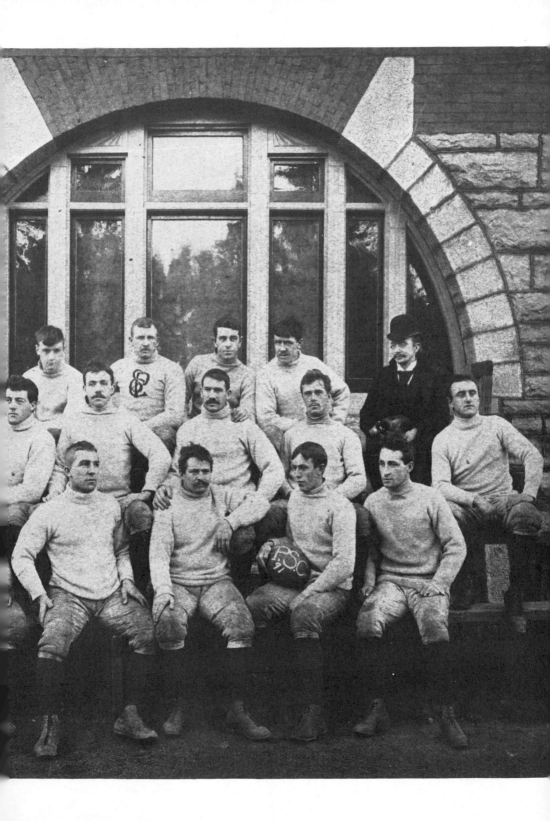

Bucknell objected to three of Penn State's players. Penn State refused to play. The only lopsided score during another 2-2 season was in Penn State's favor, 68-0 over Altoona. The Nittany Lions' schedule that year included a 200-mile trip to Philadelphia for a game with Penn, first of their long-standing rivalry. It was not worth the effort for the Nittany Lions to go all that way, however. They were beaten soundly, 20-0, by a school of richer football tradition. Penn started playing the sport in 1876.

The first of Penn State's applauded teams surfaced in 1891 when the Nittany Lions finished with a 6-2 record and won the championship of the Pennsylvania Inter-Collegiate Football Association. The league, in the first year of its existence, included Bucknell, Dickinson, Franklin and Marshall, Haverford, and Swarthmore along with Penn State.

The star of the Nittany Lions was quarterback Charles M. Atherton, the son of Penn State's seventh president, George Atherton. Because of the loose eligibility rules, Atherton played five seasons for the Nittany Lions, from 1890 through 1894. Another member of the 1891 club was Charles Hildebrand, one of the originals from 1887. Other veterans added experience that helped the Nittany Lions produce "the most brilliant and successful season in our history," according to Penn State's yearbook, *La Vie*.

Commenting on the 1891 season, *La Vie* pointed out: "Never, since the addition of football to the list of State College sports, has the team been so ably captained and so carefully managed, and, as a result of this, we have experienced the most brilliant and successful season in our history.

"Though we began the year with a number of the old players back, and our prospects for making a good record were never brighter, there were several important positions to be filled, with not a very great number of available men to choose from. When finally the men were picked, all went to work with a will, incited by a determination to win the championship of the State Football Association."

La Vie went on to list the victories scored by the team and gave minimal attention to the defeats. The article concluded: "There's a promise of a large and powerful incoming class and our prospects for again winning the pennant are even brighter than they were for last season."

Among the newcomers was George W. Hoskins, the first "coach" at Penn State.

Football, By George

Football reached glamorous status at Penn State in 1892. Newly-named Beaver Field was being fitted for a 500-seat grandstand, complete with projecting blue-and-white roof and three flagpoles. Money for improvements came out of a $15,000 allotment from the Pennsylvania legislature, a sure sign that football was rolling.

The second sign of good times was George W. Hoskins, who was hired as the first instructor of physical education at the school and a trainer for the athletic teams. This would make him the Nittany Lions' first nominal coach, although he carried no such title in his day.

"His duties as they pertained to football were rather vague," wrote Earle L. Edwards in a master's thesis about Penn State football. "Records indicate that he served as trainer rather than coach, and since the Football Committee still selected the team, this status seems to be the correct one. Hoskins himself played on the team on many occasions."

Edwards, a player at Penn State in the late 1920s and later a coach at North Carolina State, pointed out in his 1939 thesis that "Hoskins had no football experience before coming to Penn State but had been a good wrestler and was a capable athlete."

Some trends were obvious in 1892. The number of squad candidates increased and spring practice made its first appearance that year under Hoskins' direction. Apparently the spring practice helped, for the Nittany Lions won five of their six games that year.

But while Hoskins helped Penn State make a bright 17-4-4 record through four years, he eventually became a turncoat in 1896 when he left the Nittany Lions to play for the University of Pittsburgh. It was one of the more bizarre stories in Penn State football lore.

When the Nittany Lions first played Pitt (then Western University of Pittsburgh) in 1893, Hoskins was the center for Penn State. The game was scheduled for Saturday afternoon, but rain forced postponement until Monday. Meanwhile, the Pittsburgh players were welcomed into Penn State fraternity houses and "treated royally," as one oldtimer remembered.

"The game on Monday was a model of sportsmanship," recalled the oldtimer, "possibly because of the warm glow of fellowship engendered over the weekend."

The Penn State newspaper, *Free Lance,* wrote an article of football nobility after the cleanly-played game, won by Penn State 32-0: "We must compliment the players on the marked absence of slugging. Both teams behaved like gentlemen...we want the Western boys to come again and come often."

The second Penn State-Pitt game was played in 1896 and provided a little different atmosphere. This time Hoskins was playing center for Pitt and instigated one of the biggest brawls ever seen at State College as Penn State won, 10-4.

Once again *Free Lance* had something to say, but this time it was not good:

"The second game of the season on Beaver Field with Western University of Pittsburgh did more injury to the prestige of the game of football than its promoter can repair in many years. Not only did trainer and captain Hoskins (center of W.U.P.) make it a disinteresting game but he gave such an exhibition of the unmanly defiance of all fair rules which degrades the game as to make a lasting example for the 'antis' who hold up to public opinion.

"Although we believe that men from State never would allow a trainer to use such unfair and unmanly tactics, we hasten to apologize to each and every opponent that we ever met upon the gridiron if such were the means of success of our former coach."

Penn State managed to survive George Hoskins, but not the controversial hidden ball trick.

The "Gay" Nineties

Harvard and Carlisle were long given credit for originating the hidden ball trick until Pop Warner made a startling disclosure in a newspaper.

"The most unusual play I remember," wrote the coaching great in a 1932 article, "was the ball-under-the-jersey play. It was first worked on Penn State by Cornell when I was coaching at Cornell in 1897. The ball was put under the jersey of the Cornell player who ran straight for a touchdown."

Warner's statement raised doubts as to the pioneer team of the famed ruse. Only a short time before, sports writer Grantland Rice said in a national weekly that Warner had first taught the trick to the Carlisle Indians. The play was initially used in a 1903 game between Carlisle and Harvard, said Rice.

This difference of opinion touched off a spirited joint investigation by the publicity directors of Penn State and Cornell. Wes Dunlop of Penn State and Louis Boochever of Cornell concluded that the hidden ball trick was born in a match between their schools at Ithaca on October 30, 1897. Their case was clinched by one of the players who was involved in the affair, halfback Allen E. "Mike" Whiting.

Whiting, president of a Philadelphia paper company in the 1930s, recalled the circumstances in a letter to Cornell:

"As far as I know, Pop Warner absolutely originated the trick while at Cornell. It certainly had never been thought of before to my knowledge.

"One day, Pop arranged to have a strong elastic placed in the

34

bottom of my jersey. He then got us out on the field to coach us in the new play. It would be used only on kickoffs. C.V.P. 'Tar' Young, who was in the extreme middle backfield, was designated as the receiver. As he caught the ball, I placed myself directly ahead of him, with the other nine men in a circle ahead of me.

"Tar would stuff the ball up my back, and, as soon as I realized it was well placed, I would yell and the whole team would yell and start to fan-shape in all directions. I would go straight down the field; both of my hands being free, it was obvious I did not have the ball. I would go between opponents close enough to almost touch them and they would stand open-eyed wondering where the ball was. Generally, we would go straight for a touchdown. Someone would follow and extract the ball from me after I was over the line and touch it down.

"Looking over some old papers, I find that the *Cornell Daily Sun* of November 8, 1897, gives a full account of the Cornell-Penn State game, in which discreet mention of the play was made the first time it was used. I am quite sure we also played it in one or two of the later games."

The incident was further illuminated in Penn State's student monthly publication, the *Free Lance.* This description, unearthed during the 1932 investigation, was a bit more blunt than the subtle Cornell account:

"Darkness fell on the gridiron long before the end of the game, and, aided by this cloak of gloom, Cornell was able to score a final touchdown in a most novel manner. When C. A. Mechesney kicked off, the Cornellians at once bunched together, and while State was vainly searching for the ball, Whiting, with the pigskin neatly tucked beneath his sweater, was making tracks for our goal line, which he reached in safety, to the intense amusement of the cold, shivering spectators."

The ludicrous stunt was a testimony to the eccentric times. It was an era of instability, poor organization, and loose supervision. The "Gay" Nineties were not always so gay in Penn State football.

In a 6-0 victory over Virginia in 1893, there was brawling among spectators, and the game was called 12 minutes before the end. That same year a contest with the Columbia Athletic Club was ruled as "no decision" after a dispute about the score sparked mob rule. The spectators came on the field near the end of the game and joined forces with Columbia to push over a touchdown.

Schedules were disrupted in wholesale quantity. The 1894 season exemplified the tenuous circumstances as seven opponents cancelled games with Penn State after the Nittany Lions humiliated Lafayette 72-0.

Penn State's play was no less unstable. After George Hoskins left Penn State for Pitt, the Nittany Lions hired Dr. S. B. Newton in a similar capacity from 1896 through 1899, but the new "instructor of physical training" could only produce one winning team in three years. Sam Boyle took over in 1899, but had a loser, too.

Despite the presence of excellent athletes like lineman Ben Fisher, quarterback Charley Atherton, and runners Earl Hewitt, Fred Robinson, and Dave Cure, the Nittany Lions were considered second-class citizens. In the four seasons before 1900, the Nittany Lions had a 16-20 record and few bright moments. One of those came against Army in 1899 as Hewitt ran back a punt for a 6-0 Penn State decision.

Still, the football program had fallen flat and needed some new leadership. In came Pop Golden.

The Golden Years

Tape, liniment, an electric light bulb, and strong hands. These components comprised the equipment of football trainers in the early 1900s. It took a special man to make them work. Pop Golden was such a man.

"Pop was a real trainer," recalled an oldtimer. "Certainly he didn't have our present-day facilities, but he did wonders with what he had. And he was revered by the players."

W. N. "Pop" Golden made obvious use of liniment and tape for tortured bodies and utilized the light bulb as a heating lamp. There was little else for the ill-equipped times.

"We sometimes had special pads for injured ribs or bruised thighs," said the oldtimer, "but they were applied with tape and usually were discarded before game's end."

Golden's presence at Penn State not only kept athletes vigorous, but also pumped vitality into the Nittany Lions' football program. Golden was hired as director of physical training in 1900 and through the next dozen years, as trainer-coach and Penn State's first athletic director, was the architect of an unprecedented rise in football society for the school. By 1912 the Nittany Lions were rubbing elbows with some of the nation's best teams—and beating them.

When Golden first made his appearance at Penn State at the turn of the century, the Nittany Lions had finished an unimpressive era. True, there had been a scoreless tie with powerful Cornell in 1895, regular victories over arch-rival Pitt, and a 6-0 upset over Army in 1899. But Penn State was generally regarded as an upstart with no past and no future.

To make matters worse, Penn State's athletic program was losing money. In a day when coffee was going for 15 cents a pound, a dressy suit for $15, and labor was available for 25 cents an hour, it was hard to "sell" a football game. They passed the hat around at Penn State's home games and found that it was not enough to cover the annual football expense of $3,000. By 1900 the Athletic Association was in debt for $300.

Largely through Golden's efforts, the debt was cleared. He created sentiment toward an annual four-dollar athletic assessment of students, campaigned for alumni contributions, and worked to solicit donations from faculty members.

The Nittany Lions did not lose money in 1902, netting receipts of $3,022.51. Student athletic fees provided $823.14 and alumni contributions $442. The gate receipts, by passing the hat at home, totaled $81.50, and a benefit performance by a local dramatic club brought in $98.25. The balance of $1,577.62 came from guarantees at five road games. The biggest of these was a $450 guarantee from Yale University.

Golden was instrumental in uplifting Penn State football in other obvious ways. He established the first Nittany Lions' training table, rallied funds for a track house to provide quarters for athletes, and was the gadfly for a new athletic field to replace antiquated Beaver Field. His most significant contribution was humanistic, though.

"He was well-known and well-liked by the entire student body and served as guide and mentor for many of the students of his time," eulogized a memorial message after his death in Chattahoochee, Florida, in 1949. "Through Pop's intervention, many boys were able to remain in college and graduate who otherwise would not have done so."

The 1902 team, incidentally, not only did not lose money but did not lose many games, either. The Nittany Lions' record of 7-3 was the best in history until that point. Golden's teams had an inauspicious beginning in 1900 with a 4-6-1 mark, but things improved in 1901. Led by captain Earl Hewitt, Leroy

"Pop" Golden, left, was a jack of all trades at Penn State in the 1900s—trainer, coach, and the school's first athletic director Dan Reed coached in the early 1900s.

"Pop" Golden, far right in overcoat, and his 1901 Penn State team.

The boys posed for this one after winning their varsity "S."

41

"Hennie" Scholl, Andy Smith, and Fred Doge, the 1901 team won five and lost three. Victories were recorded over Susquehanna, Pitt, Lehigh, Dickinson, and Navy.

The 11-6 victory over Navy was especially significant and particularly sweet because Penn State had never beaten the Middies in a series dating back to 1894.

"The victory was a hard one," said Penn State's student newspaper, *Free Lance,* "for the Naval Cadets contested every inch of territory tooth and nail. But State's boys were equally determined to do or die and this determination, coupled with superior playing, won the day."

Penn State had an early 5-0 lead on Scholl's first-quarter field goal (field goals counted five points at this time, same as touchdowns), but Navy soon scored a TD and kicked the extra point for a 6-5 lead.

The *Free Lance* described the frenetic action in the garish style of the day: "With the ball on her own 28-yard-line, State tore the Navy line to pieces and gradually advanced to her opponent's goal. This particular series of line-bucking was one of the finest exhibitions of football ever seen on any gridiron. (Andy) Smith, in his eagerness to gain the distance from the 10-yard-line, fumbled the ball and a Cadet fell on it. At this point, the whole Naval battalion rose to their feet as one man and cheered their representatives with this inspiring yell—Navy! Navy! Navy!"

Apparently it was not inspiring enough because Penn State eventually blocked a Navy punt and recovered the ball on the enemy's five-yard line. The recovery was made by James Junk, Penn State's 220-pound guard. Scholl ran for a touchdown in two plays, and Smith kicked the extra point for the final score.

Golden's best season came the year after, when the Nittany Lions won seven games on shutouts over Dickinson Seminary, Pitt, Villanova, Susquehanna, Navy, Gettysburg, and Dickinson.

Before Smith left on November 7 to enroll at Penn, he had one of the most glamorous days in Penn State history. He scored five touchdowns and kicked two extra points as the Nittany Lions walloped Susquehanna 55-0. Another bright Penn State star began to rise in 1902, Carl Forkum. In his first season Forkum gave an indication of things to come when he returned a kickoff 100 yards for a touchdown in a 37-0 triumph over

Dan Reed's 1903 team posed with a mascot.

Gettysburg.

La Vie, Penn State's yearbook, justifiably reported: "The season of 1902 has been the most favorable one in the history of the college."

Penn State had scored 219 points, its highest production to that juncture, and held its opponents to a mere total of 34. Golden's hand could be seen in all Penn State successes that year as trainer, advisor, and father image for the athletes. He had help in the actual coaching from a former football player. E. K. Wood taught the mechanics and assumed control of the team with Golden in an overall supervisory capacity.

Following Wood in 1903 was Dan Reed and in 1904 Tom Fennell. The latter was persuaded through Reed to spend his vacation on the campus during the early part of 1904 and take charge of the football team. Fennell was a popular figure and invited to return for several seasons. He is regarded by some Penn State historians as the first bona fide Nittany Lions' football

43

coach.

Penn State had its first real coach and now was getting ready for its first all-America player.

Mother's Day

The "Mother" of Penn State football was no lady and, in fact, was not even a gentleman on certain occasions. "Mother" Dunn was 6-foot-3 and 200 pounds of violence while playing the game.

"Many critics regard Dunn as Penn State's greatest lineman," a sports writer once said in a story appraising the Nittany Lions' best athletes. "There was nothing leaden-footed about this center, who loved nothing better than to beat his ends downfield on a kickoff or punt.

"He was a powerful charger on offense...a terror to opponents on defense. Most plays directed anywhere near him ended in disaster. With it all he was a great leader, a man of unimpeachable character."

For these reasons Dunn was selected on Walter Camp's all-America team in 1906—the first such honor for a Penn State player.

Dunn played four years at Penn State and finished his career with his finest season in 1906, when the Nittany Lions achieved a glamorous 8-1-1 record. Only powerful Yale beat Penn State that season as the defense-oriented Nittany Lions shut out nine opponents. During notable 1906, Penn State defeated Lebanon Valley 24-0, Allegheny 26-0, Carlisle 4-0, Bellefonte Academy 12-0, Navy 5-0, Dickinson-at-Williamsport 6-0, West Virginia 10-0, and Pitt 6-0. The Nittany Lions tied Gettysburg 0-0 and suffered only a 10-0 loss to Yale, the sum total of opponents' points for the year.

Penn State's first all-America, W. T. "Mother" Dunn: "A powerful charger on offense...a terror on defense."

Ironically, it was the Yale loss that cinched Dunn's selection as all-America. Camp was in the stands when Dunn thoroughly outplayed his opposing center, a big but slow bruiser.

From the moment of his arrival at Penn State in 1903, Dunn took charge of things. He got his unusual nickname as freshman class president leading his mates across campus to challenge the cocky sophomores in one of the school "rushes."

A sophomore yelled, "There goes Mother Dunn and all her baby chicks," and the appellation stayed with him.

In a way the nickname was appropriate since Dunn was older than most of his classmates. He had entered college relatively late in life, at the age of 22, after working in a Youngstown, Ohio, steel mill. He finally left home with $75 savings to enroll at Penn State.

His imposing size made him a natural candidate for football. A flying tackle during scrimmage won Dunn the center job on the first day of tryout camp, and he stayed at that position, despite some serious injuries, for the next four years.

If little respect was intended in the sarcastic remark about "Mother and her baby chicks," Dunn later got plenty of respect while playing football. He played a game against Navy with a broken collarbone, discarded crutches against the advice of his coach in a career-ending game against Pitt, and had one of his biggest days against Harvard when he wore a steel brace on an injured knee.

"The Harvard boys, knowing that Mother had an injury, tried to go for the knee as soon as play started," recalls onetime Penn State Coach Rip Engle, recounting one of the more famous Dunn tales. "Instead, the big Harvard center received full treatment from the brace and was taken from the game. The substitute steered clear of Mother's injured knee."

Dunn was renowned as one of football's first roving centers.

"Dunn had found that there were many times in his center position on defense that he wouldn't be in the play at all," says Engle. "In fact, unless only a short gain was needed, the opponents seldom ran a play through center when he was there. Well, as a result, Mother became the first, or at least among the first, roving centers in the game. As a consequence, he often outplayed much heavier men than himself. He delighted in moving around the big men."

47

During Dunn's four seasons, Penn State won 27 games, lost 11, and tied 1 and grew in stature as one of the East's powers despite the presence of Yale, Harvard, and Princeton—the universally-acknowledged dominators of the day. Despite this very real success, Dunn modestly insisted that he made all-America only because of an image built by a Pittsburgh sport writer, Dale Mason. Dunn constantly shunned the limelight.

"I don't want any darned publicity," he said on several occasions.

This attitude carried over into his later life, when he became a doctor on the island of Maui in Hawaii. After several years in the crowded world of big-time football, Dunn eventually became a virtual recluse as a plantation physician. But even though there were fewer people around, he did not lose his touch with the human race. He was conscientious and never drank liquor because he was his community's only physician. He lost a finger once because he refused to wear protective gloves while working with patients under x-ray treatment. He felt he could work better with his bare hands.

Before his death at the age of 81 on November 17, 1962, Dunn made one of his rare visits to Honolulu from his Hawaiian retreat. It was for a visit with Engle, who was passing through in 1954 after conducting a football clinic in Tokyo.

"This is a night I'll remember all my life," said Engle after a four-hour talkathon with the Penn State football hero.

Engle remembers one thing, especially, that Dunn had remarked about fair play.

"One thing boys in football ought to remember is that if you play dirty, you get it right back with interest," Dunn told Engle. "If you do it against a weaker man, you are only hurting yourself."

"He's still an all-America in my book," Engle said after his warm interview.

Growing Up

Ed Yeckley wanted to go to the University of Michigan, but his father thought Dickinson would be better. He compromised and went to Penn State, a decision he never regretted. For that matter, neither did Penn State.

Yeckley was in the middle of a lot of Nittany Lions' success in the early 1900s, a period of growing up for Penn State football.

It was a time when Penn State scheduled major powers on a full-scale basis and never embarrassed itself...an era of zooming player popularity that drew adoring crowds. It looked like the 500-seat capacity at Beaver Field would be soon outmoded, and the administration turned its thoughts toward the possibility of larger facilities for the fans.

During Yeckley's four years as end and running back, 1902 through 1905, Penn State won 26 of 39 games. If you were picking an all-time Penn State team, you would have to give a hard look at some of the players from the generation around Yeckley's era: center "Mother" Dunn, running backs Carl Forkum, "Irish" McLlveen, Bull McCleary, Heff Hirshman, kicker Larry Vorhis, and tackle Andy Moscrip.

They were good students as well as good athletes. Yeckley once said: "The boys came to school with a purpose and took their school work seriously—the faculty saw to that."

Dunn, acknowledged as the best center in the country in his time, received Walter Camp's stamp of approval as an all-America in 1906. If the rest were not chosen as all-Americas, they were certainly close to that stature in the opinion of a

1905 PENN STATE FOOTBALL TEAM

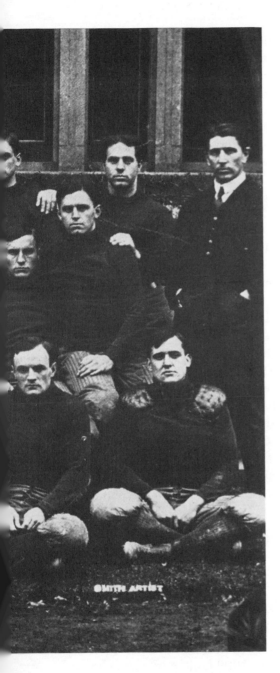

Penn State won eight games in a season for the first time with Tom Fennell's 1905 team.

51

sports writer who picked an all-time Penn State team in a 1927 newspaper article.

"McCleary, Celtic giant of the 1908 eleven, was a demon on straight smashes or thrusts off tackle," wrote George Trevor of the *New York Sun.* "His 195 pounds jolted a tackler unmercifully. Oldtimers refuse to concede that this likeable blond giant doesn't belong on Penn State's all-time first team.

"Perhaps they are right. A lethal straight arm, combined with a fadeaway pivot, made it almost impossible for a single tackler to stop McCleary. He packed a tremendous drive that carried him ahead, even when thrown off his feet. An exceptional defensive man, "Bull" could drop-kick accurately, and lead interference. McCleary's long field goal beat the Carlisle Indians (4-0) in 1906."

Trevor embellished his description of McCleary with this obvious, editorial comment: "A true Irishman, he scorned the protection of headguard and shoulder pads." Trevor must have been Irish.

The sports writer called Hirshman "a line-breaking fool when aroused. It was Heff who carried the ball on short bucks almost the entire length of the field against Navy in 1906. Hirshman, sent late into the 1909 Pennsylvania game, almost bucked his way to victory, but was cheated by the whistle."

Forkum, Trevor said, was "another temperamental line crasher who could rend opposing forwards apart, when stirred to a high pitch." It was pointed out that in a 50-0 victory over Allegheny in 1904, Forkum returned a kickoff from behind the goal line to score and wound up with five touchdowns and two extra points—one of the flashiest one-man shows in Penn State history.

"Yeckley was equally good as halfback or end and was a great player," Trevor said. "Very fast and shifty when he carried the ball. And when he didn't, he was a vicious tackler."

On Vorhis: "He was Penn State's most dependable dropkicker, as well as a cagey pilot. Vorhis rarely missed the target; even when the tension was tightest, his drop kicks being game clinchers. Vorhis scored three field goals to beat Pittsburgh in 1908, two to trim Cornell in 1907, one to tie Cornell in 1908 and one to deadlock Carlisle in 1909 and one to tie Pennsylvania the same season. That's delivering under pressure.

Vorhis was a husky 175-pounder who could run the quarter-mile in 51 seconds."

Trevor described Moscrip as a tackle in 1903 and 1904 "with an exceedingly wide range who could nail 'em out in the flanks." McLlveen was a "crackerjack" runner from 1902 through 1904, Trevor stated.

Penn State won eight games in a season for the first time in 1905, but a lot of attention was drawn to the games the Nittany Lions lost that year. They were beaten by three of the East's strongest teams—Navy, Carlisle, and Yale—but they were not mistreated. Players like Yeckley, Dunn, George McGee, Hi Henry, John Gotwals, and Bill Wray saw to that.

The Middies scored two touchdowns and an extra point for an 11-5 victory over Penn State, but the Navy knew it had been in a war. The Nittany Lions scored when Dunn blocked a punt and Yeckley ran 80 yards for the touchdown.

In the Carlisle game, before 8,000 noisy fans at Harrisburg, McGee and Frank Mt. Pleasant of the Indians waged a tremendous punting duel before the Indians made two quick scoring drives of 54 and 30 yards. Carlisle won, 11-0.

Penn State's tough line gave undefeated Yale fits most of the way, until the Elis broke through for late touchdowns and a 12-0 victory.

Going into the last month of the season, the Nittany Lions had a 5-3 record, but finished with a flourish by beating Dickinson, West Virginia, and Pitt, all by 6-0 scores.

Gotwals plunged over the goal line and was about to be thrown back when he locked his arm around the goal post for the winning score over Dickinson. Yeckley capped a 50-yard drive with an eight-yard touchdown run against West Virginia. And McGee, a substitute for Forkum for several years, scored the winning TD in the Pitt game.

Winning football games in those days was done in a manner similar to the modern era, Yeckley recalled once at a reunion of the 1905 team.

"We may think that modern football is a product of new developments," he said, "but actually there's very little under the sun that is new.

"The forward pass hadn't come in yet in my years, and line play may not have been as good. But blocking, tackling, kicking

53

and running were essentially as they are today."

The blocking, tackling, kicking, and running that the Nittany Lions were doing at that time were better than most of their opponents', at any rate. The Nittany Lions lost only one game in 1906, a 10-0 thriller to Yale and, although two mediocre seasons followed (6-4 and 5-5), a delicious treat was in store.

The Hollenback era was coming.

A Letter From Pop

Each Monday morning Bill Hollenback waited for an important letter. And each time he was not disappointed.

"Bill got a lot of his ideas in letters from Pop Warner," says Dutch Herman, one of the players under Hollenback when he took over as Penn State football coach in 1909. "Warner, of course a great coach himself at Carlisle, used to answer a lot of Bill's questions."

You could excuse Hollenback for picking Warner's brains his first year at Penn State. Hollenback was fresh out of college, in charge of a football team at the tender age of 22.

And, at the tender age of 26, he had the opportunity of looking back on three undefeated teams.

"He was a terrific fellow," recalls Herman, who was the quarterback of the 1909 team that won five games and tied two. "He was a great athlete himself. I played against him. He could run, he could throw. He was some football player."

Hollenback was an all-America at Penn and upon graduation was offered the coaching job at Penn State in an era when young players were given such positions. It was obvious that young blood was needed, since the sport had undergone vast changes. The forward pass had been legalized, and teams were given four downs to make 10 yards, instead of three downs to make five.

"The young fellows who had just graduated from college understood the new type of play better than many of the old coaches, and so they were hired," Hollenback later recalled in

55

an interview.

Hollenback was younger than some of the players on that 1909 team, Captain Alex Grey and Harry Weaver to name two. But Hollenback's inexperience bowed to his natural, youthful exuberance.

"Back in those days, pep talks were the difference between a winning and a losing football team," says Herman. "And Hollenback could really inspire a football team."

As he looked over the 60 candidates in September of 1909, Hollenback was rather pleased with what he saw. In spite of a mediocre 5-5 record the year before under Tom Fennell's part-time coaching, there was a nucleus of extremely talented players returning for the 1909 season. The 1908 team, it must be pointed out, suffered an unusual amount of injuries.

Along with Herman, Grey, and Weaver, Hollenback could deal with players like Larry Vorhis, Tom Piollet, Dick Smith, Heff Hirshman, Bull McCleary, and Fred Johnson. In addition, there were three new prospects—Dexter Very, Fritz Barrett, and Pete Mauthe.

This team opened New Beaver Field, which had a seating capacity of 1,000, by beating Grove City 31-0. Vorhis went off tackle from three yards out before the game was six minutes old to christen the place for Penn State. By halftime the Nittany Lions had a 22-0 lead, and by the second half Hollenback sent in his reserves to finish up.

Three major games were on the schedule that year—Warner-coached Carlisle, Penn, and Pitt. The Carlisle game was played in Wilkes-Barre and a large group of Penn State students paid $3.75 for a round-trip train ticket, leaving at 2 p.m. the day before to insure arrival before kickoff. A 30-piece band from Penn State also made the trip and paraded the streets of Wilkes-Barre to inspire enthusiasm for the big game.

Joe Hauser ran 38 yards through the Penn State line and stumbled into the end zone over Vorhis to give the Indians a 6-0 lead shortly after the second half started. The Nittany Lions struck back with Hirshman, McCleary, and Smith doing the ball-carrying. Smith went the final yards for a touchdown, but Vorhis' kick hit the crossbar and Carlisle still had the lead, at 6-5.

Vorhis later made good on a 30-yard field goal to give Penn

Bill Hollenback coached three undefeated teams at Penn State, including the great 1912 squad.

Fullback Pete Mauthe, third from left, front row, and quarterback "Shorty" Miller, second from left, second row, were the stars of Bill Hollenback's 1911 Penn State team.

State an 8-6 advantage, but also was a goat in the closing minutes when he fielded a Carlisle punt at the end zone. The officials ruled that he had one foot on the playing field, and when he touched the ball down in the end zone he automatically gave the Indians a two-point safety. The game ended in an 8-8 tie, but Hollenback could not feel too badly about it. He had broken even with the professorial Warner.

The game against Penn, played before 12,000 fans in Franklin Field, matched two undefeated teams. Penn had won its first five games, and Penn State had not lost in three. The cross-state rivals played the game largely between the 30-yard lines with Vorhis kicking a field goal in the second half to give the Nittany Lions a 3-3 tie.

Penn State's last game of the season, a 5-0 victory over favored Pitt, was fashioned on McCleary's touchdown run and a tough defense that held the Panthers without a first down in the opening half. Penn State students who heard the play-by-

play of the game via telephone line did not wait too long after it was over to round up all available wood and build a mammoth bonfire. Hollenback's first season was an unbeaten one, and it was worth celebrating.

The Nittany Lions received good notices in the big city newspapers, reflecting their climb into high college football circles. Said the *New York Telegram* in a review of the season: "Penn State is a team which wastes no energy. Every move is made for a purpose."

Despite his beginner's luck at Penn State, Hollenback mysteriously left for a similar job with Missouri for the 1910 season. To replace him Penn State hired his brother, Dr. Jack Hollenback, also a Penn graduate. The bizarre circumstances were never fully explained, Herman recalls.

"I never knew what the reason for that was," says Herman. "Apparently he had gone to Missouri on sort of a mutual trial basis. And for some reason or other, it didn't suit Bill and it

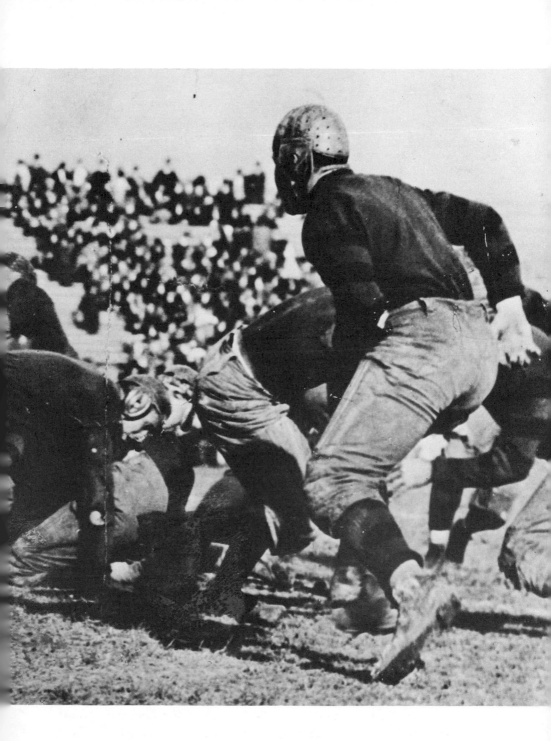

A pileup during Penn State-Penn game in 1911. Penn State won, 22-6.

didn't suit Missouri. He came back to Penn State the following year.

"But since Penn State had designated Bill's brother to take his place temporarily, apparently Bill himself was not so sure when he went out to Missouri that he'd stay."

Jack Hollenback did not have the success that brother Bill did, but did not do too badly, either. Under their lame-duck coach, the Nittany Lions had a 5-2-1 record. If the season of 1910 was not spectacular, it was notable for one thing: Penn State charged admission to a home game for the first time, on November 12 against Bucknell. The Penn State fans did not go away unhappy, either, for the Nittany Lions won, 45-3.

In 1911 Penn State's prodigal son returned and led the Nittany Lions to another undefeated season. Under Bill Hollenback, Penn State beat Geneva 57-0, Gettysburg 31-0, Cornell 5-0, Villanova 18-0, Penn 22-6, St. Bonaventure 46-0, Colgate 17-9, and Pitt 3-0 and had a scoreless tie with Navy.

"Most fans wouldn't know about the Colgate game that year because not much had been written about it," says Herman, "but Colgate came into State College as an important team with a good record. To finish the game, I recall, cars rimmed the field and their lights were turned on—probably one of the first games ever completed by artificial light."

Hollenback's job that year was made easy by the presence of "Shorty" Miller, a quarterback whom he termed "a marvelous player—one of the greatest football players of our times.

"We were playing the University of Pennsylvania in 1911 when Shorty took the opening kickoff and went through the entire Penn team, 88 yards for a touchdown. It was the most thrilling play I'd ever seen," said Hollenback years afterwards.

If Hollenback revered his fine broken-field runner, the 5-foot-5 star returned the admiration.

"Hollenback was a real leader and never had any disciplinary problems," Miller said. "He was agile and quite active but never mixed it up with the boys. He was a rough-and-ready guy who was quite a favorite with the players—a hale fellow, well met."

With Miller coming into his own and Pete Mauthe maturing as a star fullback and Dexter Very one of the country's finest pass-catchers, the Nittany Lions had teeth in their attack. They crystalized into one of Penn State's best teams in history the following year.

"That 1912 team was so good," said Miller, "that I threw nine touchdown passes and wasn't even the best passer on the team—Mauthe was."

Welcome, 1912.

The "M" Squad

"Give me a gun! Oh! Give me a gun, so I can shoot him! He's trying to hand them a touchdown on a platter!"

It was not often that Bill Hollenback's 1912 team gave him fits of anger, but it did on this occasion in the season's last game with Pitt.

Hollenback threw up his hands in dismay, faced the crowd, and exploded to the spectators in general when Shorty Miller called for a pass play deep in Penn State territory. It did not matter that Penn State was far ahead, 31-0, in the fourth quarter. It was considered a crime in those days to throw a pass from your own 20-yard line.

Watching each play intently, Hollenback first noticed that his team was lining up in a kick formation on first down. The play was changed to an end run, whereupon the Pitt defense diagnosed the switch and moved wide of the ends.

Taking in the defensive alignment, Miller decided that another change was in order—a pass play over the center of the line. That is when Hollenback exploded.

But it was too late for the coach to do anything about it, because by this time the pass had already been made to Dexter Very, and the Nittany Lions' excellent receiver ran 70 yards to the Pitt 10-yard line before he was downed.

Hollenback watched the play to completion and then turned back to his bench with a big grin and remarked without batting an eyelash: "There, by gosh! That's brains and how to use 'em!"

Things involving Miller—and Penn State in general—always

seemed to turn out all right that year. The Nittany Lions had a perfect season in 1912 with an 8-0 record and gained status as a national power. Except for momentary disenchantments like the famous Hollenback story, Penn State's 25-year-old coach had a love affair with his little star. Miller was worthy of Hollenback's admiration. His unlikely football size (5-foot-5 and 140 pounds) made him even more potent than king-size heroes.

"Shorty was one of the greatest broken-field runners ever seen at Penn State," recalls Dutch Herman, a teammate of Miller's in 1911. "He was a little fellow, but he was quick and fast. Because of his short legs he could stop and start on a dime without losing speed, and was so small that bigger fellows had a hard time stopping him.

"I can remember times when he'd get tripped up and would be almost running on his hands before he'd regain his balance. He was a tough man to bring down."

Miller was the quarterback on offense, the deep safety on defense, and the punt-return specialist of the 1912 team. He gained 801 yards on the ground, including a still-standing record of 250 yards rushing in a game against Carnegie Tech, and threw nine touchdown passes.

The number of touchdown passes was quite a lot, recalls Herman, since Miller's hands were relatively small.

"He was a left-handed passer, and because of the shape of the ball, he couldn't grip it and had to throw it off his hand," says Herman.

Miller's school record stood for 50 years before Pete Liske threw 12 TD passes in 1962.

Despite his success with the innovative forward pass, Miller felt that fullback Pete Mauthe was more adept at the maneuver.

"Mauthe, not I, was the best passer on the team," Miller insisted for years afterwards. "You must remember that the ball was more oval in those days, and even with that kind of ball, Mauthe would knock down a receiver with a pass. I'm positive he could have thrown the modern ball a mile."

Mauthe was the other half of Penn State's "M" Squad in 1912. A sports writer characterized the stocky fullback as a "plunger who could rip a line to shreds...he always got his distance under pressure.

"He was a faultless interferer, as well as the greatest backerup of the line on defense in Penn State's history. Mauthe never received the attention he deserved. Pete worked unobtrusively, thinking first of the team. As an inspirational leader of men, Mauthe never has been surpassed. He was always out front, setting the pace. Mauthe could pass 50 yards and hit a moving target. Here was a football player!"

Mauthe later became the first Penn State player to be inducted into the National Football Hall of Fame, joining immortals like Red Grange, George Gipp, Bronko Nagurski, Elmer Layden, and Jim Thorpe. While accepting the honor, his remarks were typical.

"This is a great honor for me, of course," said Mauthe, "but more important, it is also a tribute to the team of 1912. That was a fine team. It was devoid of jealousy or factionalism. Its spirit was marvelous. And it had great confidence in Shorty Miller, who called the signals. He was the boss."

When Miller called signals, he enjoyed giving the ball to his brutish backfield mate. Mauthe scored 119 points that season, producing 11 touchdowns, eight field goals and 29 extra points, and ran for a total of 710 yards.

Miller and Mauthe were instrumental as the Nittany Lions scored 285 points against a paltry sum of six for their opponents. They defeated Carnegie Tech 41-0, Washington & Jefferson 30-0, Cornell 29-6, Gettysburg 25-0, Penn 14-0, Villanova 71-0, Ohio State 37-0, and Pitt 38-0.

"The 1912 team was one of the outstanding teams in the East," said Hollenback.

And, for that matter, it could have been one of the best football teams in the world since eastern football was supreme in that era.

"It was really one of the great teams of all time," added Hollenback.

In the backfield with Miller and Mauthe were halfbacks Dan Welty and "Punk" Berryman. The ends were Dexter Very and

"Shorty" Miller quarterbacked the famous 1912 team. One of the best broken-field runners in Penn State history, Miller rushed for a school record 250 yards in one game.

66

Al Wilson, the tackles Levi Lamb and "Dad" Engle, the guards Albert Hansen and "Red" Bebout, and the center, John Clark.

It was customary in those days for graduates to return to campus and help teach fundamentals to Penn State players. One such old grad came back before the 1912 season and Hollenback asked him what he thought.

"The backfield is good," he said, "but the line is weak."

"You can imagine how the linemen took that," "Dad" Engle once recalled. "And Hollenback decided to give the visitor a chance to back it up. He put the ball on the 5-yard line and gave the guy five tries to put it over. After the third try, he was back on the 20-yard line and rather the worse for wear. He decided that he had had enough and admitted that his judgment was a little off."

Their fine season was punctuated with an historic game against Ohio State on November 16 that ended in a 37-0 Penn State victory but ruptured relations between the schools. The game between the regional powers was laced with rough play and finished in a massive brawl involving spectators as the Ohio State players walked off the field with nine minutes to go.

The Nittany Lions had come into Columbus as underdogs and did not like what they saw in the newspapers. The local writers treated the visitors with disdain, predicting an easy Ohio State victory.

"They really poured it on," remarked one Penn State man, "in fact, too much so for the Nittany Lions coaching staff."

Hollenback and Assistant Coach Dick Harlow capitalized on the provincial newspaper stories as inspiration in team meetings.

"In the pre-game pep talk," remembered Welty, "Bill and Dick did not lose a good opportunity for a little, well-directed propaganda, which effect was not lost on the boys. We left the dressing room higher than a kite."

The inspired Nittany Lions ran up a big lead at the start, and the lopsided contest had a frustrating effect on the Ohio State players. They fought back the only way they could—with fists instead of touchdowns. A couple of hard blows from the Buckeyes further inspired Penn State.

"I got up after a play when, 'bang,' a roundhouse haymaker hit me from behind right on the mouth and away went my

Pete Mauthe, one of the great fullbacks in Penn State history, had enough ferocity "to rip a line to shreds," according to one observer. He starred on the 1912 team.

front teeth," said Wilson. "When I opened my eyes the trainer was throwing water in my face. Anyhow, the Ohio State halfback was put out of the game and I finished it."

During the course of the brutal contest, an Ohio State tackle had been needling Miller, and the Penn State quarterback decided that he needed humility.

Wilson recalled the incident: "Miller walked over and said, 'Okay, Mr. Raymond. Mr. Mauthe will take the ball right through here.' Dex Very shifted over to my side, and Pete Mauthe went all the way. Ohio State never got over that, and we beat them worse than we should have done."

Another time, a Buckeye tackle named Barraklow challenged Miller: "Run one through me."

"Righto," said Shorty and then turned to Mauthe and said:

Penn State's Famous 1912 Team
Front row, left to right: Dexter Very, right end; Levi Lamb, right tackle; Albert Hansen, right guard; John Clark, center; "Red" Bebout, left guard; "Dad" Engle, left tackle; Al Wilson, left end. Back row, left to right: "Punk" Berryman, left halfback; Pete Mauthe, fullback; "Shorty" Miller, quarterback; Dan Welty, right halfback.

"Mr. Mauthe, will you kindly escort the ball through Mr. Barraklow's position?"

"Check," said Mauthe and ran eight yards for a first down.

If there was bad feeling between the teams, Miller did nothing to alleviate it, recalled a sports writer:

"This bow-legged, barrel-chested little Dutchman had a keen sense of humor and loved to josh high-strung rascals. He chattered like a magpie between signals. Against Ohio State, Shorty's banter had the Buckeyes demoralized."

Not only were the Buckeye players unhappy, but so was their coach, Jack Richards.

"The Ohio State coach had been kicking about clipping, although there were no rules against it at that time, and both sides were doing it," said Engle. "Tension kept growing as the afternoon went on—and finally, with about 10 minutes to go, Ohio State sent a play through tackle and guard.

"The runner was stopped but was trying to fight his way through the scrimmage line, and I remember I stood up out of the pile and pulled him down by putting my arm around his neck and shoulders. He claimed I hit him but I never did.

"The Ohio State players started off the field. We had no idea they were leaving, but thought they were going to try some sort of spread or trick formation. So we started following them. That was the signal for the crowd to come down out of the stands."

At this point it was apparent that the Ohio State crowd was in a malevolent mood.

"We formed a circle to protect ourselves," Engle continued. "I remember one fan in particular who came running out swinging his fists and yelling, 'Let me at 'em.' Assistant Coach Dick Harlow was on the field by that time, and when the fellow got close enough Dick let him have one along the jaw. He rolled end over end two or three times, and when he stopped he got up and lit out for the stands faster than he had run on the field a few minutes before."

The Penn State players finally escaped to their dressing room, but bad feeling lingered between the schools for some time. It took 44 years before they resumed their rivalry.

The Nittany Lions not only smothered Ohio State's strong offense but also shut out such highly-touted teams as Penn and

72

Washington & Jefferson (which had beaten powerful Yale that season). The only team to cross Penn State's goal line was Cornell, in the third game of the season. The touchdown was made when a Cornell end intercepted a Penn State pass.

"When we were lining up for the try for Cornell's extra point," said Wilson, "Engle, who never cussed and was rather quiet normally, broke out with the greatest array of cuss words you ever heard. He ended with: 'I'll be damned if I'll ever stand under another goal post like this.'

"And, the varsity never did."

Penn State finished the season on a high note with a romp over arch-rival Pitt. Miller amazed not only the crowd but his own teammates when he called for a field goal from mid-field.

"Our linemen turned around and looked at me as if I were crazy," said Miller.

But Miller repeated his orders, got the snap from center, and held it for Mauthe. The fullback kicked the ball 51 yards for a field goal, a record that still stands.

"When Captain Mauthe and his men gave the college yell at Forbes Field on Thanksgiving Day, the most successful season the Blue and White has ever had became history," proclaimed Penn State's student newspaper, the *Collegian,* on December 11. "Other great teams have represented the Blue and White on the gridiron in past years, but none accomplished quite as much."

Flowers, Birds' Eggs,
And Chippendale Chairs

"They say Dick was a holy terror when he was at Penn State, and I can believe it. I've seen him walk up to a big lineman who had been loafing, grab him by the nape of the neck, and give him a boot in the rear."

This description supplied by a friend was only one facet of Dick Harlow, a man of complex design. The coach of Penn State's football team from 1915 through 1917 was just as able to coddle a player as kick him.

And although a serious student of the violent world of football, Harlow just as easily adapted to gentler pursuits. The hobbies of this soft-spoken scholar included collecting flowers, birds' eggs, stamps, and Chippendale chairs.

Of course football was Harlow's escalator to fame. He was one of the first exceptional tackles at Penn State.

"Harlow could stand out in the fastest company," said a sports writer. "He was a 195-pound giant who used his hands more effectively on defense than any other Penn State tackle. Endowed with spartan courage, Harlow played a slashing game against Pittsburgh in 1911, with his leg in a cast. His offensive charge was cyclonic."

Upon graduation Harlow remained as assistant coach and got the top job when Bill Hollenback left after the 1914 season. Harlow had a tough act to follow, for Hollenback's teams had gone unbeaten at one point through 19 games. Even a disappointing 2-6 season in 1913 and a mediocre one of 5-3-1 in 1914 could not diminish Hollenback's high accomplishments.

74

Harlow's first year was an instant success and his second even better. The Nittany Lions had 7-2 and 8-2 records before falling to 5-4 in 1917 for an overall mark of 20-8 in the brief Harlow era. For success like that, Harlow's players did not mind trailing their enigmatic coach around over hills and valleys to pick wild flowers and rare ferns and to watch birds. These were occasional sidetrips for the football players when they were not hard at the game.

Their Pied Piper had them mesmerized.

"Everybody loved Dick Harlow," recalled an associate.

The innovative Harlow was not only given credit for inventing or developing several football plays, he also was called the pioneer of intercollegiate boxing. While doubling as the proctor of a dormitory during his years as football coach, Harlow was asked to stop a fight between his students and a group from a nearby dorm.

Instead of chastising the students, Harlow gathered the best talent from both dorms, took the boys to a gym, and started a boxing team. Then he challenged another college to a match.

His sway of human minds was downright supernatural at times.

"Dick was a great psychologist," recalled Rip Engle, the Penn State coach of a later era. "He was a marvel as a halftime orator, and in many games his dressing room talks were the difference between victory and defeat. He also had a knack of rallying the entire student body and staff behind the team, which falls in line with his abilities as a psychologist."

Engle, an end on Harlow's team when Harlow later coached at Western Maryland, recalled a "great stickler for details and a fine teacher of the technical parts of the game. I remember we used certain plays from time to time that were almost as confusing for us to learn as they were for our opponents. As you might expect, we spent an awful lot of time practicing signal drills—more than a half hour at most practices."

Harlow was superstitious, despite his sophistication.

"That was a side to Harlow that not many people knew about," recalled Engle. "Western Maryland played its home games in Baltimore, and when we rode the bus into the city from the campus at Westminster for our first game, the seats we sat in for the first trip were the seats we had to use all the rest

75

of the season."

In 1918 Harlow left Penn State to join the Army for the First World War. When he returned in 1919, Harlow was enlisted as a chief aide to Head Coach Hugo Bezdek. Before the 1922 season, Harlow left for the coach's job at Colgate and was followed by several fine Penn State players. The Nittany Lions were depleted after Harlow's departure and never the same after that. They were hoping for a third straight undefeated season in 1922, but instead lost three games.

At Colgate, Western Maryland, and later Harvard, Harlow

found countless disciples, as he had at Penn State. A little while after his retirement from coaching in 1947, Harlow reflected that he had coached 606 boys. He had time then to keep tabs of such things.

"I went over all of my old records and totaled the amount of money I loaned boys while they were in college—money they needed in a pinch for books, illness, trouble at home, or even to go home on a holiday," Harlow said. "It came to $27,000. And

The art of drop-kicking was demonstrated to some of Dick Harlow's players in 1915.

do you know how much I am still out? Just $165—a boy who was killed in World War II."

Harlow helped people in other ways. He got Engle his first coaching job, for instance.

"It was a great thing, for Dick was the man who gave me the idea that I would like to take up coaching," said Engle. "He got me a job at a high school. I used a lot of the stuff he taught me. It was sound for years afterward."

Harlow died of a heart attack on February 20, 1962, at the age of 72. Some say it was a result of hypertension that built in a complex man over the years.

"He was a sick man in his old age," remarked an acquaintance. "That was not the real Dick Harlow. The real Dick Harlow was the only man I ever came close to hero-worshipping."

Higgins And More Fat Years

Of all the stories involving Bob Higgins, one of the most often told is the time he had to duplicate a touchdown play. It happened during the 1915 season in a game with Lehigh.

Penn State and Lehigh were locked in a scoreless tie when Higgins caught a pass from Stan Ewing and ran 15 yards for a touchdown. But the happy moment quickly turned sour when Penn State was penalized for having 12 men on the field instead of the regulation 11 and lost the touchdown. A substitute, sent in to give instructions, had wandered onto the field too soon.

It was a pretty mad bunch of Nittany Lions that greeted the substitute, Chuck Yerger, when he finally arrived on the scene.

"Coach Harlow says to throw that pass," announced Yerger with a pained expression.

"We just did!" chorused the answer.

Time was running out as the Nittany Lions went into their formation. They called the same play, threw the pass to the same spot where Higgins was waiting, and he scored a replica of the first touchdown. This one counted, and Penn State had a 7-0 victory.

If you knew Higgins, he could have probably run that same play and scored touchdowns all day.

"Higgins was one of those types who played his best in big games," recalled a teammate. "It took top-notch competition to bring out the real Higgins. Always cool and heady, he was quick to diagnose formations. Bob used his hands beautifully to fight off interference, yet it is as a receiver of passes that he will

Bob Higgins, a great end for Penn State in the First World War era, made all-America in 1919.

go down in posterity."

Higgins was a fine kicker, and shone as a defensive player, too. A familiar figure with a battered leather helmet pulled snugly down to his ears, he preyed on enemy ball carriers. Sometimes he tracked an opponent halfway across the field before bringing him down. Like the proverbial Mountie, he usually got his man.

"I have never seen a yard gained inside or outside Bob, and have never failed to see him handle a tackle alone or fail to get his man downfield on punts," the teammate said.

Before battling opposing players, Higgins had to fight his own family to get into sports. They were at first against it, but he finally got his parents' consent to play football. Then he caught Dick Harlow's eye and was snapped up for Penn State.

Harlow, an assistant coach in Higgins' first year in 1914, was the head coach in 1915 after Bill Hollenback left. Hollenback had only one losing season in five while compiling an overall 28-9-4 record.

Harlow stepped into the top job during high football popularity in America. The sport was more attractive than ever. It was reflected in increasing attendance, larger gate guarantees for teams, and juicier profits. For instance, a standing-room-only crowd of 10,000 showed up to watch that Lehigh game at outmoded Beaver Field. Plans were in the wind for a larger capacity. They could only seat a little over 1,000 at the time.

While more people attended games, more players showed up for football at Penn State (candidates now numbered over 100 yearly). An eligibility code was adopted at the school for the first time, and the one-year's residence rule resulted in the first freshman team at Penn State in 1915.

With players like Higgins, Harlow's first year was an artistic success. A 7-2 record included victories over Westminster, Lebanon Valley, Penn, Gettysburg, West Virginia Wesleyan, Lehigh, and Lafayette. The Nittany Lions were beaten only by Harvard and Pitt.

In the Lehigh game, one of the highlights of the season on November 5, Pennsylvania Day, the Nittany Lions proved that "speed was superior to weight in modern football."

Reported the *New York Times:* "Outweighed 15 pounds to the man, the Blue and White team displayed an attack that

81

could not be stopped...the game was by far the best exhibition of football seen on Beaver Field this year and gave the Pennsylvania Day crowd plenty of excitement from start to finish."

After recounting the famous Ewing-to-Higgins touchdown play in the first half, the *Times* reported: "Lehigh opened the second half in a way that would not be denied and had they been able to keep up their wonderful attack, a different score might have resulted.

"Receiving the ball in their own territory they advanced it by terrific plunging to Penn State's 10-yard line. A brace by the Blue and White enabled them to take the ball on downs, and H. A. Clark kicked them out of danger.

"It was in the last period that Cahall's sterling work nearly scored for Lehigh. On long runs and wonderful plunges, he was instrumental in carrying the ball to within 10 yards of the Penn State goal post and gave the Penn State rooters several anxious

The Penn State football team of 1916 lined up before a game with arch-rival Pitt. End Bob Higgins, left, first row, was the star of the team.

moments."

Penn State held again.

"The real features of the game," added the *Times,* "was the work of Bob Higgins and (halfback) Punk Berryman and the State secondary defense."

Higgins' name was always prominent in Penn State success stories. He helped the Nittany Lions improve their record to 8-2 in 1916. That year Penn State beat Susquehanna 27-0, Westminster 55-0, Bucknell 50-7, West Virginia Wesleyan 39-0, Gettysburg 48-2, Geneva 79-0, Lehigh 10-7, and Lafayette 40-0. They were beaten 15-0 by Penn and 31-0 by Pitt.

Higgins' value to the Penn State teams of that era was dramatized by his absence as well as his presence. When he left to join the Army in 1917 for the First World War, the Nittany Lions slumped to a 5-4 mark, and then 1-2-1 in 1918. The 1917 season was highlighted by Harry Robb's school record 36-point performance on six touchdowns against Gettysburg, but it just was not the same team without Higgins.

When Higgins came back after the war, a new era of football prosperity dawned at Penn State—the Hugo Bezdek era.

Time Out: Charley Way

Charley Way was only 125 pounds in football trappings, but it was 125 pounds of talent.

"Charley was probably the best man I have ever seen running with the ball," said one of his teammates. "He weighed only one hundred and twenty-five pounds and ironically detested playing football. Head Coach Hugo Bezdek had to have an assistant manager call him from his room to practice every day. He very seldom started games as he was not rugged enough to play a full hard game and was used as a pinch-runner.

"His presence was electrical to the team, for we always went 'good' with him in the game. He would get worked up to a high pitch sitting on the bench and never could be stopped. He usually played with tears running down his cheeks and crying out loud like a small child. But he had all the nerve one man could possibly have. He used a wonderful change of pace and a good straight arm to make his long runs. He had a remarkable stride for a little fellow...I have never seen him tackled by both legs. He also was the most unassuming fellow and the most likeable fellow I have ever known."

"I was one of those quick boys, you know," says Way himself, recounting paths of glory in 1917. "I loved to go off tackle, inside. I see an opening—and I'm gone."

Way was not merely quick but nimble, able to adjust his runs in mid-flight. "The Pittsburgh people thought I was really something, even in defeat," says Way, recalling a loss to Penn State's arch-rival more than 50 years ago.

85

Way, a former Penn State all-America, warmed to the interview although he admitted that he was sometimes reticent to do so.

"I never like to talk much of my achievements," he says, his voice velvety and laced with emotion, "although I am very proud to be an all-America."

Few players worked harder to be one, certainly. Way's beginnings were humble, his future uncertain.

"My father was a carpenter and he worked only in the summer," Way explains. "It wasn't easy. We were really poor."

Because he had little money, his family sent him to Penn State for schooling. Tuition was low there.

"You could go up there without too much money in those days," recalls the 5-foot-9 Way, now 75 years old and a gentleman farmer in Thorndale, Pennsylvania, just south of Philadelphia.

A four-sports letterman at Downingtown High School, Way could not make the Penn State freshman team because of varied circumstances.

"I went out for the team, but I wasn't a scholarship boy," Way explains, fingering his gray hair. "It was the scholarship boys who got the preference. I only weighed about 125 pounds at the time and my right hand was split open from playing baseball. I just wasn't ready for football."

Once given an opportunity as a sophomore, however, he did not let go. It was this characteristic of grit that exemplified his football life.

"I didn't start out as a halfback," he recalls. "I was a quarterback—and a second-string quarterback at first. But when the first-string quarterback, Frank Wolf, got hurt, I was given the job by Coach Dick Harlow—a really nice man. Wolf never got in again after I got the job."

Way's weight was only about 125 pounds—but he does not mind telling you, "I could run like the devil. I could run like a scared rabbit."

After Penn State won five games and lost four in 1917, Way took a year off for the First World War. He was in a machine gun training camp in Augusta, Georgia, during 1918. The layoff apparently did not rust his talents, and as a matter of fact was even good for him. He returned with a little more weight.

The "original" scatback—Charley Way.

"When I came out of the Army I weighed 145 pounds," Way recalls. "I was a little heavier and perhaps a little slower. But I could still go. I was the original scatback. At least the sports writers dubbed me that. I have a newspaper clipping from a Pittsburgh writer who classified me as one of the best backs they ever had at Penn State. I never liked to run the ends, because it was too long a way around. I just liked to run inside. It was more direct that way."

Harlow, a favorite of Way's, had become a scout in the 1918 season. Hugo Bezdek was the coach when Way returned from the service, and the player found it tougher going under the new boss.

"He was a little bullish at times," says Way about Bezdek, considered a martinet by some. "He liked to order the boys around. He liked to have his thumb on everything, which was proper I suppose. And he gave you a hard time when you weren't doing the job. I still think that Harlow helped him more than some people know. He scouted a lot of the games for Bezdek and made him look pretty good. But in later years, those two had a falling out."

Way concedes certain things about Bezdek, though.

"I suppose Bez was a good coach," recalls Way. "He introduced things at Penn State they never had before—like the spinner play."

Bezdek built Penn State into a hardened football team in the 1919 season, when the Nittany Lions won the eastern championship, forerunner of the Lambert Trophy.

"We practiced every afternoon from 4 o'clock until after dark," says Way. "In those days it was three or four hours a day. The coach didn't let up any, even on Friday. It was quite a grind for a little fellow."

With Way one of the stars, Penn State won seven of eight games that year. The one loss was a 19-13 defeat by Dartmouth during which Way scored two touchdowns. Way lost a game, but gained the respect of a Dartmouth tackle, Billy Cunningham.

"He later became a sports writer with the *Boston Post*," says Way, recalling a story that Cunningham wrote about him on October 11, 1942.

Cunningham, drawing an analogy of football to war at the

time of the Second World War, recalled an incident that happened in that 1919 game.

"Three of us Dartmouth bruisers had happened to tackle simultaneously and from different directions one memorable afternoon a little halfback from Penn State, famous in his time under the name of 'Pie' Way. Almost 600 pounds of hard-conditioned, high-velocity football flesh struck him head-on at one time. It was at high speed, too, and the shock felled him like dead.

"He was only a little shaver, weighing about 150 pounds. I'll always remember him lying semi-stunned on the sod and of how he spoke when he could and of the bandsaw snarl in his voice as he said: 'I'm hurt a little now but I'll be all right in a minute. And then I'm going to get up and run you big lugs right out of the ballgame.' He almost did, too. We had a terrible time with him. That's the way you ought to carry a fight."

"The reference to 'Pie' was one of my nicknames," recalls Way, "but don't ask me what it means. There was a Pie Way at Yale before my time. I guess that's where I got the name, I don't know. I had so many nicknames, I can't remember them all."

In 1920 Penn State's fine runner received the ultimate reward for his toil—the stature of all-America on the Walter Camp team. The Nittany Lions had an undefeated season that year, whipping perennial antagonist Penn 28-7 and Nebraska 20-0 in the process.

"That was a good day for me, Nebraska," says Way. "I reeled off a couple of long runs. Bezdek used me as a spot player in that game—he had his pets. Well, the first time I had the ball, I ran for 53 yards. The next time I got my hands on the ball, I scored a touchdown."

When he left Penn State, Way had intermittent coaching jobs at the University of Dayton, Downington High School, and Virginia Polytechnical Institute. He also played professional football with the Canton Bulldogs, Philadelphia Yellowjackets, and Philadelphia Quakers. He went into the insurance and taxi business in his Downington home town, but lost all his money in the Depression. Way then spent 27 years with the Internal Revenue Service until retirement in 1963.

He has been a quiet man since.

Disappointed Penn State fans watch a 26-3 loss to Rutgers in 1918, Hugo Bezdek's first year. It got better after that.

"I loaf—I've got a little 14-acre place in the country in Chester County," says Way. "I did farm it at one time. But I don't now. I just try to keep the bushes and the grass down."

People keep admiring his youthful appearance, his rugged tan and trim physique.

"Some people say I look young, some even say 50," says Way. "But at times I don't feel that young."

He chuckles while he talks and is an easy smiler. He is an introvert, though, who sometimes finds the pace of today's world awesome and overpowering.

An uncommunicative man at times, Way admits that he does not always open up to interrogators. His brown eyes danced mischieveously when he told a story of an abortive interview once.

"The reporter came to see me and I didn't say more than six words," says Way. "I never saw him again. I don't usually like to talk about myself—but I guess I'm doing all right now."

Up, Up, And Away

It had rained most of the week, turning Forbes Field into a mud bowl, and conditions were not the best for the 1919 Thanksgiving Day game between Penn State and Pitt. Observers saw it as a definite Penn State advantage, since it would slow Pitt's explosive running game.

The battle for the unofficial title of Pennsylvania football champion would be decided in the air, the observers figured, and they were correct. The only thing was, nobody expected the kind of pass play that Penn State came up with that watery autumn afternoon.

With the game only a couple of minutes old and the Nittany Lions in an obvious kicking situation on their own seven-yard line, they pulled off a play that "will be seen perhaps once in a hundred collegiate football games," according to one newspaper account. Bill Hess took the snap from center in his own end zone and threw a short screen pass to Bob Higgins, and Penn State's all-America end ran 90 yards for a touchdown. The play broke Pittsburgh's spirit and eased the way to a 20-0 victory that capped Coach Hugh Bezdek's fine second season.

The play was so nervy for the times that sports writers praised Penn State's new coach and poked fun at Glenn "Pop" Warner, Pitt's famous leader.

"Some colleges may go to law with their claims for the title of the United States, so open is the controversy, but only Hugo Bezdek, a broad-gauge built tactician, is eligible to take the chair when Keystone state football is before the House," said one writer. "Taking liberties with Glenn Warner is almost as common as razzing Willie Hoppe into scratching at a critical moment at a billiard match. It is done about as often as Mississippi goes Republican or a landlord reduces the rent."

The credit of the play should not have actually gone to Bezdek, but to Penn State's assistant coach Dick Harlow. He had scouted the Panthers for weeks and noticed that the Panthers put nine or ten men on the line when opposing teams, deep in their own territory, went into a punt formation. Harlow decided that a screen pass was in order, and Bezdek went along, somewhat hesitatingly.

The passing attack as a whole, though, was Bezdek's idea, and the Nittany Lions dominated the Panthers that day before many disappointed fans.

"Bezdek earned his right to the first row of football field marshalls by unleashing an aerial attack today that has never had a parallel in the game," the writer continued. "There may be nothing new under the sun, but Bezdek certainly had something new under a sky over a gridiron. Bezdek has pushed Penn State back into the football sun and today by his air wizardries proves himself to be one of the great strategists of the game. He outguessed Warner and had a plan of battle that Pitt could never solve.

"There were numerous Penn State heroes. Not a man of the original eleven failed to show but the highest qualities. Several men stood out. They were Captain Higgins, Charley Way, Bill Hess, Ben Cubbage, and Larry Conover."

The "aerial attack," incidentally, was mighty for the times but not by modern standards. The Nittany Lions threw eight passes and completed five.

"State Swamps Pitt By A Wonderful Air Attack," a newspaper headline said, and Bezdek was able to savor it the next day. He not only had completed an attractive 7-1 season but did it with a rare triumph over Pitt. It was the first victory over the Panthers in seven years and would be the only one until 1939 for Penn State.

The 1919 season began a rich era at Penn State. In the ensuing years the Nittany Lions granted athletic scholarships freely, scheduled many intersectional games, and traveled to the

94

west coast for the first time. As the team enjoyed artistic success before bigger crowds, it also enjoyed financial success. Profits from football reached $50,000 a year. This was due in large measure to a bigger seating capacity at Beaver Field, which now was 5,500 with the addition of new wooden stands.

No wonder they drew loving fans. Charley Way was making spectacular kickoff returns, Bob Higgins great catches, and Hinkey Haines, Harry Robb, Bill Hess, Ben Cubbage, Larry Conover, and the rest were playing winning football.

Even in 1919's only loss, a 19-13 thriller to Dartmouth, the Nittany Lions did not look bad. Way returned the opening kickoff 90 yards to score and also picked up a fumble and ran 85 yards for Penn State's other touchdown. In a 48-7 victory over Ursinus, Way was at it again—racing 95 yards on the opening kickoff for a TD.

That season Penn State also defeated Gettysburg 33-0, Bucknell 9-0, Penn 10-0, Lehigh 20-7, Cornell 20-0 and, of course, Pitt in the Thanksgiving Day game highlighted by Higgins' fancy pass play.

Victories over both Penn and Pitt in one season meant status in that era, for both of Penn State's arch-rivals were perennially ranked among the leading teams in the country. Robert Maxwell, the sports editor of the *Philadelphia Public Ledger*, made Penn State No. 1 in the East, and the triumph over powerful Penn helped him in his judgment.

"Bezdek has developed a powerful attack and a strong defense," said Maxwell. "And with the men to carry out his ideas, the team just HAD to win."

Penn was favored in the November 1 meeting before a crowd of 23,000 at Philadelphia's Franklin Field. The playing surface was dripping wet after a morning rain, and Penn State proved to be the better of the "mudders" on that day. After a fumbled kick had given the Nittany Lions the ball on Penn's two-yard line, Robb went over for the game's only touchdown in the second period. Conover kicked a 25-yard field goal in the final period for the other three points.

"Pennsylvania's aspirations for a football championship were drowned in a sea of mud and rain on Franklin Field when Penn State's fighting eleven literally slipped over an unexpected victory," reported the *New York Times.*

It was unexpected, in more ways than one. Not only did Penn theoretically have greater scoring punch, but insiders revealed that Penn State was having morale problems.

"Bezdek and Captain Higgins recognized for several reasons unknown to the public that Penn State, although having an abundance of material, was an unsettled machine," said Walter F. Dunn, a writer for the *Philadelphia Public Ledger*.

"This uncertainty was being caused by some friction which had been a campus secret. Bezdek, when reporting, had found one or two factions, these being more or less responsible for the loss of the Dartmouth game two weeks ago.

"But within a week prior to the game with old Penn, Bezdek and Higgins called a mass meeting which, of course, was attended by all disgruntled candidates, students, and members of the faculty. The coach apparently succeeded in ironing out the difficulties between the various members of the squad and made it known to them that the success of the present season depended upon the cooperation necessarily given him by each and all of the large group of candidates, the majority of whom were former varsity men."

In 1920 the Nittany Lions had their first undefeated season since the glory years of 1911-12. It included victories over Lebanon Valley, Muhlenberg, Gettysburg, Dartmouth, North Carolina State, Penn, and Nebraska and ties with Lehigh and Pitt.

"We were really beat up in the Dartmouth game," recalls Glenn Killinger, a future all-America. "We won 14-7 but what a bunch of cripples turned out Monday! That game was a dandy. No one gave us a chance. We stood 7-7 near the end. I intercepted a pass at midfield and went to the Dartmouth seven. Joe Lightner scored the big one."

The contest was described as "a thrilling, gripping, intense game" in Penn State's *Alumni News.* It was a good one to have for the first official Alumni Homecoming Day on October 9, 1920.

The practice of setting aside football weekends for the return of old grads actually began several years before with Pennsylvania Day. The Pennsylvania Day festivities brought alumni back to University Park for political speeches, military reviews, and parades in addition to the football game. In 1920 the promotion of the first official Alumni Homecoming brought 1,500

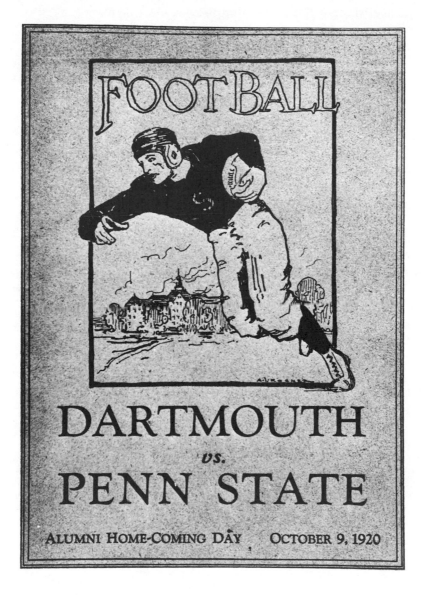

A program cover worth saving: The first Homecoming Day in Penn State history.

former students back to watch Bezdek's strong team.

Taking train, bus, and gas-buggy the alumni flocked into town. They were met by the Penn State college band.

"The sidewalks were lined with people watching the hilarious mob invade the town," wrote Edward N. "Mike" Sullivan, the Alumni secretary.

A mass meeting, no doubt the forerunner of today's pep rallies, was held by the visitors in the school auditorium. It was followed by a concert, given by the New York Chamber Music Society. On Saturday morning more than 4,000 persons gathered in front of Old Main, the administration building, to hear speeches. Then they marched to Beaver Field for the game.

The victory over Dartmouth was celebrated by fraternity dinners and other gatherings Saturday night.

"After these," wrote Sullivan, "the alumni came up to the Armory to enjoy the cider, pretzels, and smokes."

Officials spoke, the glee club sang, and the proverbial good time was had by all. Such a good time, Sullivan noted, that it was decided that an annual occasion should be "set aside purely for alumni and everything turned over in the advancement of their interests."

The proud alumni had more happy occasions to look forward to, for Penn State was not going to lose another football game for a while.

Going Places

Writer Ring Lardner asked the logical question: "Does Penn State have any home grounds this season?" The answer was, yes, but they're hardly home anymore.

The Nittany Lions did play games at Beaver Field in 1921, but their schedule also was one of the most adventurous and far-reaching in college football that year. They traveled 8,500 miles and visited Seattle, Washington; Cambridge, Massachusetts; Philadelphia; New York; and Pittsburgh.

The Nittany Lions were starting to be called the "Nittany Nomads."

"State College is located in Center County, and Center County can be located by means of a large map, a compass, and an experienced guide...it is a very hard place to get to and for that reason, most of the big games are played away from home," wrote Robert Maxwell, sports editor of the *Philadelphia Public Ledger.* "Penn State is doing a lot of touring, but not from choice. It is impossible to get good teams on the home grounds, so it is necessary to go someplace else."

The Nittany Lions, in the midst of a 30-game undefeated streak, won eight games that year and tied two. They beat Lebanon Valley 53-0, Gettysburg 24-0, North Carolina State 35-0, Lehigh 28-7, Georgia Tech 28-7, Carnegie Tech 28-7, Navy 13-7, and Washington 21-7. They tied Harvard 21-21 and Pitt 0-0.

Penn State players carried superstition to a ridiculous extreme in 1921. Quarterback Glenn Killinger got out of bed on

"Rigorous self-denial and intense application" made Glenn Killinger one of Penn State's greatest quarterbacks.

the same side every morning, and players wore the same neckties all year. But if they were lucky, they were also good.

Killinger, once fully recovered from a pre-season injury, was definitely the star of the team.

A Penn State alumnus who was close to the great back provides this personal insight:

"The big thing in Killinger's career was his determination to win an all-America berth. As a kid in Harrisburg High School, he was too small for the team and didn't make it. Neither did he make the freshman team. In 1918 Coach Hugo Bezdek came to Penn State and found not a single veteran football player in college because of the war. He called for candidates, and Killinger was among the youngsters who reported.

"In 1920 the stars were gone to some extent, and Killinger was turned into a quarterback, a new position for him. He played regularly that season with only moderate success. Toward the close he slumped, and student opinion began to pick his successor for 1921. But Bezdek still remained with the youngster. When 1921 rolled around, Killinger was a regular but was injured before the season opened. He missed the first game, but in the second he found himself.

"One afternoon in practice he tore up and down the field like a whirlwind, drove the team like a Napoleon, and in general brought down Bezdek's commendation. 'If you play like that, Killie, I'll guarantee you an all-America berth,' said Bezdek. And he did.

"In New York, he turned what appeared to be a Georgia Tech victory into a rout. The Southerners went through Penn State for a touchdown right in the first quarter and appeared to have the situation well in hand. However, on the kickoff Killinger caught the ball on his 15-yard line and dashed 85 yards through the entire team for a touchdown that tied the score. Not a single Tech man touched him on that run according to those on the sidelines.

"Bezdek has classed this run as the greatest play that he has ever seen—for several reasons. First, it was not just an accident, it was a rehearsed play that actually worked from kickoff formation. Second, it was perfectly carried out by Killinger and the Penn State interference. Third, it changed the whole complexion of the contest, took the starch out of the Tech team, and from its moral effect enabled Penn State to score subsequently three more touchdowns."

Arthur Robinson, a writer for the *New York American,* was duly impressed with Killinger's performance, as were the fans at the Polo Grounds that day. This is what he said:

"Out of the Nittany Mountains of Pennsylvania a young man who hopped and skipped and wriggled like a frog came to the Polo Grounds and throughout a wonderful Autumnal afternoon, some 30,000 fans had his name in their hearts and throats.

" 'There he goes again!' they roared. 'Killinger—again.' And in and out of a golden maze of yellow-jerseyed southern giants the man who hopped and skipped and wriggled like a frog wove a phantom wreath as the members of Georgia Tech's football team lunged desperately and vainly at his wraith-like form. 'Killinger again!'

"It seemed that it was Killinger always. And largely because of his spectacular and elusive running in an open field, Penn State beat Georgia Tech, the Golden Tornado of the South, 28 to 7."

Killinger's name, along with Joe Lightner and Harry Wilson, also was on the lips of those who saw the famous Harvard game, cited in football anthologies as one of the most exciting in college history. "It will always remain in the minds of those who saw it as one of the greatest of football contests," said Bob Harron, a top Boston football writer.

Harvard football had been revitalized by returning servicemen, and the Crimson rivaled Penn State for national honors in this era. The two, certainly, were among the best in the East.

Penn State students gave their football heroes a royal sendoff to Cambridge. "The entire student body gathered at the old Track House (the team's living quarters) to wish the Lions bon voyage," a newspaper reported. "After the signal drills, the players all visited the infirmary to say goodbye to George Snell because their fullback would miss the game because of a throat infection."

When they arrived at Cambridge, the Penn State players were greeted by this story in the *Boston Globe:* "There is no sign of over-confidence among the Blue and White players, and they realize they are facing their hardest test of the season against the Crimson."

The newspaper's buildup to the season's biggest game in the East also pointed to "huge interest in Boston."

"State College, too, is greatly wrought up over the contest," the story added.

Penn State's own newspaper approached the key game cautiously. "Chances are not exceptionally large," said the *Collegian*. "With Captain Snell out, the team is not in the best of shape."

That looked like a fair assessment from the way the game started out before a vociferous audience of 30,000. Harvard drove 48 yards for a quick touchdown and then went in for another after a bad punt by Penn State left the ball on the Nittany Lions' 25-yard line. It was 14-0 Harvard early in the first quarter, and the unruly crowd screamed for more touchdowns.

To make matters worse an unlikely string of injuries hit the Nittany Lions' backfield. Runners kept hurting their legs, and Bezdek was forced at one point to use a third-string back, A. H. Knabb. He fumbled on his first carry and never was allowed to touch the ball again.

Harry Wilson (arrow) on a 56-yard run against Harvard. Penn State's 21-21 tie with the Crimson in 1921 was a memorable game.

*A typical Forbes Field "mud
bowl." This one in 1921 ended in a
scoreless tie between Penn State
and Pitt.*

Glenn Killinger (arrow) goes up the middle against Georgia Tech. The 1921 game was one of the biggest for the star runner, and Penn State won, 28-7.

However, Killinger artfully manuevered Penn State through Harvard in the second quarter and sent Joe Lightner over for a touchdown from close in. The first half ended with Harvard holding a 14-7 advantage.

When starting left halfback Pete Redinger was hurt, Bezdek wondered aloud whether the gods had conspired against him. "Wilson, warm up!" the leader screamed to Harry Wilson, who was sitting with the other reserves in a bleacher section. Wilson warmed up on the sidelines and then lit a fire under the Nittany Lions on the field. On his first run from scrimmage he took a handoff from Killinger and ran 56 yards to the Harvard four, easily the most spectacular play of the game. Killinger handed the ball to Lightner, and the right halfback carried it over for the tying score.

Killinger kept the Penn State momentum flowing, leading the team to the Harvard 19 as the third period ended. Killinger ran

Glenn Killinger (second from left, back row) and Harry Wilson (far right, back row) were the running stars of Hugo Bezdek's well-traveled 1921 team.

through Harvard for 10 yards, and Lightner plunged for 5 before scoring his third touchdown of the day to give the visitors a 21-14 margin.

There were seven minutes remaining, and darkness was settling on Harvard Stadium, when Crimson quarterback Charlie Buell threw a 15-yard touchdown pass. The Harvard star then kicked the extra point and the game was thrown into a 21-21 tie.

The contest, which still had plenty of excitement left, was now being played in semi-darkness because of a rule at Harvard that "no football game can start at the stadium earlier than three o'clock before November 1st."

"The match, with its fifteen-minute quarters, carried the contest into darkness," reported the Penn State *Alumni News.* "It was darkness and time the Penn State eleven were fighting against in the last few minutes of play."

Killinger completed two passes to Lightner, Wilson added 10 yards to the Harvard 43, and Killinger raced 25 more to the 18-yard line. Penn State was able to gain only 4 yards in two plays, and then Lightner was thrown for a 10-yard loss. Killinger's pass to Lightner was grounded just as the game ended.

The game inspired a long and melodramatic lead by a sports writer covering the event for a Philadelphia newspaper:

"In an October gloaming, whose gathering gloom covered the vast stadium with a fleecy veil of dusk, Harvard, her Crimson back plastered squarely against the wall and trembling on the threshold· of her first defeat in five years, awakened and quickened into a fury like a tigress robbed of her cubs today, drove back Penn State's magnificent warriors with a savage attack and scored a touchdown that evened a 21 to 21 contest in a game as spectacular as any gridiron has known in the past 20 years."

In short, it was a whale of a game.

Time Out: Harry Wilson

"Dear Ken:

"You asked me to tell you if there were any instances I recall of my early playing days. Before the Harvard game of 1921, they had gone to a great deal of pains to convince us that the Harvard boys would steal the ball from you at every opportunity. Shortly after getting in the game, I managed to get loose for about 60 yards to about Harvard's five-yard line, where it seemed like the whole Harvard team fell on me at once. Remembering the warnings, I shut my eyes and clung onto the ball with both arms. Sure enough, there seemed to be a dozen hands tugging at it, and it felt like they were never going to stop. Finally, I heard Glenn Killinger's voice saying, 'Come on, Harry, give the referee the ball.'

"On another occasion in the same game, someone kicked out one of my front teeth. I tried to call time out, but someone said, 'What for? We can't stop for a little thing like that!' So we didn't. Later that night at the railroad station in Boston, the referee came up to me and said: 'Here, Wilson, here is that tooth you were looking for this afternoon.'

"If I had to write about our times, one of the men I would like to see honored is Dutch Herman, who coached varsity basketball and freshman football and scouted opponents for the varsity. He was a good coach and quite a character.

"I remember playing in a basketball game one night, and we were doing so poorly that Dutch left the bench, went up to the stands, and started booing us from the bleachers. If things were

109

"Lighthorse" Harry Wilson, Penn State running star of the 1920s: "It took courage to play football."

going wrong on the football field, he would relieve his feelings by yelling, spitting, and tearing his hat from front to rear on his head—the hat he saved especially for the games, knowing how worked up he might get. Nevertheless, he was a dignified professor of history and a good coach and was respected and liked by all the players.

"I remember on one occasion I was walking down across campus sneaking a few puffs on a cigarette when I ran into Dutch. I quickly stuck my hand and cigarette into my coat pocket! Well, he stopped and talked and talked until the lining of my pocket was well burned out, and while he never said anything about the cigarette I am sure he knew exactly what he was doing as well as what I had been doing.

"If you can send this letter back when you're through with it, I'd appreciate it. If it gets lost in the shuffle, don't worry. It is just that I'll never write it again and would like to have it.

"Sincerely,

"Harry Wilson."

His once-rich blond hair now is a thinning silver, and 200 pounds are packed on a 5-foot-8 frame. That is 30 pounds over his playing weight of the 1920s, when he was an all-America halfback for Penn State.

Away from the crowd's hurrahs, Harry "Lighthorse" Wilson lives a blissful life of retirement in New Smyrna Beach, Florida, with his wife, Patricia. He fishes, goes boating and swimming, and is pretty good at shuffleboard. When he needs excitement, he can drive to the "big city"—Daytona Beach—about 10 miles down the road.

Of course, he is always ready to talk football. That is his favorite pastime.

"The players today are bigger and faster, but not any smarter than in my day," says Wilson. "And they don't have any more heart or guts than we did, either.

"It took courage to play football in the 1920s in those uniforms we had. There wasn't much protection, I'll tell you. I wish I could show you the headgear I wore. It was a little padded thing that sat on top of my head with a chin strap."

No one knows more about courage than Wilson. He had two football careers—one with Penn State and the other with Army—and then served in a bomber squadron in the Pacific

111

during the Second World War when he won the Distinguished Flying Cross.

It took courage, also, to play under Hugo Bezdek, Wilson recalls.

"He was a tough man," Wilson says of his football coach at Penn State in 1921. "I think he owed his success to keeping people in condition and teaching fundamentals. Bezdek's idea was to get you in shape—and I don't think I was in any harder or better shape in my life than under Bezdek."

Wilson, who went to two Pennsylvania prep schools and graduated from Sharon High in 1920, decided to go to Penn State because his brother, Lloyd, was an alumnus. Wilson made several all-America teams later in his career, but as a sophomore could not make Penn State's first team, he remembered.

"I was a substitute who just went along for the ride whenever we had road games," says Wilson. "The first time I got into a game, in fact, was up at Harvard, halfway through the 1921 season. They had scored twice real quick, and Bezdek didn't look too happy about it. We subs were sitting in open bleachers at the time, and Bezdek turned to me and growled: 'Wilson, warm up.' I got a little nervous. I got up and ran around and around until I got pooped. I was so tired that I had to sit down and rest. And just as I sat down, Bezdek screamed: 'Where's Wilson?' "

"Lighthorse" Harry showed Bezdek where he was immediately, carrying the ball for big yardage despite his tired condition.

"I managed to run 60 yards or so shortly after I got in—I don't know how," Wilson says. "Up to that point it was the longest run ever at Harvard Stadium. Funny thing, though, Centre College came in to play the Crimson the very next week and their great back, Bo McMillan, ran twice as far as I did.

"We tied a fine Harvard team at 21-21, but I always said afterwards that we softened them up for Centre and McMillan, because they beat Harvard by a point the week after. After our game, Harvard had so many injuries they almost had to use their cheerleaders against Centre.

"I played again that year, but I wasn't a regular. Gosh, how could I be with people like Glenn Killinger on the team? As a leader and a halfback, he was the best I ever played with."

112

Killinger, an all-America that season, impressed Wilson with his poise.

"He never let mistakes bother him," Wilson recalls. "In the 1921 Georgia Tech game, they kicked off and the ball went to Killinger. He fumbled and they recovered on the 20-yard line and went in for a touchdown. The next time they kicked off, they sent the ball Killinger's way. This time he grabbed it and ran it back for a touchdown. They were never the same again. We beat 'em good."

The 1923 Rose Bowl was another highlight for Wilson, even though Penn State lost. "I still think we were better than Southern California," says Wilson, recalling the 14-3 defeat in Pasadena, California, in the 1922-23 season.

Wilson blames the weather for the Nittany Lions' lackluster showing.

"It was awfully warm out there, and we weren't used to it," Wilson explains. "After practicing in that California heat for a while, I found that I couldn't stand up. All of us were pretty pooped. I remember we practiced in a foot of snow in the East and then took a train out to California for the bowl game. We left a week early so we could get acclimated to the weather, but it didn't do any good."

A young man's first trip to California was a Rose garden.

"Gee, it was terrific," says Wilson. "I really enjoyed it. We had a special coach on the train and were treated like kings."

Events leading up to the game included a visit with movie stars and a look at the glamorous Parade of Roses.

"We got to meet Douglas Fairbanks, Sr., and Mary Pickford," says Wilson. "You know, he was a nut for keeping in shape. He showed us his parallel bars and rings, where he'd condition himself. Miss Pickford wasn't as receptive. She just said hello."

Wilson became an overnight actor, he recalls.

"There was this movie star—Arthur Rankin," says Wilson. "He asked all of us football players if we wanted to be in a movie of his. Our job was to play the cheering crowd at a fight scene. Of course we didn't get paid for it. He just wanted to know if we wanted to have some fun. Well, we did it—but you know, I never did see that picture!"

There were other things on Wilson's mind—most importantly, Southern Cal. Not only was the Trojan team difficult for the

Nittany Lions, but Wilson remembers that Penn State players had trouble getting to the game.

"Some of the Rose Bowl people took us down to see the Parade of Roses on the day of the game, and it was so jammed at the parade that we had a hard time getting out when we had to leave," Wilson recalls. "We had to drive our cars on the sidewalks.

"By the time we got back to our quarters and went to the stadium, we were late. Boy, was the Southern Cal coach mad about it! He thought that we were late on purpose. Well, we finally played—but we didn't play well. I remember that our quarterback, Mike Palm, played a good game, and Dick Shuster kicked a field goal—but no one else did much of anything."

Bezdek tried to inspire the Nittany Lions at halftime, but to no avail.

"He tried to fire you up," says Wilson, "Play on your emotions. He wasn't a tear-jerker in the Knute Rockne style, though. However, not even Rockne could help us that day."

From the disappointing Rose Bowl loss, Harry the Light Horse went on to better things. His all-America selection on the 500 Coaches team in 1923 brought him joy.

"I thought it was the greatest honor that I could receive," says Wilson, who later was to receive many more laurels in a much-honored career at West Point and in the Army Air Force.

Penn State in Wilson's era had a spotty schedule, playing some easy teams along with the powerhouses. Wilson explains why.

"People always used to needle us that we didn't play the kind of schedule that Notre Dame played," says Wilson. "But Bezdek used to schedule those soft teams as a warmup for the stronger ones. He'd give us only four plays or so to polish, and we'd run them over and over again at the weak clubs. The opposition knew what was coming time after time, but couldn't do much about it. We just wore them down eventually."

The big rivalry of the day, of course, was Pitt. That was usually at the end, or near the end, of the season.

"Pitt always had good teams and excellent coaching, you know, and did a pretty good job of scouting you," says Wilson. "Seemed they always had a pretty good defense. (In Wilson's three years, Penn State scored a total of 3 points against the

114

Harry Wilson (No. 15) goes up the middle for Penn State in the famous 21-21 tie with Harvard in 1921.

Panthers—that for a team that scored 592 points altogether).

"Some of the coaches got together to try to stop Bezdek, exchanging information about us. Navy would ask Pitt or Pitt would ask Navy."

Specifically, Pitt wanted to know how to contain Wilson. He had scored three touchdowns, one on a 95-yard kickoff return, against the Midshipmen as the Nittany Lions won 21-3 in 1923.

"That Navy game was really a thrill for me because I had never run a kick back for a touchdown," recalls Wilson. "It was even more exciting because I scored another touchdown on a 40 or 50-yard run from scrimmage right after the first one. I scored two TDs in less than a minute, and I was feeling pretty darned good about it, I'll tell you!"

Wilson left Penn State after the 1923-24 season and went to West Point at a time when the Military Academy allowed him to continue his college football career.

"Of course you can't do it now," Wilson explains, "but in those years they let me play football at West Point even though I had finished a full career with Penn State. I think that West Point was the only school where I could do that. I know that Navy wouldn't let you do it."

He made several all-America teams while at Army, but not only in football. He also was a basketball and lacrosse all-America.

After graduation Wilson spent 28 years in the service until retirement as an Air Force colonel on August 31, 1956. In that period he served in the Second World War and commanded a B-25 bombing group in the Pacific. He flew 48 missions and won the Air Medal with six oak-leaf clusters and the Distinguished Flying Cross.

In his 70th year he was voted into the Football Hall of Fame.

Time has not blurred the memory, though. He still recalls a Philadelphia sports writer who gave him the nickname, "Light Horse."

"I really can't tell you why, either," says Wilson with a grin. "I know that it wasn't because my name was Harry."

Time Out: Joe Bedenk

Joe Bedenk sometimes wakes up in the middle of the night and has a 50-year-old daydream.

"There was one game in the Polo Grounds against Syracuse that I'll always remember," he says. "We punted downfield and I knocked over my defensive man and headed straight down the middle.

"Our ends would squeeze the receiving ball carrier toward the center of the field for me. I remember, like it was yesterday, the Syracuse back on this particular play was a boy named Roy Simmons.

"Well, I hit him real hard, just as he fumbled. I rolled on the ball and thought I did a great job. I fell on the ball on the four-yard line and set up a great scoring opportunity for us. But we didn't get a touchdown on that particular series and wound up with a scoreless tie against Syracuse."

Moments of glory stay with a 75-year-old man, especially one who did not have a glamorous position with the Penn State football team. In the 1920s Bedenk was in the trenches as a guard, running interference for heroes like Glenn Killinger and Harry "Lighthorse" Wilson.

"We were running guards in those days," says Bedenk. "I used to open holes for Killinger and Wilson. They were probably the best runners I ever teamed with. Not that they were that fast, you understand. I was just as fast. But they had great change of pace. They could go fast and slow in almost one step, stop on a dime. Killinger was more of a daredevil type than

Rugged Joe Bedenk led the interference for Penn State's great runners of the 1920s.

Wilson. He always pulled the unexpected. He was a real opportunist on a football field."

Bedenk's contributions, although not considered magical in the general public's eye, received due recognition in his senior year, 1923, when he was awarded all-America honors on the Walter Camp team. After graduation he stayed in sports as a coach in both football and baseball before retirement in 1962.

While at Penn State in varied capacities, he had the opportunity to play for Hugo Bezdek and work with Bob Higgins, two coaches who encompass three decades of Nittany Lion football history from 1918 to 1948.

They were on opposite ends of the personality spectrum, Bedenk recalled.

"Bezdek was an iron-hand type, and he didn't have too many friends," says Bedenk. "You could never get close to him. Higgins, on the other hand, was an awfully nice fellow who had a nice personality and was loved by all of his players."

Bedenk, born in Williamsport, Pennsylvania, had gone to a prep school in Mansfield before a year's service in the Army in 1918. He was lured to Penn State in the fall of 1919 by the prospect of playing baseball for Bezdek, the former Pittsburgh Pirate manager who had left the major leagues for college life. Bedenk's muscled 192-pound frame was also ideal for football, and he decided to go out for the varsity in 1920 but broke a collarbone and had to wait until next year.

In 1921 he made the team and was almost sorry he did.

"Those scrimmages under Bezdek were brutal," says Bedenk, recalling something called "Bloody Tuesday" when the players would scrimmage "until we were almost dead."

"Bezdek's philosophy was the harder you work, the more success you have on Saturday."

Bezdek had something there, because Penn State compiled an unbeaten streak of 30 games from midway through the 1919 season to the middle of 1922. That gaudy record earned them a Rose Bowl bid in the 1922-23 season.

However, the club that played Southern Cal in the prestigious post-season affair on January 1, 1923, was not truly representative of the undefeated string. The Nittany Lions had lost three of their last four games of the year.

"We were selected by the Rose Bowl committee in early

November, on the strength of that undefeated streak, but a lot of our best players had left in the 1922 season," Bedenk remembers. "They had gotten dissatisfied with Bezdek, and when Dick Harlow left to go to Colgate he took several good players with him. The players loved Harlow."

Harlow, a former coach, was a scout under Bezdek and was given credit for a lot of the Penn State success during that undefeated period.

The Nittany Lions lost to Southern Cal 14-3 on New Year's Day, and it was even more frustrating for Bedenk. He could not play because of injury.

"We scrimmaged the first day we got to California, and I broke three ribs," says Bedenk. "Naturally I couldn't play. I couldn't even get up."

The sweet-and-sour memories of the Rose Bowl trip still linger.

"It took us three days and nights to get out there on a train and, every night we stopped, Bezdek had us running up and down the train platform for conditioning," says Bedenk.

Once in California, Bedenk recalled a whirlwind week of red-carpet treatment.

"We practiced every afternoon, but every morning they took us around to visit the movie studios and meet the stars. We met Douglas Fairbanks, Sr., and his wife, Mary Pickford, and Mr. Fairbanks entertained us at his studio. I also remember seeing Viola Dana—she was quite a star of the day—I can't remember all the names, but there were plenty."

In 1923 Bedenk became an all-America on the strength of strong performances such as the one in the Navy game, when he opened touchdown paths for Wilson.

"Probably my greatest game as a senior was when we beat Navy 21-3 and Wilson scored three touchdowns," says Bedenk, who was responsible for knocking down a lot of enemy defenders that day. "They had 19 first downs and we only had 4—and we beat them, nevertheless. It was amazing!"

Associated with great players in school, Bedenk was later fortunate to couple with a towering football figure afterwards —John Heisman.

"My first job was as a line coach when Heisman was head coach at Rice," says Bedenk, remembering his association with

120

the man whose name marks college football's most coveted trophy. "I got very well acquainted with him when we worked together in 1924, 1925, and 1926. It's a shame, people don't know enough about him. He was quite a man."

Bedenk spent a few years as line coach in football and head coach in baseball at the University of Florida before returning to Penn State to hook up with Higgins. Along with his football job as Penn State line coach from 1931 to 1948, Bedenk simultaneously was the Nittany Lions' baseball coach. When Higgins departed, Bedenk spent a lame-duck term as Penn State's head football coach in 1949, compiling a 5-4 record, and then turned to baseball until his retirement.

"I tell you, Higgins was a good coach but he didn't have too much material," says Bedenk. "We didn't have scholarships in those days like some of the other schools. Right after I came back here and Bezdek went out, they eliminated scholarships. We had to get the kids jobs, but that was the only thing we could do for them."

The Higgins-Bedenk era started slowly with only one winning season in eight. But it ended with a flourish with no losing seasons starting from 1939. The highlight was an undefeated year in 1947 ("when we had a very good team with a lot of returning GIs from the Second World War"). Penn State went to the Cotton Bowl and tied SMU 13-13.

"Bob and I had a very nice relationship in those years, win or lose," says Bedenk. "We were very close. And Bob was the sort of a guy who cared about people. Everyone loved him."

Although some of the seasons were dark for Penn State, they had some bright individual players during Bedenk's coaching era.

"We had a lot of good ones, all right," says Bedenk, naming Steve Suhey, Leo Nobel, Fran Rogel, Elwood Petchel, and Sam Tamburo among them.

Most of the aforementioned players were linemen, of course. Bedenk is partial to that kind of animal.

Cozy in the living room of his State College, Pennsylvania, home, his relaxed conversation intermittently drifted back to the playing part of his career.

"I was always nervous," he recalls. "I was nervous in the first game and nervous in the last one."

It did not show on a football field, though. He was characterized as a tough cookie.

"They said I had two personalities, a sort of Jekyll-and-Hyde, you know," says Bedenk. "I was a nice person off the field, I'm told, but a son-of-a-gun when I played football."

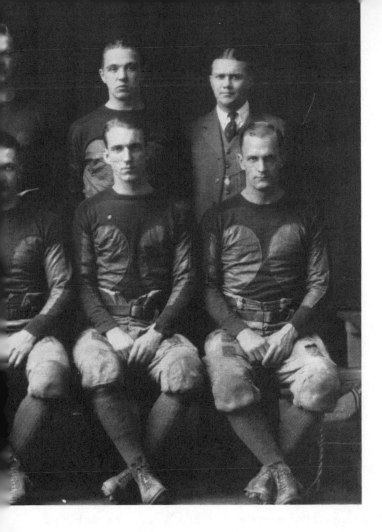

Penn State's 1922 Team Went To Rose Bowl
Front row, left to right: Harry Wilson, Ross "Squeek" Hufford, Jay "Tiny" McMahon, H. N. "Newsh" Bentz, Joe Bedenk, J. C. "Hap" Frank, and Myron Palm. Back row: Coach Hugo Bezdek, L. Harold Logue, William Hamilton, Ted Artelt, Fred Flock, Barney Wentz, and Manager Parsons.

Rose Bowl Day

"Beautiful" Pasadena did not look so beautiful to Penn State's football players on Rose Bowl Day, January 1, 1923. They had been squeezed in traffic, slandered by the opposing coach, and then soundly beaten 14-3 in the first official game played in the sparkling new Pasadena stadium.

In fact, football authorities questioned their presence there in the first place. Walter Camp, who selected all-America teams in those days, wondered in a newspaper article whether the Nittany Lions were worthy of the Rose Bowl honor after some losses during the 1922 season.

"Penn State has been given an invitation to visit Pasadena at the time of the Carnival of Roses and meet a Western team, but how the Western team will feel about the invitation after the defeat of Hugo Bezdek's warriors by the Navy is a question," wrote Camp. "It is a tradition that an unbeaten team is the only one sure of a welcome amidst the orange groves during the period of carnival."

Not only was Penn State beaten by the Navy that year, but the Nittany Lions also lost games to Penn and Pitt and were tied by Syracuse. However, invitations were extended in early November, and the Rose Bowl selection committee obviously admired Penn State's 30-game unbeaten streak at the time. The 14-0 loss to Navy in Washington, D.C., on November 3 broke the string but did not turn off the Rose Bowl committee.

Of course while making their selection, Rose Bowl committee members possibly were unaware that this was a Penn

State team shorn of some rich talent. Several of the players who helped make the 1921 club so strong had left after the season to follow their beloved Dick Harlow to Colgate when he was given the coach's job there.

Penn State detractors pointed out that the 30-game undefeated streak was helped by a soft schedule at the beginning of the 1922 season. St. Bonaventure, William and Mary, Gettysburg, Lebanon Valley, and Middlebury were the first five victims of the year before a scoreless tie with powerful Syracuse. The Nittany Lions, however, were loved at home despite questions raised by outsiders, and the *Alumni News* had this to say about Penn State's first bowl bid:

"The selection of Penn State comes as a direct tribute to the great record compiled in the past four years under the coaching of Hugo Bezdek, wizard mentor of the Blue and White aggregation, and is made regardless of victory or defeat during the present season. Penn State's record of the past three seasons ranks the Nittany Lion as the king of the eastern football machines."

The "king" did not roar too loudly the rest of the 1922 season, however. Following the loss to Navy, Penn State defeated Carnegie Tech 10-0 but lost to Penn 7-6 and to Pitt 14-0.

After a brief rest following the season-ending loss to Pitt on November 30, Bezdek took a squadron of over 30 people with him on the train to Pasadena.

It took three days and nights and was a nice trip, reported a Pennsylvania newspaper: "According to word that reached State College this morning (Dec. 23) from Williams, Ariz., the Penn State football players are standing the long trip to the coast in fine fashion and they are glad of the arrangements whereby they are to spend a day in sight-seeing up the Grand Canyon. The trip will then be continued tonight, reaching Pasadena shortly after noon tomorrow."

Penn State's first strenuous workout under the intense Pasadena sun cost the Nittany Lions one of their best players, guard Joe Bedenk. He broke three ribs during a particularly vicious scrimmage and had to miss the game. During that December 26 practice, Bezdek himself got into the action and permitted his men to charge and block him savagely.

After a week of such brutal training, the big odds had van-

The 1922 team and the famous Nittany Lion. The boys went to the Rose Bowl that season; the lion stayed home.

ished against the eastern intruders. In fact, some observers even predicted a victory for a team that previously was given no chance against Southern Cal. Reported a newspaper:

"Since the Nittany Lions have been working out here, the impression that was so general before their arrival—that the easterners were merely a setup for the coast team—has disappeared almost completely. Now, the Bezdek machine is looked upon as a more powerful outfit, likely to more than hold its own against Southern California."

The same newspaper also reported that Southern Cal Coach Elmer (Gloomy Gus) Henderson was so agitated by reports of the savage Penn State workouts that he took a plane trip to Palo Alto to get advice from Pop Warner, whose Pitt team was playing Stanford. Henderson's hopes of beating Penn State apparently were based on a good passing attack and adept punt returning. A running attack against the Nittany Lions' terrific line

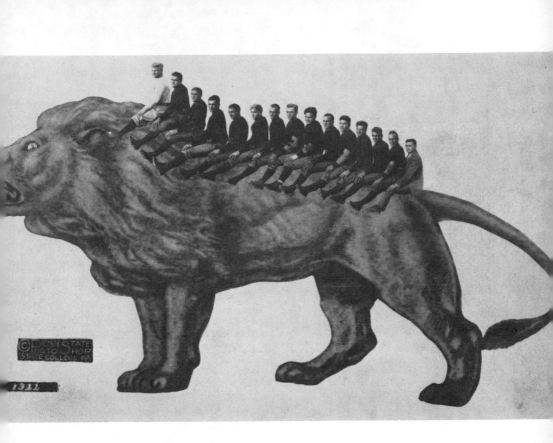

was considered useless.

"The Nittany Lions from the fastnesses of the Alleghenies and the Trojan horde from Los Angeles go to grips on an even-money proposition," said the *Los Angeles Times* on the day of the game. The Penn State starting lineup was given as follows: Hap Frank and Ted Artelt at the ends: Tiny McMahon and Dick Johnson at the tackles; Jules Prevost and Tom Ellwood at guards; William Hamilton at center; Mike Palm at quarterback; halfbacks Harry Wilson and John Patton and fullback Barney Wentz.

What the *Times* did not know was that these players would be late showing up for the game, leaving 43,000 fans fidgeting nervously at the newly-opened playground. The Penn State aggregation had attended the Parade of Roses and got locked into a mammoth traffic jam. By the time Bezdek and his boys arrived at the Rose Bowl, the Southern California coach was boiling mad. Henderson challenged Bezdek at midfield, in full

Penn State opened the 1922 season with a 54-0 "laugher" over St. Bonaventure.

The forward pass—a rarity of the times—was used in the 1922 game with William & Mary. Penn State won, 27-7.

view of the crowd, and the pair almost came to blows. Henderson charged that Bezdek purposely delayed the start of the contest because he wanted the hot day to cool off a bit for his players. They played football, but not until Bezdek had gotten in a few choice remarks of his own.

The first game played at the present Pasadena site before the largest gathering to see a football match until that point was "replete with thrills," according to the *Pasadena Evening Post.*

Palm's 20-yard field goal in the first quarter gave Penn State a 3-0 lead, but it was all Southern California after that. The Trojans were able to move through Penn State's highly-touted line —and it did not matter how, straight smashes or end runs. Their first touchdown was made near the end of the second quarter when long end runs put the ball on Penn State's one-yard line. Fullback Don Campbell carried the ball over for a 7-3 Southern Cal lead.

"Blaring bands, full-throated cheers from the rooting sections, and waving banners gave a wealth of color and sound to the scene between halves," said the Pasadena newspaper.

A 14-0 loss to Navy at Washington, D.C., in 1922 broke Penn State's 30-game unbeaten string, but the Nittany Lions still went to the Rose Bowl that season.

Campbell and halfback "Ironsides" Baker did the leg work for Southern Cal in the third period. After Penn State failed to move the ball on the first series of downs, the Nittany Lions had to punt. Baker gobbled up 22 yards with a run to the Penn State 35. Baker made 12 yards on the next play, a run through center, and then advanced 4 yards over right guard. Baker and Campbell combined to move the ball to Penn State's 1-yard line, and Baker finally carried it over for Southern Cal's second touchdown.

Southern Cal had the ball in the shadow of the Penn State goal almost the entire last quarter, and it took a strong defensive effort by the Nittany Lions to hold off more touchdowns. At the end, as shadows lengthened over the field and players were indistinct in the early-evening dusk, Penn State was in possession of the ball on its own 30-yard line.

The Nittany Lions had no alibi, said Bezdek, they were

beaten by a better team. "Southern California was too fast for us, they played better football. They said the climate was a big factor in our downfall. I don't think it had anything to do with the outcome of the game. Their line was stronger and faster than ours, and their backfield men were exceedingly fast."

The Trojans took advantage of a Penn State line weakened by the loss of Bedenk and Dick Shuster, another top player. Shuster had been declared ineligible earlier in the year because of a violation of the one-year residence rule.

"We had a weakness, and I know it," said Bezdek. "The coast team aimed its first play at our weak spot and kept aiming their thrusts there throughout the game. And we were unable to hold them."

The Arch Rivals

A Penn State-Penn game always had an aura of intensity and attracted people from faraway places. A crowd of 56,000 showed up at Franklin Field for the 1923 meeting, but they were not all from Philadelphia. The Nittany Lions had their camp followers, students who traveled by any means—from hitch-hiking to bicycling. Some fortunates had cars and jammed a load of friends in for the 200-mile trip from State College to Philadelphia.

"Football fandom will witness a game of football as she should be played," predicted an observer.

Penn State rooters were just wild about Harry after Harry Wilson scored touchdowns on runs of 24 and 46 yards and another on a 51-yard pass play.

"Too much Wilson is the only way to say it—unless one cares to say it with flowers," was the way a clever sports writer said it. "Penn State was the winner; Penn the loser, and the bitter statistics 21 to 0."

After the Penn game, Penn State played its traditional Thanksgiving Day battle with the Pitt Panthers. A crowd of 33,000, largest ever to see a football game in Pittsburgh at that time, watched a predictable result—a Penn State loss. The Nittany Lions simply had an awful time with Pitt in those years. In fact, from 1913 through 1938 the teams played 23 times, and Penn State only won one game. There were two ties in that stretch. The series became so lopsided that there was an outcry from Penn State in the 1920s to move the game to a neutral site, Franklin Field in Philadelphia. Penn State always played at Pittsburgh, giving the Panthers the home field advantage each year. Nothing was done about the protest, however,

The Nittany Lions lost with such regularity to Pitt that they were finally taken off the holiday date because of dwindling interest in the late 1920s and early 1930s. The series was even discontinued for three years, 1932 through 1934.

Hugo Bezdek's bad luck in the Pitt series was complicated by a personal feud with Pop Warner, the Panther coach. The fact that Bezdek could only beat Pitt once in his tenure was one of the great frustrations of his Penn State coaching career.

A typical feud shaped up in the 1923 game, which incidentally was Warner's last with Pittsburgh. He was leaving for Stanford the following season and hoped for a going-away present by beating his longtime adversaries. Warner instigated a psychological war before the game started by protesting Penn State's use of leather pads on the sleeves and chests. The pads were sewn there for protection, but Warner objected to the fact that they were deceptive because they gave the appearance of footballs tucked under the arm. There is no record that the objection was sustained. Warner, it was said, also liked to water down the field to slow Penn State runners. It was not needed on this particular day, however, since it rained all day. The Nittany Lions lost 20-3.

The Lions could lose some tough ones in those years, but they showed sportsmanship in the meantime. In a 1927 game with Bucknell, a recently-broken ankle kept Bucknell fullback Walter Diehl out of the starting lineup. Even so, the Bisons managed to take a 7-0 lead at the half. In the second half Penn State came back to tie the score, and it was at this point that Diehl decided his services were needed.

"Captain Diehl was sent in to encourage the team," said a newspaper story by the Associated Press. "With the big fullback at his post, Bucknell appeared 25 percent stronger."

The Penn State players, of course, realized that they could cripple the Bucknell star simply by hitting his injured ankle. But when Diehl was dropped for the first time, the Penn State tackler said: "Don't worry, Wally, we'll be careful of your bad ankle."

And each time that Diehl was tackled in that game, Penn State players actually went out of their way to avoid hurting his ankle. Inspired by the presence of their star, the Bisons went on to beat the Nittany Lions and break a string of Penn State victories that started in 1899.

A spokesman for Bucknell was especially impressed with the way Penn State players handled themselves that day. "Whether or not Penn State's fine sportsmanship cost them a victory is hard to say. But if it did, the loss was not commensurable with the gift it made to American football," he said.

Perhaps in payment for their sportsmanship, fate let Penn State bounce back from Bucknell and beat Syracuse for the first time. The 9-6 victory at Syracuse was fashioned on Johnny Roepke's dramatic field goal in the final three minutes. Earlier, Cy Lungren had scored a touchdown for Penn State to even the score at 6-6. The Orangemen were among the few remaining undefeated teams in the East before losing to the Nittany Lions. Penn State-Syracuse games were always heady defensive struggles at the start, years before they met to settle national titles. It took 11 years before one team could score two touchdowns in a game and 16 years before both teams could score twice. And it took a war before either team could make 40 points in a game.

Reopke, incidentally, was one of the brightest stars of the late 1920s, a period of decline in Penn State football power. This dashing runner turned in some explosive scoring performances—including a 28-point performance against Gettysburg and 27 against Lafayette in the 1927 season. Both were Penn State victories. Roepke was known as the "Masked Marvel" because he wore a headgear with a leather face guard. Roepke's departure after 1927 left Penn State with little scoring punch. Low scores were common in Penn State games—such as the "baseball" victories of 6-3 and 6-4 over Lafayette and Syracuse in 1929.

Cooper French took a deliberate safety in the closing minutes to help Penn State win the Syracuse game. The ball was deep in Penn State territory with the Nittany Lions holding a tenuous 6-2 lead and time running out. French stepped back in his end zone as if to kick, but when he got the ball he touched it down

135

and gave Syracuse an automatic two points. The strategy worked, for Penn State then was able to kick from its own 20-yard line and booted the ball out of danger. Syracuse had the ball at midfield, but failed to move it with desperation passes.

The Lafayette game, played on Alumni Homecoming Day at State College, was appropriately won by Penn State—but not until after time had run out! The Nittany Lions had scored a touchdown earlier, but it was called back because of a penalty. Another time a Penn State pass play had provided an excellent opportunity to score, but the Nittany Lions were not able to

Penn State and Syracuse battle through one of their typical low-scoring games. This one ended in a scoreless tie in 1922.

get the final yards.

So, with Lafayette winning 3-0 and one second remaining, the Maroons got set to punt. The kick was in the air when the final whistle blew. French, Penn State's safety, caught the ball on his 40-yard line but was surrounded by three Lafayette players. He tossed a lateral pass to Frank Diedrich, who ran 60 yards for the winning touchdown.

"The play left some 15,000 persons dumbfounded," reported a newspaper. "Efforts to describe it were kept up for several days. The near-riot which ensued found both of the men carried off the field on the shoulders of admiring students. Half-crazed alumni could talk of nothing else during their stay at the Homecoming celebration."

The story of a lost coat testified to the wild celebration that followed the spectacular victory at Beaver Field. A classified advertisement later appeared in Penn State's student newspaper, the *Collegian*.

The advertisement, signed by varsity cheerleader Izzy Heicklen, read: "LOST—Cheerleader's jacket at game Saturday. Return to Athletic Association Office."

Bulletin No. 23

It was called simply "Bulletin No. 23" but had widespread impact on college football in America. It was warmly received by some, coolly evaded by others, and hotly denied by still more. At Penn State the revolutionary Carnegie Report of October 23, 1929, had deep meaning.

After almost four years of investigation, the Carnegie Foundation for the Advancement of Teaching issued a 383-page report from New York condemning the popular practice of subsidizing athletes.

The report, based on visits to 130 schools in America and Canada, focused principally on what the investigators called "the deepest shadow that darkens American college and school athletics"—the practice of giving athletic scholarships.

The controversial bulletin, prepared by Howard J. Savage, Harold W. Bentley, John T. McGovern, and Dean F. Smiley after interviews with 2,000 persons, branded college officials who allow the practice as "the Fagins of American sport and American higher education. They tempt young men to barter their honesty for the supposed advantage of a college course, dishonestly achieved. The schoolboy notion that athletic ability can be turned to advantage is so widespread that the mercenary athlete seldom waits for solicitation."

The Carnegie Report, in short, proclaimed it was immoral to have a professional atmosphere in amateur sports. Penn State, among a minority group, heartily endorsed the report and urged a cleanup in amateur athletics.

"It will bring to light conditions at various colleges which will put them in a position to deal with a matter that has been exceedingly elusive," said Penn State President Ralph D. Hetzel. "I hope it will result in united effort of all colleges to clear themselves of any questionable athletic practices."

As a matter of record, Penn State had endorsed this position a couple of years before the Carnegie Report was made public. A movement to abolish athletic scholarships at Penn State was started in January, 1926, and completed in August, 1927. The university made an announcement that no additional scholarships would be granted after October 1, 1927. The program drew commendation from officials of several other schools.

Dean R. L. Sackett, chairman of the College Senate Committee on Athletics and vice president of the Penn State Athletic Board of Control, told reporters of the Carnegie investigation at University Park:

"Early last year (1928), we received a preliminary report from the foundation, based on their 1926 investigation here. It did not mention the scholarship abolition movement, which we had started here. We sought and obtained their permission to revise the report. Upon receipt of this revision, Dr. Savage wrote:

" 'We are especially happy to note the favorable changes which your memorandum sets forth.' At present, there are only 23 athletic scholarships here and these will not be renewed as they lapse."

While of noble intention, the new "purity wave" at Penn State did nothing for the football team. Because of an inability to lure good athletes, the football program began to slide and cause unrest at Penn State. The once-popular Hugo Bezdek was not as popular anymore when Penn State had a mediocre .500 season in 1925 (4-4-1) and a losing one in 1928 (3-5-1). Bezdek's golden years were considered to be in the 1919-1924 period and the era of his decline shortly thereafter. Winning seasons in 1924 (6-3-1), 1926 (5-4), 1927 (6-2-1), and 1929 (6-3) did not keep the wolves away. The intensity of the unrest was disclosed by Philadelphia sports writer Gordon MacKay, who revealed the presence of the "Ohio Gang."

"Like all college scraps, the air of 'hush-hush' is always thrown over the situation at Penn State," MacKay said. "The college is divided, roughly speaking, into the Bezdek and

Hugo Bezdek was football coach and athletic director at Penn State for nearly two decades. Under him the Nittany Lions reached the heights and the depths.

anti-Bezdek camps. The latter centers largely around the element known as the 'Ohio Gang,' who virtually control the athletic destinies of the Nittany Lions. These Westerners are after Bezdek's scalp because he hasn't been able to lick Pitt. This 'Ohio Gang' dictates elections through fraternities, although this statement probably will be denied with vehemence.

"The 'Ohio Gang' has control of vital spots in the structure of the college. But it hasn't been able to date to oust Hugo. The latter is a fighter. He won't quit under fire. Bez has a contract with two or three years more to run. Like one of the Old Guard, he'll never surrender. The usual 'nothing but harmony'

141

will be voiced when this story is read by those who are part and parcel of the rival camps. To this, the writer says 'hooey' and 'baloney.' Every student knows the inside. Some of 'em will talk."

MacKay was right about one thing—Bezdek did not go down easily. But he did go down eventually.

This period of uncertainty in Penn State football history had ironic sidelights. At one point the Nittany Lions could not decide which color to wear. They opened one season by appearing in brilliant cardinal, the following season a blue and white variation using a white stripe running around the chest and white shoulder coverings on a blue background. The year after, the Nittany Lions used a white jersey with blue numbers on front and back. Finally they returned to a traditional blue shirt at home.

In 1929, Bezdek's final season as coach, even the highlight of the year had a negative touch to it. A 19-7 victory over Penn was particularly brutal and ruptured relations with the Philadelphia rival. Fights broke out, several players were crippled in the roughest game seen at Franklin Field in 10 years. And Penn State did not meet Penn again on a football field until 1933.

In accordance with the policy to eliminate athletic scholarships, Penn State created a new School of Physical Education and Athletics and put Bezdek in charge of it. A Penn State announcement on January 20, 1930, said that Bezdek had "volunteered" to retire from coaching to take the new position, which entailed command of the complete athletic program. It was the beginning of intramural sports, a unique plan that opened athletic activities to the entire student body.

"Professor Bezdek (he was promoted) has recognized the great opportunity that lies in the program of this new school and has asked to be relieved of his coaching duties in order that he may devote his full time and energy to the promotion of this program," said Penn State President Ralph D. Hetzel in his announcement.

It was most certainly a step up for the new professor, but one could not help thinking that some pressures were brought to bear in the action.

Said one sports writer: "It cannot be said that the withdrawal of the veteran pigskin tutor came wholly as a surprise. The only feature of it that might be termed unexpected was the fact that it came before the expiration of Bezdek's 10-year contract. For some time his failure to get better results with Blue and White elevens have been openly criticized by Penn State men, and plans for a change in coaches as soon as possible were frequently rumored."

Bezdek was given a voice in the selection of his successor. His choice was Bob Higgins.

Time Out: Hugo Bezdek

The Czechoslovakian-born Hugo Bezdek inspired Penn State to euphorious football heights before a humiliating downfall in his last year. He was both respected and hated, simultaneously pictured as a savior and a dictator, usually controversial and innovative, but never dull in his 19 years as the power behind Penn State's athletic program. He was to have many successes as coach and after that as athletic director of Penn State from 1918 through 1936.

"I feel that Bezdek deserves more credit than some will give him," says "Lighthorse" Harry Wilson, a running star under Bezdek in the early 1920s. "He was tough, but he put out and demanded that others put out, too. He taught good football and he insured that you were in condition to play 60 minutes.

"He would be the first to tell you that he was not running a popularity contest. Even so, he was good to me as a young man and I always held him in high esteem."

"If you worked hard and played fair and square with Bez, you got along with him," recalls Dutch Ricker, who was a Penn State tackle in the late 1920s. "But if you were a chisler, he'd make life miserable for you. I don't think he ever tried to be loved."

Before making post-war football at Penn State a rousing success, Bezdek had glamorous years at Oregon and Arkansas universities and also worked as an assistant coach to the famous Amos Alonzo Stagg at the University of Chicago. In 1917 Bezdek's Oregon team defeated Penn 14-0 in the Rose Bowl.

During his early coaching years, Bezdek kept busy in a lot of areas. Along with football he coached basketball, baseball, and track and also found time to scout for the Pittsburgh National League baseball team. From this latter association he eventually became manager of the Pirates. But he severed that relationship in 1919 to devote his full attention to Penn State.

His ruthless training tactics instilled fear in his players, for Bezdek was a martinet during the arduously-long sessions. The season was a snap, it was jokingly said, if you got through the brutal training period. Football was not fun, but it was profitable under the swaggering little man.

"Bez didn't only teach football, he taught boys to become men," remembers Glenn Killinger, another of the Penn State running stars of the 1920s. "He could instill responsibility and manliness.

"Bez taught me something that is still in my mind—never underestimate an opponent. I respected every team we played. That's the way Bez taught us. He'd say, 'They're good. They can hurt you. But you're good, too. You can hurt them and you can beat them. Now, go out and do it.'"

With this philosophy Bezdek welcomed back the boys from the First World War in 1919 and began to construct one of the most powerful teams in Penn State history. From a 1-2-1 record in lackluster 1918, the Nittany Lions went to 7-1 in 1919, 7-0-2 in 1920, and 8-0-2 in 1921.

Bezdek's post-war teams included all-Americas Bob Higgins, Charley Way, Glenn Killinger, and Joe Bedenk, as well as Hinkey Haines, Duke Osborne, Mike Palm, and Dick Rauch and were easily among the best in the country. The Nittany Lions were invited to the Rose Bowl, their first bowl game, at the end of the 1922 season in the midst of unprecedented football success at University Park. During the period of 1919 through 1924 Penn State won 40 games, lost but 10, and tied 7. In one period the Nittany Lions were undefeated in 30 games.

Bezdek always came up with a new twist, sometimes dismissing book-taught football.

"The first of the so-called spinner plays I recall seeing was used at Penn State," reported a newspaper story by Pop Warner, the well-known coach. "So successful were these plays that for several years after Hugo Bezdek originated the play, Penn State raised havoc with nearly every team it met. As early as 1921 Glenn Killinger made all-America halfback largely on the long runs that developed from this play. Later, Harry Wilson ran wild for Penn State on the same play."

In Bezdek's version of the spinner, the quarterback took the ball from center, turned his back on the opponents, and with the ball hidden in his arms made several fakes to the backs. He would give the ball to one, while all dived into the line.

Dick Harlow, who coached Penn State for three seasons before going into the Army in 1918, returned to University Park in 1919 and saw his first fake reverse. Bezdek, of course, was the innovator, albeit an accidental innovator.

"A signal was missed and the wingback did not take the ball from Harry Robb," recalled Harlow in an article in 1951. "Being a smart back, Robb turned toward the line and a huge hole developed. This was talked over but nothing was done until the same thing happened again...and Bezdek put it in as a play."

It was said that Bezdek developed the screen pass to such a point that it had to be outlawed for a while. Penn State's maverick coach also polished the quick kick and the on-side kick to such an extent that rules had to be changed. Bezdek was also credited with developing the roving center and the staggered ends on defense.

Even practice sessions were unique with the imaginative Bezdek. They used a "ghost ball"—painted white for late practices in the near-dark. And the "Charleston" jazz dance was included as part of the training to improve footwork, the players performing an adaptation of the popular refrain in cleated shoes on a noisy tanbark pavilion.

If Bezdek was unique, he was also controversial. Before he came to Penn State stories preceded him about his rough-and-ready style. He had the reputation of a tough guy after battling a baseball pitcher on a train all the way from Pittsburgh to New York. When they got off he and Burleigh Grimes shook hands, so the story goes.

He was reputed to be the only man to hold up a Rose Bowl game. The Penn State team arrived late for the January 1, 1923, game, and Bezdek was accused of dirty tactics by Southern California's coach, Elmer Henderson. He claimed Bezdek wanted to wait until the sun went down a bit so the Nittany

Lions would better be able to play in the California heat. The two got into a violent argument at mid-field, while thousands waited impatiently for the contest to begin. All the while Bezdek maintained hotly that his team was held up in a Rose Bowl Parade traffic jam. They had to drag "Bez" away from the scene.

Bezdek's longtime feud with Pop Warner, the coach at cross-state rival Pitt, is legendary.

"Bezdek was one of the most complicated men I had ever seen," says Dutch Herman, one of Bezdek's assistants.

He was also one of the most unusual men that Herman, and everyone else, had ever seen at University Park. He built character in his pupils by setting an example himself, but ironically his moralistic posture eventually caused his own downfall.

Bezdek once turned down a $20,000 yearly salary, twice what he was making, to manage Philadelphia's National League baseball team. It was a matter of ideals. He wanted to stay at Penn State, where he felt he could help young athletes.

Always an advocate of simon-pure athletics, he vociferously supported and put into effect guidelines laid down by the sensational Carnegie Report, which proclaimed athletic scholarships immoral. Bezdek was in the eye of the hurricane, shutting off all subsidization of athletes.

The movement was at first popular, reflecting Penn State's noble intentions to keep college football "clean and unprofessional." But when the Nittany Lions began to lose games to teams they used to beat, it was not so popular.

Bezdek's loss of popularity coincided with the downward trend of Penn State's football fortunes in the late 1920s. From 1925 through 1928 the team had a mediocre 18-15-3 record, certainly a comedown from former glittering seasons. And it did not help Bezdek's image, either, when he lost to Pitt for eight straight years.

"The same people who were in his favor in the early part of the 1920s were the ones who turned on him at the end," says Joe Bedenk, meaning the students, the Alumni Association, and the Athletic Committee.

"When he was up for a new contract after the great 1921 season, I remember we woke up one morning and there were these signs all over the trees—'Don't Leave Us Hugo,' and 'We

147

Go Where Hugo,'" recalls Bedenk. "Then they had this mass meeting where one of the cheerleaders, Buck Taylor, got down on his knees at Schwab Auditorium and prayed with the whole student body, 'Bez, don't leave us."

At one time Bezdek was so popular that he was not only prized by Penn State but also coveted by other universities. He once got a telegram from Minnesota which said: "Bez, we want you. Come out and name your own terms." Other schools like Boston University and Syracuse also were interested, but Bezdek turned his back on all offers and remained at Penn State.

Bezdek later was to regret his decision.

He coached his last season in 1929, giving way to former all-America Bob Higgins, and took the newly-created position of dean of the School of Physical Education and Athletics.

On October 3, 1936, Bezdek was virtually thrown out on his ear by the Board of Trustees after the Nittany Lions suffered through seven straight non-winning seasons. Higgins remained as coach, however.

Penn State's student newspaper, the *Collegian,* could not contain its joy. It had been pushing for Bezdek's ouster for a long time.

"The removal from office of Hugo Bezdek is a major victory for the alumni of Penn State," the newspaper said in a front-page editorial the day of his release. "While there is hardly a student, coach or faculty member interested in athletics here who will not greet the announcement with a sigh of relief, it is the alumni who will be most glad to hear the news.

"It has been expected for about four months, but as the weeks passed with no announcements, many were beginning to feel that Bezdek had again managed to obtain a reprieve from the trustees. But Bezdek is gone now and it seems unnecessary —as well as a little unsportsmanlike—to continue to malign him. The trustees' report merely stated that a 'want of confidence in the leadership of the Director, particularly in his relation to the administration of intercollegiate athletics,' questioned seriously the 'value of his services in that office.'

"Like most committee reports, this is a classic of understatement, but if it suited the trustees it suits us. Bezdek is gone. That is the important thing. His dismissal, however, will not be

148

a cure-all for the athletic troubles of the college. While there is no doubt that it will result in a better morale, it will not be a guarantee of winning football teams. And that is the principal interest of the alumni. The alumni got what they wanted with the removal of Bezdek. If that does not produce results, they will try again."

He coached the Cleveland Rams professional football team one year, then retired to a chicken farm in Doylestown, Pennsylvania. The chicken farm failed, and he came out of retirement in 1949 to act as coach and athletic director at the National Agricultural College in Doylestown.

Bezdek died three years later. His friends said it was a broken heart that killed him.

Time Out: Bob Higgins

Bob Higgins was a stately gentleman, but his wife was not above kicking the student editor of the *Collegian* in the pants. It happened in 1939, several weeks after her husband had taken an unmerciful beating from the school newspaper for losing a 47-0 decision to Cornell.

When Higgins coached the Nittany Lions to their first victory over Pitt in 20 years in the last game of the season, Virginia Higgins provided the perfect end to the year by booting the editor for picking on her husband.

You could excuse Mrs. Higgins' intense feelings. Bob Higgins had been through hell at Penn State.

Higgins walked into an uncomfortable situation when he took over as football coach in 1930. The combination of Penn State's "purity" campaign against athletic scholarships and the Depression had plunged the Nittany Lions into their darkest period of history.

As a player 11 years before, Higgins had been applauded, punctuating an all-America year with an often-remembered touchdown play against Penn. But the guy who caught the legendary pass in 1919 now was a maligned coach working with a severe handicap—few talented players.

As a result Higgins did not have a winning season for seven years and lost to the likes of little Waynesburg College.

"When you get licked as often as I did in those terrible 1930s," Higgins once recalled, "you get over being a tough guy."

Bob Higgins coached for nearly two decades and in 1947 developed one of the strongest defensive teams in Penn State history.

Higgins' combined record in the period from 1930 through 1936 was 21-33-3, including a disastrous 2-8 showing in 1931 when the *Collegian*—and the alumni—were ready to throw him out on his ear.

His coaching career was checkered with later disappointments, too. In 1940 a weak Pitt team which had been booed off the stage of a pep rally by its own students upset undefeated Penn State and spoiled a certain bowl bid.

Higgins was criticized through many of his years for using an "outmoded" single wing and "old-fashioned" defensive ideas. His teams constantly won games they were not supposed to and lost the easy ones.

But in 1947 Higgins attained a coach's dream—an undefeated, untied season—and at last gained widespread acceptance. Seven years later he was inducted into the Hall of Fame.

"He was a good teacher and a good coach," recalls a close friend, Dutch Herman. "He knew football inside and out. He knew his players well, and he had a knack of getting the most out of the talent on hand. He had a tremendous personality. Everybody liked him."

Herman, who coached freshman football 18 years and varsity basketball for 15, had one of the closest relationships of anybody with Higgins.

"Higgins never had much to say about his greatest victories," recalls Herman. "We'd rehash some old games. Actually, he liked to talk more about the so-called dark days when Penn State was getting licked."

Higgins began coaching immediately after graduation from Penn State in 1920. He started at West Virginia Wesleyan and then moved to Washington University in St. Louis.

During his formative coaching years he played professional football with the Canton Bulldogs and was always kidded about the time he pinch-hit for the legendary Jim Thorpe.

Thorpe failed to appear for a game on this occasion. The management of the Canton team did not want to disappoint the crowd, so Higgins was asked to impersonate the great runner. Taped heavily by teammates so he could fill out Thorpe's uniform, Higgins appeared on the field before a large audience.

But the ruse ended quickly when Higgins went back to punt on one play and a fan shouted: "Who's that bum in Thorpe's uniform?"

Higgins returned to Penn State as an assistant coach in 1928 and was an aide to Hugo Bezdek for two years before getting the top job. At first a strict disciplinarian who was known to drop players quickly from the squad, Higgins soon mellowed after going through the agonies of several losing seasons.

The 1931 season was his worst. That year Penn State defeated Lebanon Valley 19-6 in the second game of the season and Lehigh 31-0 at the end. They did not score more than one touchdown in any of the other games and lost to Waynesburg 7-0, Temple 12-0, Dickinson 10-6, Syracuse 7-0, Pitt 41-6, Colgate 32-7, Lafayette 33-0, and West Virginia 19-0.

He needed a sense of humor in those days, and—fortunately —he had one.

"He could raise the devil with the players, but he could also be comical at times," remembers Jim O'Hora, who played for Higgins and was later one of his assistants. "He was a very sharp individual."

Higgins told this story on himself: "One time, after losing our annual game at Pitt, I approached a Penn State rooter and asked him for a nickel to call a friend. He gave me a disgusted look, tossed me a dime, and muttered: 'Here, call both your friends!'"

Losing or winning Higgins always expected the proper decorum from his players. He did not stand for profanity and always insisted that his players be properly dressed, on or off the field. Once he chewed out a student manager because a player reported for practice wearing apparently oversized brogans.

"Get this boy a pair of shoes that fit him," snapped the finicky Higgins. "Get rid of these gun boats."

The player intervened quietly: "Thanks, coach, but these 'gunboats' fit fine. I wear size 14, you see."

"Ike" Gilbert, former graduate manager at Penn State, recalled another Higgins story concerning attire.

"Michigan State was playing Colgate and stayed in Syracuse the night before," said Gilbert. "We were playing Syracuse and stayed at the same hotel. We checked in and were standing around the lobby when several Michigan State players came down the stairs. Bob looked up and saw those huge athletes with the big "M" on their coat sweaters.

"He said, 'Boys, let that be an important lesson to you. Those gentlemen are always dressed properly.' "

Higgins found it easy to build character in those days. Being a loser always builds character.

"Our football team was really low," recalls Joe Bedenk, Higgins' assistant. "I could tell you about some of those boys who played for us, oh, boy! We had guards weighing 148 pounds. Hell, our blocking back was only 138. We couldn't beat a good high school team!"

Referring to the scholarship ban, Bedenk says, "We couldn't even buy a meal for players. That's the way things were."

But the alumni were around the corner and so were better years. The school, of course, could not officially sanction it, but some of Penn State's well-to-do graduates offered summer jobs as an enticement to prospective football players.

"That was about 1935 or 1936," Bedenk says. "We had no organization with the alumni at that time to even collect any money, but things began to pick up and along about 1938 and 1939 we got going pretty good."

One of the friends of the school who helped Higgins build stronger teams was Casey Jones. A former teammate and longtime friend of the coach, Jones served as an unofficial scout for Higgins and supplied several good players. Higgins' adherence to good, old-fashioned power football did the rest. His "unimaginative" formations drew harsh criticism from detractors, but Higgins unswervingly stayed with the single-wing offense and time-tested defensive setups. ("A good coach can do just as much with the single wing as he can with the T-Formation," he said.) And the victories began to come.

The Nittany Lions had their last losing season in 1938 (3-4-1) and then began one of the most glamorous eras in college football history. Higgins' 1939 team won five, lost one, and tied two and started a string of non-losing seasons that has lasted until today. Higgins was credited with building the foundation for Penn State's modern power teams.

His greatest accomplishment was the 1947 season when his team made national defensive records that still stand. The Nittany Lions allowed a total of only 27 points to their nine regular-season opponents, but were not totally defense-oriented for they scored 319 themselves.

154

The 1947 Nittany Lions' team was the first to win the Lambert Trophy, annually awarded to the best team in the East, and was ranked No. 4 in the country in the final Associated Press poll. Higgins took Penn State to its first bowl game in 25 years, too. The Nittany Lions visited the Cotton Bowl and tied favored SMU 13-13 with a late comeback.

After another good season in 1948 during which Penn State lost only once, Higgins was forced to retire from coaching because of failing health. He had a history of heart trouble.

In retirement for two decades in the shadow of Beaver Field, he and his successor, Rip Engle, met often.

"I admired Higgins because after he stepped down he never put a coach on the spot, and he never tried to make anybody look bad," Engle says.

Higgins did show up occasionally for practice sessions, but always with grandchildren on one arm and a dog on the other.

"Who can look for coaching or player mistakes and still watch children?" he would say.

When he died at the age of 75 on June 6, 1969, Penn State lost a dear friend.

"He was a fine example of how a coach should lead his life," says Joe Paterno, the present coach. "When history about Penn State football is written, his contributions will be the lead."

Downright Humiliatin'

"If Jock Sutherland had been an unkind man, the score up on Beaver Field might have been 141 to 6 instead of a mere 41 to 6. For Jock started his second team, advanced to the third by the second quarter, and finished up with the thirds and fourths.

"It was a horrid experience for Penn State, but the worst was yet to come. After the final whistle, as we were filing out of the stands, out came Pitt's regulars for a warmup signal drill. Let me tell you, it was downright humiliatin'."

This was a common account of Penn State fortunes in the early 1930s, a period when the Nittany Lions had no bite. Not only did Penn State continue to lose to Pitt by scores similar to the 1931 game, but to just about everyone else. Somebody complained that they had "a nerve" charging $1.10 for their games.

The Depression described the nation's financial status, but Penn State backers were sure it also meant football at University Park. The Nittany Lions were not only embarrassed at home, they also traveled to places like Iowa City to be embarrassed.

Like most every school in the country, however, optimism was high in the spring. Said an Associated Press pre-season story on April 1, 1930:

"It's a fairly safe bet that the Nittany Lions will bob up on gridirons with a new measure of three prime football requisites—craftiness, fight, and ability to think fast under fire. If there is anything in leadership, they should acquire these

156

characteristics from the large stock of Bob Higgins, a big smiling Irishman who last week took the Penn State head coaching problems from the ample shoulders of squat Hugo Bezdek."

Higgins also predicted a good season: "We'll be tricky. I've got some smart boys. We'll lick more teams than will lick us next fall."

Turned out, both the AP and Higgins were wrong.

Higgins' first season, not unexpectedly, was a losing one because he was rebuilding. The second year was even worse for Penn State's energetic new coach. "Highlights" of the 1930 season, therefore, must be discussed in terms of landmark occurrences rather than wins and losses.

The season was significant for the trip to Iowa and a Thanksgiving Day game with Pitt. The trip to Iowa marked the first invasion of Iowa City by an eastern football team. The traditional Thanksgiving Day battle with Pitt was the last played with Pitt on that particular holiday for a while. Pitt decided that Penn State simply was no longer a drawing card and scheduled Nebraska for Thanksgiving Day in 1931 and 1932. Pitt and Penn State later broke off relations for three years until 1935 after a disagreement on financial arrangements.

As long as the Nittany Lions were going to lose, they might as well have enjoyed themselves. And that is what they did when they traveled to Iowa City near the end of the 1930 season.

The first leg of the trip on the Pennsylvania Railroad to Chicago included a sumptuous breakfast with grilled fish, ham omelets, and roast beef hash with green peppers. The next day, after switching to the Rock Island line in Chicago, the Nittany Lions dined on an elegant lunch that included Consomme Belle-Vue en Tasse, and a choice of Filet of Halibut au Beurre Noir, Braised Spring Lamb au Jus, or Roast Young Duck with Gooseberry Sauce. Apparently, all training rules were ignored on this trip.

The game was considered a toss-up because Iowa was not having a particularly good season, either. The Nittany Lions, with a few holdovers from Bezdek's era like Mike Kaplan, Joe Miller, Earle Edwards, Frank Diedrich, and Cooper French, played Iowa almost even for three periods before losing 19-0.

Iowans celebrated the Homecoming victory over Penn State by burning a huge "I" constructed of corn husks. While several

157

thousand Iowa alumni whooped it up Saturday night, the Nittany Lions were back in their hotel, some asleep and some drowning their sorrows in near-beer.

Penn State's 3-4-1 record in Higgins' first year was deceiving, for the Nittany Lions were probably worse than even that shows. They won all their games at the beginning from three soft touches—Niagara, Lebanon Valley, and Marshall.

They did pull off an "upset," however, by holding Syracuse to a scoreless tie on November 8, Pennsylvania Day. A crowd of 8,000, 10,000, or 12,000 saw the game at Beaver Field, depending on which newspaper account you read. In that one Diedrich missed two field goal attempts by narrow margins. Or was it Diedrich and Kaplan who each tried a field goal? That, too, depended on which newspaper account you read.

Higgins' first season ended on a familiar refrain. Pitt beat Penn State on November 26, 19-12.

Casey At The Bat

A newspaper cartoon showing a battered lion humorously depicted Penn State's plight in the 1931 football season. The lion had bandages on its body, a disgusted look on its face, and its tail tied to a stake in the ground. Clipped to the tail by clothespins were eight socks, each embroidered with the name of a different team.

"The season was just one sock after another," said the frowning lion.

It was funny to some readers, perhaps, but not to the folks at Penn State. The year had been a washout with those eight defeats and victories only over Lebanon Valley and a post-season charity success over Lehigh.

"The once-proud Nittany Lion, the same lord of the jungle that used to rule the roost, that once was chosen to represent the East in the Rose Bowl is now a mere hearth-rug for teams that would have only been a warmup in the days of Hugo Bezdek," said the story under the cartoon.

Caustic letters from readers appeared in newspapers. "I understand that Bob Higgins has had to play half of the glee club this year and if I also understand correctly, Penn State will be playing cheerleaders next year."

Things were mighty low in 1931, if not quite in the drastic situation described by the sarcastic letter writer. Only six lettermen were left after the 1930 season—fullback George Lasich, guards Tom Curry and Chuck Gillard, tackles Stan Stempeck and Bill McMillen, and quarterback Bob Snyder.

"Coaching a football team is the craziest, most baffling business in the world," said Higgins, who also found it the most frustrating in 1931.

The Nittany Lions' worst season in history was characterized by their longest losing streak—seven games. Even charity took a beating that year when they defeated Lehigh on November 28. Only 2,500 fans appeared in nasty weather at Philadelphia's Franklin Field to watch the game, which gave the meager proceeds to unemployment funds.

During the boring charity affair an early women's libber got her licks in at the "chauvinistic male." Betty Starr, one of the few women sports writers around at the time, was covering for the *Philadelphia Record.* She apparently found the game as uninteresting as everyone else, for she directed a lot of her story at the male sports writers.

"In the secluded spot of the press box (secluded for the ladies) where our well-known newspapermen uncork their virile words and spit on the floor with impunity, we wouldn't think of invading this last stand of the lordly male," she wrote. "But we would like to know what lies within those black cages that is kept so secret from the females."

She apparently tried to crack the press box but had been rebuked, for she added: "As one person, who stood the blinding drizzle about as long as is possible, and sought refuge in the covered part of the stand remarked as she looked up at the multitude of steps leading to the Sacred Press—'No wonder the sports writers are so lithe and handsome, climbing all those steps must be good for the figure!' "

She apparently did not see the game the same way the men did, either, commending Penn State halfback George Collins for playing "a stellar role." Male sports writers covering the event hardly mentioned Collins, but rather singled out Lasich, Snyder, and Phil Moonves as the Nittany Lions' heroes.

"Lasich, one of the best backs seen on Franklin Field this season, was the high scorer with two touchdowns and one goal after touchdown," wrote Ed Pollock of the *Philadelphia Public Ledger.* "Moonves also crossed the Lehigh goal twice. The first touchdown of the afternoon was pegged to Bob Snyder on a forward pass from Moonves."

"Five touchdowns were annexed by the lads from Center

Hugo Bezdek, a once-popular football coach, was the object of scorn in his later years as athletic director. Penn State had seven straight non-winning seasons—and Bezdek got booted in 1936.

County and in each of these markers, Lasich figured largely and to a dominating extent," reported Gordon MacKay of the *Philadelphia Record.*

Because the power was not there, Higgins' teams relied on speed, deception, and passing out of the single-wing formation. Higgins' new style included use of the "Military Shift" made famous by New York University. The idea was to confuse the opposing teams by shifting into assorted formations while calling signals. Sometimes the line ended up unbalanced with the formation to the left or right, and the manuever also changed the orientation of backfield players.

It did not help much, of course, except in rare instances like the Lehigh game. When tiny Waynesburg College whipped the Nittany Lions in 1931, the entire community of Waynesburg celebrated with a big bonfire. It was the first time that the school had beaten a major college opponent in its history, and observers wondered whether Penn State itself should not be clustered with small college teams from then on. Also, sports writers began to question the worth of Penn State's "Grand Experiment" banning subsidization.

In 1932 two victories and five defeats did not make Higgins' position any more comfortable, nor Penn State backers any happier. The Nittany Lions defeated only Lebanon Valley and Sewanee. Using 135-pound centers and 150-pound guards, they lost to Waynesburg again, not to mention bigger schools like Harvard, Syracuse, Colgate, and Temple.

In 1933 a 6-6 tie with Penn and Jim Boring's 100-yard punt return against Johns Hopkins highlighted a mediocre 3-3-1 season. In 1934 and 1935 Penn State had 4-4 seasons each year, but the Nittany Lions began to show signs of awakening. They were competitive with several major teams of the day. They only lost 3-0 to Penn and 13-7 to Bucknell in 1934 and in 1935 defeated Villanova 27-13 and barely went under to Syracuse 7-3. In the Syracuse game, Vannie "Iron Man" Albanese carried the ball 19 straight times for the Orange and took a pass for a late touchdown that beat Penn State.

During this period alumni were working backstage in the Penn State cause. One of them was "Casey" Jones, a former teammate and close friend of Higgins. Casey worked for a power company in western Pennsylvania but found time to scout players for Penn State. In the middle of the 1930s his work paid off because Jones uncovered several prospects, including three of his finest—Joe Metro, Alex Barantovich, and Sever Toretti. These players made Higgins' job a little easier during the 1936, 1937, and 1938 seasons.

"He darned near got killed walking down railroad tracks to

162

The removal of Athletic Director Hugo Bezdek was acidly portrayed in this cartoon in the October 3, 1936, issue of the Penn State newspaper, The Collegian.

find the boys," said Higgins, who explained that Jones literally beat the bushes for talent.

On October 3, 1936, an old era ended at Penn State when the college's Board of Trustees fired Hugo Bezdek.

The Penn State *Collegian* put out an "Extra" with Bezdek's removal the lead story. The story was an epitaph for the Bezdek era, as it had been for Bezdek himself:

"Hugo Bezdek, director of the School of Physical Education and Athletics since its organization in 1930, was relieved of his position this morning by the action of the College Board of Trustees meeting here today with President Ralph D. Hetzel.

"In recommending that Bezdek be relieved of his position, the Committee said that they had studied the problem because of the criticism directed against Bezdek by student publications and the alumni. While they found that many of the specific complaints against him could not be justified, they felt that there had developed such a want of confidence in his leadership as to question the value of his services."

In those days when a team was going bad, they apparently fired the athletic director instead of the coach. But whether or not Bezdek was to blame, Penn State's football fortunes took a positive turn upon his departure. The Nittany Lions were to have their first winning season in eight years in 1937, a period when the school symbolically finished a new section of steel stands, 20 rows high, that replaced the old wooden stands at Beaver Field.

A Winning Season — At Last!

In the late 1930s Bob Higgins could finally come out of hiding, literally and figuratively.

Higgins, who usually went into seclusion on the eve of big games, mellowed after several bad years and decided not to be so unsociable.

Of course, he was not afraid to show his face after the 1937 season, anyway, because the Nittany Lions won more games than they lost that year. And while the 5-3 record was not especially distinctive, it was a winning season, something that had not been seen at Penn State since 1929.

The Nittany Lions began their domination of Penn in this period with a 7-0 victory over the Quakers in 1937. A Higgins-coached team never lost to Penn after that, something the coach could not explain logically.

However, Higgins did have an explanation of sorts for the four Penn State victories and one tie in five games with Penn from 1937 through 1948.

"Here we were, hidden away in the mountains, far from the bright city lights, just waiting for an invitation to play at Franklin Field," said Higgins. "It was inevitable that our kids would be fired up. They just lived for that trip to Philadelphia. Coaching the team for a game at Franklin Field was one of my easier assignments."

The 1937 season began with a 26-19 loss to Cornell, and pessimists braced for an eighth straight non-winning year. However, victories followed over Gettysburg (32-6), Bucknell

165

(20-14), and Lehigh (14-7), and things did not look so bad after all. There was a 19-13 loss to Syracuse before the Penn victory. Penn State then defeated Maryland 21-14 and wound up with the inevitable loss to Pitt, this time by a 28-7 score.

The Nittany Lions had a losing season in 1938 (3-4-1) but it included some impressive victories—33-0 over Maryland, 59-6 over Lehigh, and 33-6 over Syracuse. Chuck Peters was a big man for Penn State that year. Against Syracuse he scored two touchdowns, including an 80-yard run off tackle, and passed to Spike Alter for a 14-yard touchdown play.

The season of 1938 was also distinguished by the first of Higgins' outstanding defensive clubs. Penn State set a few national pass defense records that year, including fewest passing yards allowed per game (an average of 13.1 in eight games); lowest average per pass (1.78, 105 yards allowed on 59 attempts); and lowest completion percentage allowed (16.9 percent, 10 completions on 59 attempts).

"It was strictly a team that was defense-minded," says Leon Gajecki, the Penn State center of that era who became an all-America as a senior in 1940.

The Nittany Lions did not look particularly "defense-minded" in the third game of 1939, losing an embarrassing 47-0 decision to nationally-ranked Cornell after opening with victories over Bucknell and Lehigh. Not only did Penn State get beaten badly, but Higgins took a severe lacing from the campus newspaper.

A 6-6 tie with Syracuse the week after took some of the heat off Higgins and started a 12-game undefeated string that continued until the last game of the 1940 season. In between there was a 5-1-2 season in 1939, including a 10-0 victory over Penn State's longtime tormentors, the Pitt Panthers. It was the first triumph over Pitt in 20 years. The last time the Nittany Lions defeated their dominating neighbor to the west was 1919, when Higgins was a player.

The triumph was such a rarity that Alumni Secretary Ridge Riley wrote a rather exuberant piece in his weekly *Football Letter*:

"Twenty football seasons have been played. Twenty hopeful Nittany Lions teams have taken the field against the Golden Panthers of Pittsburgh. Nineteen have left the gridiron without

166

victory. Small wonder that Penn State's delirious student body last Saturday became so confused that it stormed out on the field and captured its own goalposts and bore them triumphantly down campus to the main gate."

After unexpectedly winning that game, Penn State was expected to win the following season against a much inferior Pitt team but lost, 20-7. It was their only defeat in a 6-1-1 year in 1940, and cost the Nittany Lions a certain bowl bid.

The *Alumni Letter* reacted eloquently to the drama of the moment, one of the saddest in Higgins' tenure:

"Within the grimness of Pitt Stadium, Penn State's visions of an undefeated season went up in the murky Pittsburgh sky, and heavy Penn State hearts finished out a weekend in the Smoky City with forced gaiety and dreams of what might have been."

Riley added some salve at the bottom of the note, however:

"Well, anyway, the varsity soccer team finished its eighth consecutive season without defeat."

"We were terribly overconfident in that game," recalls Gajecki. "We should have never underestimated them. They deserved to beat us. They were better on that day. But on another day, we felt we could have won. We had a tremendous football team at the time."

It was a team that not only had Gajecki but also one of the slickest passing combinations in Penn State history, Bill Smaltz to Len Krouse, and outstanding runners in "Pepper" Petrella and Chuck Peters. Before losing to Pitt on the final day of the 1940 season, Penn State defeated Bucknell 9-0, West Virginia 17-13, Lehigh 34-0, Temple 18-0, South Carolina 12-0, New York University 25-0, and tied Syracuse 13-13. The West Virginia victory typified an ability to bounce back as Petrella led a long touchdown march to pull the game out in the second half.

With the Smaltz-to-Krouse combination in high gear, the 1941 club won seven of nine games. The Nittany Lions defeated Pitt for the second time in three years, and Riley recalled "an anecdote worth retelling" in the 31-7 victory.

"I was sitting next to "Zez" (Howard W.) Cohen, an old Nittany Lion who was the drama critic for the *Pittsburgh Post Gazette*," says Riley. "Next to him was Bob Lane, a young Penn State graduate. Bob was then serving as our sports assistant. He was born and brought up in Pittsburgh and had never seen a Penn State triumph in the Pitt Stadium.

"As the score mounted, in youthful ecstasy, with eyes shining, Bob turned to Zez and said: 'Oh, boy, I've been waiting a long time for this.' I'll never forget the look of utter scorn and pity on Zez's face as he turned vehemently on the youth: 'You've been waiting a long time?'" he said. 'YOU'VE been waiting a long time?'"

The years of the Second World War provided a tenuous situation at Penn State, with players shuttling in and out of the campus at irregular intervals. It did not stop Higgins from producing winning teams, however. The Nittany Lions had a 6-1-1 record in 1942, 5-3-1 in 1943, 6-3 in 1944, and 5-3 in 1945.

"We talked to these kids," recalls Joe Bedenk, Higgins' lieutenant, "and told them to please come back after the war. We knew if they did, we'd have some pretty good teams at Penn State."

Things were going so well for Higgins that he even "dreamed" about winning plays, almost as if he had aid from a supernatural source. After beating Colgate 13-10 in the 1942 Homecoming game at Penn State, Higgins told the story.

"I had this dream two nights before the game," he said. "It wasn't a new play, but it worked so perfectly in my dreams that I decided to use it Saturday.

"It was rather a simple thing. Our fullback passed sharply to our end, who was standing on the 40-yard line with his back to the Colgate defender. And just as the Colgate man closed in on him, one of our halfbacks drifted by, took the ball on a passoff, and outran the Colgate secondary to the goal line.

"It worked just as I had visualized it. The Colgate boys did just what I had hoped they would do. Our timing was perfect. Everybody in the dream—Colgate and Penn State players alike—cooperated. It was a beautiful thing."

West Virginia and Penn State continued their hot rivalry during the wartime and produced a beauty in 1944. The Mountaineers defeated the Nittany Lions 28-27 in a wild finish as Penn State's Johnny Chuckran and West Virginia's Jimmy Walthall waged a war of great individual talents.

The war years were also noted for extremely young Penn

State teams that sometimes drove Higgins to the lunatic fringe. Higgins was riding along the highway en route to Syracuse for a game when he spotted a half dozen of his best players—all freshmen—fighting a farmhouse fire.

"Not content to stay on the ground, they were dangling from the roof of a nearby barn, their hands occupied with buckets, and their heads completely barren of everything, including the game on the next day," remembered a Penn State man.

The going was just as bad for Higgins once he reached Syracuse with his crew of wild, exuberant yearlings. Before he had gotten them all into their hotel rooms, the freshmen had purchased all the chocolate bars in the lobby, had tried to talk their way into a jitterbug contest, and had risked their health by racing full speed through revolving doors.

"I hope once the war is over that someone will someday erect a monument to freshmen football coaches," said Higgins.

Time Out: Leon Gajecki

A country boy recalls his first appearance in a goldfish bowl. It seemed like yesterday, but actually it was the winter of 1938.

"There must have been 50,000 fans watching us in Franklin Field," Leon Gajecki remembers. "I'd never played before that kind of crowd before. I was really awed. I told myself that there was no way I could have a good game that day. I had so many butterflies in my stomach."

The roar of the crowd was forgotten once Gajecki leaned over the ball and snapped it back from his center position. "I had one of the best games of my college life" as Penn State played powerful Penn to a 7-7 tie.

"I wanted to impress people that I could play," says Gajecki.

Throughout his football career at Penn State, Gajecki continued to be impressed by big-time football—but at the same time never failed to impress other people. He became one of the finest centers in Nittany Lions' history.

His college career finished in glory during the 1940 season when he was chosen team captain, applauded as an all-America, and selected as one of the all-stars in the East-West Shrine Game in San Francisco.

Not bad for a onetime 96-pound weakling from Colver, a tiny western Pennsylvania coal-mining town.

"When he was a freshman in Ebensburg High School, he was so small that they didn't have a football uniform to fit him...they had to go to a hardware store to get one of those kids' play suits," recalls his wife, Mrs. Gajecki, sitting in on the conversation. "Well, it was really funny—because my husband went from 96 pounds to 160 over one summer. And when he reported for football practice the next year, the coach almost didn't know who he was."

The "coach" was Earle Edwards, one of the inspirations of Gajecki's life.

"He was very influential in my going to Penn State," says Gajecki. "Earle took a job as an assistant coach at Penn State when I graduated from high school, and I followed him up there. He took a few of us with him and indoctrinated us in the Penn State background. I wouldn't have gone up there without him. I'll always thank Earle for that."

In 1938 Gajecki also began his association with another adored figure in his life—head coach Bob Higgins.

"I liked Bob very much," says Gajecki. "I was impressed with his background. He was a very good coach and a very good fundamentalist. He was inspiring to play for. I have to give him a lot of credit for helping me and guiding me along."

If Higgins was a good coach, though, he was not very good in pronunciation. He had a terrible time with the names on his team, rich in ethnic qualities.

"He couldn't say, 'Gajecki'," interjected Mrs. Gajecki, "so he told my husband, 'You're 'Gates'. ''

There were tongue-twisters like Frketich, Garbinski, Stravinski, and Petrella. Even Morey was too much for Higgins.

"So Frketich became Ferguson to Higgins, Garbinski became Garber, Stavinski became Stevens, Petrella was Pete, and Morey became More," says Mrs. Gajecki.

"We had a big tackle named John Michael Leo Kerns, Jr.," recalls Gajecki. "He had an easy Irish name so he didn't have to change it for Higgins."

As a college sophomore, Gajecki felt somewhat lost in new surroundings.

"I'd never been away from home," he says. "When I went to Penn State, it was like going into a different world. I had to realign my entire life. After all, I had lived in this small coal-mining town all my life. But I wasn't the only one, I soon found. Every other player on the team had the same feeling. The atmosphere at Penn State was beautiful, though. It was like a big fraternity and we soon learned to love it."

At 180 pounds Gajecki was the smallest man on the team. It did not prevent him from pulling his weight, though.

"I averaged 58 minutes a game," says Gajecki. "You know, we played both ways in those days—not like today's age of specialization. In those days we had to spend half our time practicing defense and half our time practicing offense. It was really rough. You had to be good at both positions."

The 1938 season was Penn State's last losing one through the present day, and Gajecki helped the Nittany Lions welcome an era of football prosperity rare in college history. The Nittany Lions, whose forte was defense, lost only one game in 1939—and that by an outrageous 47-0 score to Cornell.

"It shouldn't have happened, since our team was strictly defense-minded," says Gajecki "But it was a game of mistakes, obviously. The ball bounced the wrong way for us. The oddity about the Cornell game was that the first two plays we ran, they made touchdowns. We fumbled both times, and they went in for TDs and we were never able to recover."

However, they defeated Pitt and Penn that year, both by 10-0 scores, so their season was a success. Both were perennial Penn State rivals and usually national powers in that era.

"We had a hard-nosed team," remembers Gajecki. "It wasn't a team of offensive power—but then, not too many clubs had a lot of offense in those days. You didn't find much wide-open football until Stanford later opened up the game."

Gajecki's bulk increased in 1940, his senior year, and his six-foot frame held 225 pounds. It helped him push people around a little easier and gained him notice on the Newspaper Enterprise Association's all-America team.

Recognized as one of the best centers in the country, Gajecki accompanied other football luminaries from the East to San Francisco for the Shrine Game. It was one of the highlights of his career, he recalls.

"We lost 20-14 in Kezar Stadium, but the game wasn't the thing I remember," says Gajecki. "The real highlight of my trip west was visiting the Shriners Hospital to meet the crippled kiddies."

The affair, which raises funds for crippled children, lingers in a 55-year-old mind.

"We walked through the hospital to meet the young

patients," says Gajecki. "We signed autographs and played catch with them. It was quite an experience."

"When Leon talks to me about the East-West game," recalls his wife, "that's the thing that got to him the most—the crippled children."

Gajecki had thoughts of turning professional after college. He was drafted by the Pittsburgh Steelers but did not take the bait.

"Pro football at that time was not as enticing financially as it is now," he explains.

Anyway, the Second World War put a stop to any glamorous football thoughts. He worked in a western Pennsylvania munitions plant, where he met his wife, changed to another powder plant in Missouri for a while, and then after the war came back to the East to join the Humble Oil & Refinery Co. in Pitman, New Jersey, his present job.

In the post-war years Gajecki had a brief professional fling with the Jersey City Giants, but then stuck to bird-dogging players for Penn State. In the intervening years Gajecki's sharp scouting eye helped produce several glittering Nittany names: Milt Plum, Dave Rowe, Dave Robinson, Lydell Mitchell, and Franco Harris. Gajecki also helped resurrect the Glassboro State College football program and officiated games and worked with youngsters in various capacities.

Gajecki suffered a stroke in 1968, but got back on his feet and became an active figure again. He was honored with a place in the All-Sports Hall of Fame at Johnstown, Pennsylvania, alongside such bright names as golf superstar Arnold Palmer and swimmer Johnny Weismuller.

"People mean more to Leon than awards, though," his wife says. "His years at Penn State were a very important part of his life. That's where his heart is."

Utopia

A big, mobile line, running backs with the rare combination of power and speed, and a record-breaking defense. These were the ingredients for one of Penn State's greatest football teams—the team of 1947. This wrecking crew provided an undefeated, untied regular season, a berth in the Cotton Bowl, and a place in the sun for Penn State.

"It was nice to know for a change that the other team wouldn't run over you at will," said Coach Bob Higgins, who recalled the early lean years when things were not this much fun.

The "other team" did not run over Penn State at all in 1947. The Nittany Lions established three national defensive records that still stand.

En route to a 9-0 regular season record, the nation's top defensive team broke standards for fewest yards allowed in a game (minus 47 against Syracuse), fewest average yards allowed rushing per game (17.0), and lowest average allowed per rush (0.64).

The players mainly responsible for the sparkling defense included a line that was one of the biggest and toughest in the land during the post-war years. John Wolosky was the center, Joe Drazenovich and Steve Suhey were the guards, Negley Norton and John Nolan the tackles, and Sam Tamburo and John Potsklan the ends.

These brutes averaged 203 pounds, with Nolan the heaviest at 228. Line coach Joe Bedenk considered Suhey the best guard he

Guard Steve Suhey was an important part of the line that helped Penn State establish three national defensive records in 1947.

ever coached. An all-America that year, the 210-pounder was remarkably fast and a key blocker who led the ball carrier on most plays.

Jeff Durkota, the team's top scorer with 10 touchdowns, starred in a backfield that averaged 190 pounds despite the presence of 145-pound Elwood Petchel. Durkota was one of the starting halfbacks along with Larry Joe, the team's quickest runner who made a 95-yard kickoff return for a touchdown against Bucknell. The quarterback was Joe Drazenovich's brother, Charles, an exceptional blocker who made Higgin's single-wing function properly, and the starting fullback was Joe

Penn State's 1947 Powerhouse
Front row, left to right: Rogel, Tamburo, J. Drazenovich, Nolan, Suhey, C. Drazenovich, Gorinski, Ulinski, Czekaj, LaFleur, Hicks, Durkota, Smith, Misiewicz. Second row: Hoggard, Kyle, Finley, Weitzel, Murray, Cooney, Chuckran,

Colone.

It was a backfield of many interchangeable parts, however, and also included Petchel, a small wonder whom Higgins called "the best back of his weight in the country," fullback Fran Rogel, and halfbacks Wally Triplett, Larry Cooney, Bill Luther, and Bobby Williams. Their comparative values were measured in the fact that Rogel was a reserve, yet still led the team in rushing with 554 yards. This multi-talented backfield put Penn State among the top five offensive teams in America.

Ed Czekaj, Penn State's present Director of Athletics, had played an important role in the 1946 season when Penn State

Bell, Norton, Luther, Beatty. Third row: Williams, Joe, Colone, Triplett, Kelly, Wolosky, Potsklan, Petchel, Palmer, Erickson, Cullings, Ross, Cominsky. Back row: Coach Higgins, James, Hedderick, Hummel, Felbaum, Simon, Barron (manager).

posted a 6-2 record and was the place-kicking specialist on the fabled 1947 squad.

"After the boys came back from the war, we had a good ball club in 1946 but we couldn't get completely together," recalls Tamburo, who was an all-America in 1948. "Then things sort of fell into place in 1947. We were loose and just tried to go out and have a good time. We weren't shooting for an undefeated season—we weren't worried about breaking records, just playing football to our best capabilities."

Those were some capabilities, to be sure, and the best explanation for the Utopian season was provided in a news release from Penn State's sports information office. It pointed to "an abundance of experience gained over the years, good spirit and the school's good fortune in finding some of its best talent of the last six years on the campus, all at one and the same time."

Penn State defeated Washington State 27-6, Bucknell 54-0, Fordham 75-0, Syracuse 40-0, West Virginia 21-14, Colgate 46-0, Temple 7-0, Navy 20-7, and Pitt 29-0. This is the year the Nittany Lions went to the Cotton Bowl and battled favored SMU to a 13-13 tie with a second-half comeback and finished No. 4 in the country in the Associated Press poll. And Penn State for the first time won the Lambert Trophy, emblematic of eastern supremacy.

Higgins violated his own rules by openly predicting a good season. At the end he confessed that it was easily his best team in three decades of coaching. Some observers felt it was the best team ever at Penn State.

In the opening game a touchdown pass from Petchel to Chuck Drazenovich gave the Nittany Lions an early 7-0 lead over Washington State and started them on their wonder year. Triplett and Rogel also scored touchdowns, and the tough defense provided another, smothering an attempted Washington State punt in the end zone.

Joe's spectacular kickoff return sparked the rout of Bucknell in Game No. 2. Behind beautiful blocking, he took the ball 95 yards up the middle of the field.

Highlighted by Petchel's 78-yard end run for a touchdown, Penn State racked up 40 points in the second period while trouncing Fordham in a game that Tamburo called "no pleasure...you can't enjoy a ballgame when it's that much of a runaway."

Petchel threw a touchdown pass and scored another TD on a run, and Rogel powered over two touchdowns as Penn State walloped Syracuse. Penn State took over after a scoreless first quarter.

The Nittany Lions came closest to losing in the West Virginia game when breaks helped the Mountaineers. West Virginia scored one touchdown after two interference penalties put the ball on the Penn State two-yard line and another after blocking a mishandled punt. Penn State broke a 14-14 tie in the third period, scoring the winning touchdown on a long pass play from Petchel to Triplett.

One of the outstanding plays of the game occurred in the fourth period when Petchel executed a fake field goal. While Czekaj apparently stood ready to kick, Petchel kneeled down in the holding position on the 20-yard line. Petchel took the snap from center, jumped up, spun to his right, and ran to the one-yard line. Penn State could not score, though, and had to be content with a one-touchdown victory.

For the sixth straight time Penn State won the opening toss and elected to receive in the Colgate game. The Nittany Lions took the opening kickoff for a long drive that was eventually stopped by the Red Raiders. But that was one of the few times that Colgate could contain the Penn State offense, as Durkota and Luther scored two touchdowns apiece.

Slowed by a sea of mud, neither Penn State nor Temple could get untracked in the first half of their game in Philadelphia. Colone's superb punting helped put the ball deep in Temple territory, but the Nittany Lions were not able to take advantage of the situation. Penn State scored the only touchdown of the game in the third period. Williams was the star of the touchdown drive which started at midfield.

The Nittany Lions' impressive triumph over Navy on another rainy Saturday the next week made them a Cotton Bowl possibility. The story goes that the Midshipmen played the Nittany Lions evenly for the first period until a Navy lineman was complimented by Potsklan for a particularly good block.

"Sure, it was a good block," the Navy player replied. "You're playing in the big league today."

When Potsklan returned to the Penn State huddle and reported the disparaging remark, it inspired an awesome Penn State attack that easily swept Navy aside. Durkota scored two touchdowns.

The Nittany Lions completed their first undefeated, untied season since 1912 by disposing of Pitt on November 22. Penn State scored on its first possession with Williams' short run capping a 55-yard touchdown drive. Czekaj completed the rout with a field goal in the dying minutes of the game, and Penn State got its cherished Cotton Bowl invitation.

They thus became the first Nittany Lions' team to win nine games in a season, an accomplishment not wholly unexpected considering the way they played football in 1947.

"They like to keep the ball," reported Chester L. Smith, sports editor of the *Pittsburgh Press*, in a program piece for the Cotton Bowl on January 1, 1948. "They have a theory, quaint but sound, that if they have possession their opponents aren't going to score.

"In one quarter of an important game, the ball was theirs almost 11 minutes of the 15. They made only two touchdowns, but the other fellow, naturally, didn't score at all. That will be a part of their strategy today and will be worth watching by you grandstand quarterbacks."

Smith also informed the Cotton Bowl crowd to keep an eye on Petchel:

"He will be the smallest man on the field and that, no doubt, includes the waterboys. He weighs only 145 pounds and Higgins worried about him all the way down until he learned there were no gopher holes in Dallas.

"With that 145 on the hoof, Elwood can do about all there is to be done with a football. He is one of the most remarkable little men I have ever seen in football, and he could, possibly, steal the show."

He did, too.

Trouble In Dallas

"It was a most unusual bowl trip because of the situation with blacks in the South."

Ed Czekaj and the rest of the Penn State players who went to Dallas for the Cotton Bowl on January 1, 1948, remembered it for a long time. The Nittany Lions' superb team of that season carried a contingent of more than 40 players. However, 2 of them were Negro—and that started trouble in Dallas.

"In those days, that was a first...the first black boys to set foot in the Cotton Bowl," recalls Czekaj, referring to Wally Triplett and Dennie Hoggard. "The manager of athletics at that time went down to Dallas in advance, like you normally do for any bowl game, to make all the arrangements.

"When he got down there he found out that nobody would house the football team because we had two blacks on the squad. So we got hold of a couple of alumni in the area, and they had a few contacts with the people at a Naval base between Dallas and Fort Worth. The Navy people consented to house the team—right at the Naval barracks. Thank God they did, or I don't know where we would have stayed!"

But it was 18 miles outside of Dallas and a tough place to stay, recalls Czekaj, now the Athletic Director at Penn State.

"We were all 26, 27, 28 years old, four or five years in the service, you know, and we went down there for a bowl game and had to sleep in double-decker bunks," recalls Czekaj. It was just like our World War II days...we even dined on Navy chow."

Ironically, Triplett and Hoggard had the time of their lives,

Larry Cooney is away on a 36-yard touchdown play after taking a pass from Elwood Petchell in the 1948 Cotton Bowl game. Penn State tied SMU, 13-13.

while the whites suffered.

"The thing we couldn't understand was we all stayed at the barracks, but every evening blacks would come out in limousines and escort Triplett and Hoggard into town for good times," recalls Czekaj. "They really exploited the situation.

"Meanwhile, the rest of the team was locked up in the barracks, and they showed old movies that we had seen three or four times. We had no entertainment whatsoever. The players became disgruntled, and Steve Suhey finally went to the coach and said, 'Hey, you've got to get these guys off the base! These aren't kids, these are grown men.'

"So they decided to take us out one night, and they took us to the top of a bank building. It was supposed to be the tallest building in Dallas. That was our big sightseeing trip for the week. But, to be honest, not all the guys went up, and some of them even disappeared for the night.

"As you can see, there was a lack of cooperation between the administration, the coaches, and players at that particular time."

To make things doubly hard on the Nittany Lions, practices were hindered by bad weather. It was not easy tuning up for the biggest game of the year in rain, sleet, and snow.

"I don't know if the situation did us any good or not," says Czekaj. "I don't like to second-guess any game. I do know that SMU had a real fine football team with Doak Walker. They threw long passes twice on Jeff Durkota, and before you knew it the score was 13-0 in their favor.

"But after we got squared away we settled back and tied the ball game 13-13. Hoggard was in the end zone, and Elwood Petchel threw a pass in the final seconds that hit him about here (Czekaj holds his stomach), but he dropped it. We would have won."

Hoggard was not the only one embarrassed in that game. So was Czekaj.

"My only claim to fame is that I missed the extra point that would have won the Cotton Bowl game," says Czekaj. "No matter where I go, they always remember that. Of course Walker missed one for them, too, but they've forgotten that. I get it wherever I go in my travels."

Before throwing that desperation pass to Hoggard at the

end, Petchel was just about the whole Penn State offense. He passed for both touchdowns, completed seven throws in all for 93 yards, and rushed for 25 more yards. Fran Rogel, the Penn State fullback, led all rushers with 95 yards, outgaining even the redoubtable Walker.

The Mustangs scored the first touchdown of the game on an eight-play, 82-yard drive in the first quarter. Walker threw a 50-yard pass to Paul Page for the score, then kicked the extra point for a 7-0 SMU lead. In the second quarter the Mustangs took the ball on their 37-yard line and drove for another touchdown. After Dick McKissack had driven 19 yards up the middle, Walker went over on a short plunge to give the Mustangs a 13-0 lead. The SMU star missed the extra-point try this time.

With less than two minutes left in the half, Larry Cooney returned the kickoff 22 yards to the Penn State 35. Petchell moved the Nittany Lions downfield with a 17-yard pass and a 16-yard run. A penalty and two incomplete passes put Penn State in a tough situation, but Petchel threw a 36-yard scoring pass to Cooney to cut the SMU lead to 13-7 at halftime.

Powered by the running of Rogel and Petchel late in the third period, Penn State moved the ball 44 yards to SMU's one-inch line. But the Texas team held and kicked. This time Petchel received the ball and ran it back to the SMU nine-yard line. Rogel carried two times for five yards, and Petchel fired a running pass to Triplett in the end zone. Czekaj missed the extra point and the score was tied, 13-13.

In the final seconds Petchel tried desperately to move the Nittany Lions and looked as if he would provide a miraculous finish. He completed a 24-yard pass to Bob Hicks. Then, with two seconds remaining, he fired one to Hoggard in the end zone, but the player was too well covered to see the pass. The ball hit his hands near his stomach and fell to the ground.

As the final gun sounded, Czekaj was one of the most dejected players on the field. Wishing to console his blond kicker who had missed the crucial extra point, Higgins approached Czekaj and asked: "Did you think your kick was good, Ed?"

"I don't know, coach," said Czekaj. "You always told me to keep my head down."

High Diddle Diddle, Rogel Up The Middle

A funny thing happened to the Nittany Lions on the way to another bowl trip and the Lambert Trophy in 1948. They lost to Pitt when they were not supposed to.

Even Fran Rogel could not save the day. The player Bob Higgins called the best fullback he ever coached bucked almost the length of the field in the Pittsburgh fog but was stopped at the goal line as the final gun went off.

The score was 7-0 in favor of Pitt, and it should never have happened as far as Sam Tamburo was concerned.

"We should have beaten Pitt," insisted the all-America end. "We had a good ball carrier in Larry Joe but kept running Rogel up the middle. You know, 'High diddle diddle, run up the middle.'

"Joe, a speedster who could run outside, sat on the bench because they were afraid of his fumbling. We had the horses, we were supposed to beat them by three touchdowns. We ended up getting beat on a pass interception...their tackle intercepted and went for a touchdown."

The interception of an Elwood Petchell pass by Nick Bolkovac handed the Nittany Lions their only defeat of the season on the next-to-the-last week. It was fitting, though, that if anyone was to beat Penn State that year, it would be the Panthers. Their overall domination of the series prior to the 1950s had been downright uncanny.

They beat a pretty good Penn State team in 1948, too. Except for some losses on the line, this was virtually the same

Fullback Fran Rogel: "I'm never down."

honored squad of 1947, with a year's experience to boot. However, for some reason, the same chemistry did not happen in 1948.

Even Higgins himself was not so sure about a second straight unbeaten season. When asked at the start what he thought about Penn State's chances for another perfect year, the white-haired coach replied: "A team must not only be good, it also must be lucky to win all its games."

It was a fighting team, to be sure. And a wacky one, too, with people like Petchel around. Perhaps because of his size, the diminutive halfback was usually the source of funny stories. In his earlier days Petchel tried to tackle a Navy player but wound up as a piggy-back rider because he was not strong enough to bring him down. As he passed the Penn State bench on the back of the runner, Petchel shouted "Hi, ho, Silver!" to Higgins.

Rogel was another in the cast of characters. His teammates nicknamed him "Punchy" because he appeared oblivious to everything while running. He was always the last one to hear the referee's whistle blowing a play dead. He just kept straight ahead.

"I never hear anything when I'm on the field except signals," he would say.

Rogel was not only known for his eccentricities, but also for a perfect pair of football legs that gave him superb balance. Rogel stayed on his feet longer than anyone else in the lineup.

"I don't know how he did it," says Joe Bedenk, the line coach. "I've never seen another back who could do it quite the same."

Rogel's legs were so spectacular that when he used to audition for college coaches in high school, he was always told to pull his pants down so visitors could see his showpieces.

"You'd think that it was only because of my legs that they were interested in me," Rogel said.

Because of those fabulous legs, Rogel was virtually irrepressible at full steam. He was always distressed by what he called a referee's "fast whistle."

One time as he walked back to the huddle he pulled at the referee's sleeve and said, "Hey, Mister, don't blow that thing so fast. I'm never down."

Despite the big difference in girth, Rogel and Petchel were in

187

the same class as fighters. They never ran away from a brawl, especially on a football field. They were involved in a lulu in a pre-season scrimmage against St. Bonaventure.

The Nittany Lions had been giving the Bonnies a particularly tough time in this practice game. The St. Bonaventure frustration exploded into a punching bout after a play ended in a pileup.

Higgins took the fight in stride until he saw the dwarfish Petchel run in the direction of the free-for-all. The coach leaped to his feet and shouted at his little halfback, "Hey, Petchel, get out of there. Do you want to get hurt?" Later, Higgins reflected, "The fellow's too small to get mixed up with those big linemen."

If the season of 1948 ended as a bust, it started with a bang.

Penn State opened with three routs—35-0 over Bucknell, 34-14 over Syracuse, and 37-7 over West Virginia. Dreams of another perfect season were spoiled, however, when Michigan State tied the Nittany Lions 14-14 in the fourth week of the year. Not only was the game a significant turning point in a less-glamorous season for Penn State, it was also indirectly responsible for creating more elbow room at Beaver Field.

Penn State's home stadium only seated 17,700 at the time, and it was not enough to hold the crowd that showed for the battle of intersectional powers.

"Biggie Munn was then in his early years as Michigan State's coach, and the Spartans were beginning to entertain ideas of grandeur," recalled a Penn State historian. "The game was a natural, and naturally we had a big crowd for it.

"What a game it was and what a sight Beaver Field was! Twenty-three thousand fans poured into the little stands, edged up to the sideline, climbed trees, sat on top of cars, and even brought stepladders. There was hardly room on the benches for the players and coaches, and Munn did not like it one bit. His temper was not helped any when a 100-yard run by one of his halfbacks, George Guerre, was called back because of clipping.

"Munn blasted us from coast to coast and so did a pack of writers who came from the Midwest to report the game. You never saw so much debris in your life as that crowd left. On Sunday morning the place looked like a dump heap. Then and there Penn State officials decided to expand their stadium. The result was a new plant that could accommodate a few more than 30,000."

The enlarged seating capacity came in handy, and eventually grew almost twice that size as Penn State went to a schedule that was more nationally oriented. The man responsible for this movement was Ernie McCoy, the Penn State athletic director who insisted that there should be less provincialism in Penn State's future plans.

After the Michigan State game, which Penn State tied on a complicated pass-and-lateral play involving Petchel, Tamburo, and John Simon, the Nittany Lions swept by Colgate 32-13, Penn 13-0, and Temple 47-0.,

Then came Pitt on an appropriately gloomy Saturday. The

Sam Tamburo, Penn State's all-America end: "We should have beaten Pitt."

loss stopped a 17-game Penn State unbeaten streak.

"It was just one of those games," said Higgins, whose long history of heart trouble was not helped by the tense 7-0 loss. "It happens in every sport. We figured to win and should have won.

"We drove close in the first five minutes, and an offside penalty stopped us. We drove again, and a pass went awry. And so it went. We should have won the game, but I don't think we felt that the pressure of a long undefeated string was responsible for the loss. Another year and it might have been.

"Every coach will tell you he wins games he figures to lose, and vice versa. We had the horses that season—there wasn't any lack of experienced players. I'd be inclined to agree that the offense will feel the pressure first, but in the Pitt game I don't feel that the pressure resulted in our failure to score."

Rogel had one of the best days of his career, accounting for 116 of Penn State's 188 yards rushing. But his fine performance was lost in the significance of the defeat. It cost Penn State both a bowl bid and the Lambert Trophy.

It did not matter that Penn State defeated Washington State 7-0 on the last game of the season and finished with an excellent 7-1-1 record. The year had a downbeat ending because of the loss to Pitt, a longtime nemesis. As it turned out, it was Higgins' last hurrah, too. Because of failing health, he was forced to retire in his mid-50s.

The retirement left an uncomfortable situation at Penn State and mushroomed into a power struggle for the top job between two of Higgin's assistants, Joe Bedenk and Earle Edwards.

The once-cozy football family soon split in half with factions backing each candidate. Edwards' supporters were from the present coaching staff while Bedenk was backed by the university establishment. Because of Bedenk's long association with the school, and the powerful forces working behind the scene for him, he eventually was named head coach. Edwards resigned and left for an assistant's job at Michigan State. Later he became the head coach at North Carolina State and revisited University Park for one of the most memorable games of the 1960s.

The 51-year-old Bedenk, Penn State's "New Dealer," instituted an immediate change of policy. Perhaps because he was already the baseball coach he dismissed the traditional spring football practice for veterans. He urged the experienced football players to go out for other sports in the spring, like track or baseball, for instance.

"Spring football practice is used to teach the fundamentals of the game to the boys," said Bedenk. "If some of the more experienced letter-winners go out for other sports, the boys who need the practice will have a better chance to learn the things the seniors already know."

Bedenk also made some significant changes in the Penn State offensive style.

"Although we'll stick to the single wing, you may see us adopting a new man-in-motion flanker system to our style of play, come the '49 season," said Bedenk. "Football is growing a little more wide open."

Apparently content to be a line coach for 24 years, Bedenk viewed his new position with a bit of trepidation.

"There's very little difference about me from last year or any year," he said. "I'm still the same pure-bred country boy. The only thing is that I have more troubles now."

He did not know the half of it. There was still some resentment among the coaching staff about his appointment, since a lot of the men were Edwards' backers. It was not a happy season at all for the 1949 Penn State football "family."

It did not help, either, that Bedenk's hands were tied in the department of athlete subsidization. Scholarships were still taboo at Penn State, and Bedenk recalls that "they wouldn't even give us a night meal for the athletes."

Penn State had a winning season, but not by much. The Nittany Lions won five games and lost four, their worst season since 1938, and Bedenk returned to his former job as line coach after just one year as boss.

The situation was rather muddled for a while at the mountain-bound retreat, and Penn State was not even able to find a coach by the time of spring practice. Earl Bruce, one of the assistants, was named interim coach in this period while the school continued to search for the right man. It was a time of confusion and tension.

The Nittany Lions needed a unique individual to straighten their wobbly ship, and the university came up with Rip Engle.

191

Of Mules And Men

"Rip Engle's here."

A secretary with a pleasant face stuck her head in the door of Penn State's sports information office and announced the news.

Charles A. "Rip" Engle waited in an office across the hall. He offered a warm greeting and suggested that perhaps it would be nice to talk in the football trophy room.

He said, "I hope I didn't keep you waiting too long," and settled into a chair next to a low-slung coffee table. And while spring warmth flooded the historical room, one of the most famous coaches in Penn State football history told stories about mules and men.

"I've come from as far down as people can come," said Engle, "that's why I'm so grateful for everything that's happened to me."

Engle said that he learned a lot about life from driving a mule in the Pennsylvania coal mines at the age of 14.

"That's the most prominent mule I ever knew," Engle said, his voice barely above a whisper. "That mule taught me a lot of lessons. He was the greatest mule...a small mule...but I always thought, 'What a wonderful animal.' He was always happy working. He could outwork all the rest of the mules put together. That mule taught me how to work."

The white-haired Engle paused, scanning the trophy-laden walls as he reflected on boyhood days.

"When that mule died, we skinned it," said Engle. "We would have liked to stuff it—but we didn't have the money. You know, my brother and I had that skin for 20 years?"

While driving mules in Elk Lick, Pennsylvania (now Salisbury), Engle naturally did not have time for football. In fact he never saw a game until he was a freshman in college.

"I think they had a team in Somerset, but Somerset was 30 miles away and hard to get to," he said. "I'd read about football, and my uncle, who played at Penn State, had talked to me about it. I had a real interest in trying to find out what it was."

Engle did not get the chance right away, though, because he continued to mine for coal. Engle was a mine supervisor at 19, but desperately wanted to further his education.

"My brother didn't want to go back to school, but I was going to get back to school somehow," he said.

Engle went to Blue Ridge College in Maryland and participated in the first football game he saw. Later he attended Western Maryland College and was applauded as an all-Maryland end in 1929, leading the team to an unbeaten, untied 11-game season. Incidentally, the coach of the team was Dick Harlow, the former Penn State coach.

Upon graduation in 1930 Engle went right into coaching. Actually, he had no choice.

"I never expected to be a coach," said Engle. "I got out of school right after the Depression and that was the only kind of job I could get. Coach Harlow had two jobs for me coaching, and I couldn't find another job to save me. Otherwise I would have never been a coach."

It was a good thing for Waynesboro (Pennsylvania) High School that Engle took the job there. His clubs won 8 conference titles and finished with 86 victories and only 17 losses and 5 ties in 11 years. After a year of graduate work at his alma mater in 1941, Engle moved to Brown University as an assistant football coach in 1942 and 1943.

In 1944 he was named head coach at Brown and became one of the pioneers of the Wing-T offense. He spent his first two years as Brown's head coach perfecting it, and his teams operated out of the formation almost exclusively until 1959 when he expanded into the Multiple-T at Penn State.

The first couple of years at Brown were tough, Engle recalled, but there were some good days too.

Rip Engle: "I've come from as far down as people can come."

"One of my earliest thrills came in 1944," he said. "We had a group consisting of 17-year-olds and wartime rejects, and it was a lean year for victories as we played the 'loaded' Yales, Armys, Boston U.'s, and Holy Crosses. We met Colgate in our final game, and Brown had not beaten Colgate for 20 years and had never defeated an Andy Kerr-coached team.

"Relying on a series of quick traps and quarterback-keeper plays we upset Colgate 32-20. It was at this time that I learned to know and admire Coach Kerr. He was a great gentleman in defeat and complimented our team and Wing-T offense. It was a lesson I tried never to forget.

"On our team that day we had Pat O'Brien at quarterback, Roger Williams at wingback, Tommy Dorsey at halfback, and Dick Tracy at end. A very imposing list of celebrities it was—but they weren't the originals."

Engle teams won 28, lost 20, and tied 4 in six years at Brown. Then came an offer from Penn State in 1950. Engle said, "Yes," but walked into a peculiar situation.

"When coaches come into a new school, they usually bring four or five of their own people with them," said Engle. "But I couldn't."

One of the stipulations of Engle's new job was that he retain the entire Penn State coaching staff, including Joe Bedenk, who had served as head coach for one season and then stepped down after 1949. Engle arrived only with a young assistant, Joe Paterno. The brash 23-year-old, assigned as a coach of quarterbacks at first, would later be heard from as Engle's eventual successor.

Engle was excited about joining a school that could become a national power, but came to Penn State "with a lot of misgivings."

"I had never met these coaches," he explained. "They were all Single Wing coaches. The whole staff that was here had been here long before me...and then Joe (Paterno) — had never coached, although I knew he had great possibilities. It was a pretty precarious situation, and I just wondered how smart I was, really.

"But we worked real hard together, and it was the greatest thing that could have happened. I always say I owe so much to these coaches here."

Engle rallied his staff and explained in no uncertain terms what he needed for a winning football team—full cooperation.

"I'll never forget that talk I had with my new staff," said Engle, leaning forward to emphasize the point. "I thought it over and knew I had to talk with them.

"I told them all that I didn't know what their loyalties were, and neither did I care. But if we were going to win we could never make it without certain things.

"I told them I wanted them to go home and talk it over and think it over with their wives. I said, number one, I needed their

Rip Engle (right) and Joe Paterno stayed together since their days at Brown and became a winning team at Penn State.

196

complete loyalty. Number two, I needed them to work as hard as it took to get the job done. If they were willing to do those two things, then we'd have a deal.

"Well, they went home and talked to their wives, and then I talked to each one in the morning. And everything worked out so well."

Engle credited former Coach Bob Higgins with helping him over the rough spots in the early years. "He deserves an awful lot of credit," said Engle, thankful that Higgins never embarrassed him with any second-guessing.

"Bob was a good, solid football coach, and I'm so glad he was the man who was here," said Engle.

With a new football coach came a new change of policy. The school gave out full scholarships during Engle's first year in order to help him build a national power. The days of the "Grand Experiment" were gone but apparently not forgotten since the amount of scholarships was not particularly large. Engle was allowed 45, less that half of the roaring '70s.

After comfortable seasons of 5-3-1 and 5-4, Engle started to show something solid in 1952 with a 7-2-1 record that included a 17-0 victory over powerful Pitt.

"That was the first one that got us moving," Engle recalled. "Pitt had one of its great teams that year. They had beaten Ohio State, Notre Dame, Army, and a lot of fine football teams and they were on their way to the Orange Bowl. In fact they had packed already.

"But we went out there and broke loose for a touchdown in the first half and went on to beat them by seventeen points. At the end of the game the Pitt students started throwing oranges at their bench from the stands. I thought, maybe, they were going to throw them at us. It was too bad. I felt sorry for the Panthers from that standpoint. But it was a great victory for Penn State."

Another significant victory came in 1954, when Penn State beat Illinois 14-12. It opened the season with a flourish and raised some eyebrows.

"Illinois was picked No. 1 in the country in pre-season polls," Engle said. "They had three great backs—Mel Bates, J. C. Caroline, and Abe Woodson. It looked like our ride to Champaign was futile, although we had some great players, too—Rosey Grier and a halfback named Lenny Moore.

"Don Bailey, our quarterback, was outstanding that day, and he had a great pass-target in Jim Garrity. It was a battle down to the wire, and we came away with a tremendous win. It was my first coaching victory over a Big Ten team and a great boost to our morale. Illinois never seemed to recover and ended up with a dismal record. We just broke their hearts, I guess."

A 21-20 victory over Syracuse featuring a running duel between Moore and the Orangemen's Jimmy Brown was a highlight in an otherwise disappointing 5-4 season in 1955. In 1956 Engle's crew upset Ohio State 7-6. The coach remembered that one, almost play-for-play.

"I'll never forget it," said Engle. "The score was 0-0 with about five minutes to play, and Milt Plum kicked the ball 72 yards dead on the Ohio State three-yard line. I told him when they went back in to hold them in there and we'd get one chance to score. So they held them on downs and made the Buckeyes kick out, and we went in and scored. And in 30 seconds they had a touchdown and missed the extra point, and it ended with us in front by one point. So you have to be lucky in this game, too."

Engle teams also beat Ohio State in 1963 by a 10-7 score and in 1964 by 27-0, continuing a domination over the Big Ten club. In four meetings, dating back to 1912, the Nittany Lions have never lost to Ohio State.

Under Engle's guidance Penn State played four bowl games—twice as many as the rest of the Nittany Lions' teams did prior to 1950. Penn State won the Liberty Bowl twice, 7-0 over Alabama in 1959 and 41-12 over Oregon in 1960. The Nittany Lions split two games in the Gator Bowl, beating Georgia Tech 30-15 in 1961 and losing to Florida 17-7 in 1962. Ironically, the year that the Nittany Lions lost their only bowl game under Engle, they had their best season with a 9-1 record.

Engle went out a winner, retiring in 1965 with a 19-7 victory over Maryland that he termed "the most perfect football game I've ever been connected with." It gave him a career record of 104-48-4 at Penn State.

"Both offense and defense were perfectly planned and

Rip Engle shouts encouragement from the Penn State sidelines.

perfectly executed in my last game," he said, "and we just happened to guess right with everything we did. Usually something goes wrong some place in a game. But not that one."

Engle lit up with a smile as he recalled special moments in Penn State history. He spoke in a low monotone, leaning forward and cupping his cherubic, tanned face in two fists. His bright eyes traced the cluttered, paneled, brown walls and the plush green carpet as he reflected on a question. When talking he usually looks you in the eye.

In the center of the artistic trophy room, Engle was surrounded by football history—some of it made by himself. Pictures of Penn State heroes lined the wall, and certain games were denoted in a variety of manners. Engle's Liberty Bowl triumphs, for instance, were dramatized by the footballs used in those games. They each had the scores and a little Liberty Bell painted in white near the football's laces.

But you knew, while speaking to Engle, that victories were not the important thing in his career. People were.

"I didn't want anyone to enjoy losing, naturally, but on the other hand I didn't want my players to break their hearts losing," he said.

Engle perhaps used the word "grateful" more than any other in the 90-minute conversation.

"I came up the hard way, and I appreciate everything that people have done for me," he said. "Everybody has been so good to me, and I have never really had any bad experiences in the game. I only held three coaching jobs, and each step was a bigger challenge and it all turned out so well. I'm grateful to football and the people I've known in the game."

He knew when to leave, too. Engle is among that rare breed of coaches who always make moves on their own initiative. He never had to be told to get out.

"I knew when it came time to retire," he said. "I felt it. When football began to lose its charm and began to lose its fun, I went to the president of the school (Dr. Eric A. Walker) and said I wanted to leave. And he said, well, you can still be our coach five more years. And I said, yes, that's when I want to get out—when I can still be your coach."

Thirteen Is A Lucky Number

Rip Engle and the college football renaissance arrived just about at the same time at Penn State. The 1950s signaled a significant change in the sport.

Previously dominated by wartime veterans, the GI's eventually drained out of the college football system and gave way to teenagers. The "boys" had replaced the "men."

This was one of the main reasons for an unusual amount of upsets, particularly in 1950. The dramatic readjustments at most universities provided a series of turnabouts such as Purdue's defeat of Notre Dame and Maryland's victory over Michigan State.

It did not surprise Engle, however. The 13th coach in Penn State's football history expected it.

"The GI's rounded out their eligibility in 1949," said Engle. "Only a few war veterans were left behind. Now, high school boys are representing colleges again. There'll be more and more upsets as the season progresses. Unbeaten teams will be few in number. The men are gone. Boys have taken over college football again."

Along with the change in the makeup of college football came a change in the Penn State style. The Single Wing was out, the Wing-T in.

But the arrival of a new offensive system caused headaches. For one thing, Engle needed a quarterback to work out of the mod T-Formation. The period of adjustment was reflected in the early-season record, which got progressively worse after an opening-day 34-14 victory over Georgetown. The Nittany Lions lost to Army, Syracuse, and Nebraska after that.

The emergence of Vince O'Bara as a competent quarterback helped Penn State become a winner in the second half of the season, though. Erratic at the start of the year because he had never played any other position than tailback in the Single Wing, O'Bara learned his new job quite well after a while. The Nittany Lions tied Temple after the three-game losing streak and then finished the season with victories over Boston College, West Virginia, Rutgers, and Pitt.

O'Bara was Penn State's leading offensive player that year, combining his passing and running for 692 yards. Another convert, Tony Orsini, made the shift from wingback in the Single Wing to left halfback in the Wing-T and led the 1950 team in rushing with 563 yards. Paul Anders and Ted Shattuck also adapted extremely well to the Engle approach and became fine runners as sophomores.

Anders, a power runner called a reasonable facsimile of Fran Rogel, ended the 1950 season with a star performance as Penn State defeated Pitt in a thriller, 21-20. Anders scored two touchdowns to help the Nittany Lions run up a 21-7 halftime lead. O'Bara did the rest after Pitt got too close for comfort, running conservative plays at the end that insured the one-point decision.

Engle thus ignored the Pitt jinx in his first season. The only bad thing that happened to the 42-year-old coach on that icy Saturday was that he fell into a snow drift on the sidelines and almost lost his wallet.

Engle's record of 5-3-1 was a slight improvement over the previous season. But the new coach was still in a rebuilding process and was not too optimistic about 1951.

"If we equal last year's record, I'll be eminently satisfied," said the ever-cautious Engle. "Any improvement will make it a tremendous success."

The Nittany Lions still appeared to be a couple of years away from distinction. The crop of new faces was quite imposing, though. Jesse Arnelle and Roosevelt Grier were among them, but unfortunately did not get much playing time right away. Tony Rados and Bob Szajna operated as the Penn State quarterbacks in a lackluster 5-4 season that appeared to be a comedown for the Nittany Lions. Engle did not think so, however, pointing out that Penn State's schedule was much tougher with the addition of Purdue and Boston University and the resumption of series with Michigan State and Villanova.

It was a season highlighted by great individual performances, such as Bob Pollard's 248 yards rushing against Rutgers. And Arnelle, a 6-foot-5 end with enormous hands, showed great promise in the season's finale, a 13-7 loss to Pitt. Arnelle caught four passes in a drive for Penn State's only touchdown, including a spectacular, twisting, diving grab of a long one by Rados. Arnelle finally outran and outmaneuvered the Pitt defensemen in the end zone to take Szajna's perfect pass and temporarily tie the score at 7-7. Grier also saw action in this one and was cited for his standout defensive play.

Despite the presence of these two, and several more good players, Engle was characteristically pessimistic for 1952. After all, he pointed out, opponents like Purdue, West Virginia, Nebraska, Penn, Syracuse, and Pitt all showed evidence of greater improvement than Penn State. For a change he was wrong. Penn State showed definite signs of awakening with a glamorous record of seven victories, two losses, and one tie in 1952. The tie, a 20-20 game with Purdue, and one of the victories, 17-0 over Pitt, were dramatic turning points in the early 1950s for Engle.

The Purdue game, before 22,000 wildly cheering fans at Beaver Field, featured a passing duel between Rados and Dale Samuels of the Boilermakers. The Penn State quarterback completed 17 out of 30 passes for a total of 179 yards. Samuels made good on 14 of 28 for 130. The star of the game, though, as far as Engle was concerned, was Grier, the 6-foot-4, 260-pound tackle.

"Grier made a key play in the game," said Engle. "He blocked a 240-pound Purdue lineman on the five-yard line and carried him into the end zone. Purdue was in a goal line defense, and our halfback followed Grier's block to score."

Penn State even had a 13-7 lead at one point over the highly-favored visitors from the Big Ten after Rados threw a touchdown pass early in the third quarter. After Purdue had gone ahead 20-13, Penn State tied the game with a late interception by Don Eyer on the Boilermaker 31-yard line. With less than

Penn State players carry Rip Engle from the field after their dramatic 21-20 victory over longtime nemesis Pitt in 1950.

four minutes remaining, the Nittany Lions scored the tying touchdown on nine plays, with Rados sneaking over at the end.

The victory over Pitt Engle called one of his "biggest thrills." It no doubt was also one of the most significant of his career.

"It was a great upset victory for us, and the winter was much shorter because of it," said Engle. "Our defensive line, anchored by Grier and Danny DeFalco and Pete Schoderbek, stopped Pitt cold and they couldn't score."

The Panthers had national status and a bowl bid in the offing, and the Nittany Lions had nothing to lose.

"A Pitt win over us would get them a bid to the Orange Bowl," said Engle, who recalled that Pitt officials were so certain of victory over Penn State that "many of their wives had already done their packing for a year-end vacation in sunny Florida."

Most of the crowd of 53,766 came out in Pittsburgh to wish the local heroes bon voyage to the Orange Bowl, but instead watched the Panthers turn to goats. Intercepted passes played a big part in the Penn State victory. They provided the spark for both touchdowns and helped turn back a Pitt drive in the

second quarter.

Jack Sherry picked off a Pittsburgh pass on the 49-yard line and ran it back to the Panther 29. Don Eyer was thrown for a big loss just as the quarter ended, but Penn State renewed its drive at the start of the second period. Rados threw a pass to Jim Garrity on the 16-yard line, Keith Vesling went up the middle for eight yards, Rados passed to Arnelle at the three, and then Buddy Rowell plunged for the touchdown and a 7-0 Penn State lead.

Pitt made two sustained drives in the second quarter, but the deepest one—to the Penn State 18—was stopped when Schoderbek intercepted a pass at the 10-yard line.

In the second half a field goal by Bill Leonard gave the Nittany Lions a 10-0 lead. And then they finished off the tough Panthers after another interception by Sherry set the ball up on the Pitt 10. The ball was moved to the one on a roughing foul by Pitt, and Rados took it the final yard.

With the victory went the "Old Ironsides" trophy, symbolic of the district's annual Big Three battle between Penn State, Pitt, and West Virginia. The Nittany Lions earlier had beaten the Mountaineers 35-21.

The huge crowd at Pitt Stadium also gave Penn State's 1952 team another distinction of sorts. For the first time in 66 years of collegiate football, the Nittany Lions played before crowds totalling 300,000 in a season. A crowd of 67,000 had showed up for the Penn game at Franklin Field and 51,000 for the Michigan State game at East Lansing. A new home attendance mark was also established at Beaver Field, where Penn State drew more than 100,000 fans.

Interesting things were beginning to happen at University Park. Even though Syracuse had beaten the Nittany Lions 25-7 in 1952 to clinch the Lambert Trophy, it appeared that the 13th coach in Penn State's history was a lucky number.

What's New?

The 1953 season was a year of surprises for the Penn State football team. The arrival of Lenny Moore as an instant star. The emergence of Roosevelt Grier as a team leader. And, perhaps the most unexpected of all, the big snowfall before the Fordham game.

Of course, the weatherman had not predicted such a snowfall. "Cool and dry" was the forecast.

So, although snow had already begun falling, Coach Rip Engle herded his players into buses, and they made a 20-mile trip to their mountain retreat that Friday, as was customary on the eve of a home game. The purpose of the monastic hideaway was to assure no distractions and plenty of rest the night before the game.

The complacent contingent ate a big meal, watched television for a few hours, and then tucked into bed, no doubt dreaming about Saturday's contest with the Rams. Everybody, that is, but two assistant coaches—Jim O'Hora and Joe Paterno. They stirred around after midnight, nervously noticing that the snowfall was not letting up. Finally about 2 a.m., Engle himself was up. The coach ordered his assistants to sleep, and he sat by himself at a fireplace, pondering the problems that would arise if it did continue to snow at its present fast rate.

The extremely heavy precipitation began to make college officials nervous, as well. Athletic Director Ernie McCoy and his assistants mapped snow removal strategy on campus. Ike Gilbert rounded up some heavy snow removal equipment, and Ralph

Ricker visited dormitories seeking volunteer help.

McCoy, Gilbert, and Ricker were at Beaver Field shortly after dawn, heavily bundled and in command of a small army of students, evolving their plan of attack. A dozen trucks roared into the area, and all hands went about the task of clearing the football field and stands of a night-long snowfall that had now amounted to 10 inches.

The work of the makeshift task force went so well that by midmorning officials decided to go on with the game. The Fordham aggregation, safe and sound in nearby Lewistown, readily agreed.

Meanwhile, Penn State's athletic office had its hands full with several details, like ordering food for the working crew, starting program sales, and checking that the game officials would arrive in time for the kickoff. People who usually travel to Penn State games from neighboring towns were warned by radio announcement to stay off the treacherous highways. And the athletic office had to contact some 60 high school bands and tell them to stay home, despite the traditional Band Day outing.

The working crew had made some headway by noon. The field was cleared to ground level, a place smoothed on the sidelines for each team, and many seats in 30,000-seat Beaver Field dusted off for an expected crowd of 5,000. The Fordham team, starting early and encountering no difficulty on the highways, comfortably arrived shortly after noon and began dressing for the game. Meanwhile, the stadium started to fill and eventually attracted 15,000 people, an amazing crowd considering that few believed the game would be played in the first place.

At about this juncture, with game time drawing near, somebody noticed that the Penn State football team had not yet made an appearance. The Athletic Office, naturally, had been in touch with Engle and also asked the State Police to perhaps escort the Penn State team bus from camp. However, the bus was not even able to get into the camp area because it ran into trouble plowing through snowy back roads. O'Hora and Paterno, fortified with a good night's sleep and a lusty brunch, put on sweat suits and jogged about a mile through heavy snow in search of the missing bus.

By this time Engle was fidgety. And when O'Hora and Paterno returned to report that their mission was unsuccessful, the head coach instructed two rifle-armed cooks to serve as lookouts and fire shots if and when the bus appeared. Then he formulated a plan of attack.

An advance contingent—eleven players least likely to see game action—moved out on foot and cleared a path for the regulars. The players fell in line by order of importance, and O'Hora and Paterno held up the rear.

This bedraggled group trundled through the drifts until a rifle's crack informed them that the bus had been found. The fatigued party boarded the vehicle and slowly made its way to Beaver Field. The bus arrived just about at kickoff time, tooting its way through a crowd filling the gateway to the stadium.

While his players dressed, Engle sought out Fordham Coach Ed Danowski and apologized for being late. Danowski was receptive to a belated start, 2 p.m. instead of the normal 1:30 p.m. starting time.

Danowski thoroughly sympathized with Engle's sad story. Take more than 30 minutes to get ready if you need it, Danowski insisted. Please, don't worry about Fordham, he said. "The delay won't lessen our desire to win," he told Engle.

As Engle was about to leave, Danowski asked: "By the way, what did you say the name of the camp was?"

"Camp Hate-To-Leave-It," replied a grim Engle, retiring hastily to his own dressing room.

If the experience at Camp-Hate-To-Leave-It was unpleasant to Engle, he found some consolation in the result of the match with Fordham. The Nittany Lions defeated the Rams 28-21 on that icy November 7. And Engle got further satisfaction watching deeds of two of the players he eventually placed on his personal "all-time" team—Lenny Moore and Roosevelt Grier.

Moore, one of the greatest of Penn State halfbacks, was a flashy runner even as a sophomore, when he rushed for more than 600 yards. An idea of his ability came in Moore's first game, the 1953 opener against Wisconsin, when he ran 65 yards for a touchdown around end. It was called back because of a penalty, and Penn State eventually lost 20-0, but Engle knew that he had found the breakaway threat he so desperately needed. Moore's singular presence changed Penn State's offensive orientation from passing to running.

Against Fordham that day, after the "Camp-Hate-To-Leave-

Lenny Moore signed a lot of autographs.

It" incident, Moore scored a touchdown on a typically long run, taking off straight up the middle on a draw play.

"Moore was the finest back I've ever known," said Engle. "His ability to be moving at full speed after two steps helped to make football look easy. He seemed to be able to change directions in mid-air and this assured him of a long career in pro football, for no one ever got a clear shot at him. (He later starred for the Baltimore Colts.)

"He had great mental toughness and the coordination necessary to be the best. You would get an idea of his ability if you

Tackle Roosevelt Grier, "big and agile as a cat."

could have seen him walk over to the broad jump pit one evening, after a hard practice, and with his uniform on, broad jump 22 feet. Lenny was just as good on defense as offense, too. He could block with anyone, was a great pass defender, and had no superior as a ball carrier."

The 6-foot, 175-pounder had his top day against Rutgers in 1955, when he rushed for 179 yards. Except for penalties nullifying some long runs, he would have been well over the 200-yard mark. In 1955 his ground-gaining yardage totaled 697, his pass receiving 37, his punt returning 45, and his kickoff returns 122. From 1953 through 1955 Moore rushed for a total of 2,380 yards, the second best career figure in the school's history. His best year was 1954, when he rushed for 1,082 yards.

Engle was not his only booster. Opposing coaches were duly impressed with the star from Reading, Pennsylvania.

After facing Moore one game, Art Lewis of West Virginia described him as terrifying.

"Moore scared you every time he got the ball," said Lewis. "That man sure could go. Our boys did a good job of stopping him—never letting him get started. But he looked good even when he was being thrown for a loss."

Bob Higgins, the former Penn State player and coach who had seen just about every fine runner in the school's history, had the supreme compliment.

"He's probably a better runner than anybody we've had—even better than Shorty Miller, Charley Way, and 'Lighthorse' Harry Wilson," said Higgins. "They could do some other things, perhaps, but I doubt whether any of them could run with this fellow."

Moore was Engle's favorite as a runner, and if the coach had a favorite person it was Grier—his beloved "Rosey."

"Rosey was a great human being," said Engle. "He had a sense of humor that contributed greatly to our squad morale. Everyone who knew him loved and admired him. He always knew when to insert a little humor into a dull practice session or give someone a lift when it was needed most."

One of Engle's favorite "Rosey" stories happened long after the big brute left Penn State and had gone on to successes in professional football and later show business. Engle had undergone some extensive surgery when he received a get-well card

212

from his former tackle.

"I had always insisted to the squad that you can never make the team sitting in the training room or in the whirlpool bath," said Engle. "Fifteen years later, I got his version of my statement of facts on a telegram after the surgery. It read: 'Dear Rip, you can't make the club sitting in the tub. Get well. Signed, 'Rosey.' "

"It was great for my morale, just as many of his remarks lifted the team in the '50s."

Grier "had a tendency to be lazy as a player," according to Engle. "He could never drive himself to obliterate the easy opponent.

"But," Engle added, "he was at his best against the good ones...he was big and agile as a cat."

Grier and Moore helped Penn State win six of nine games in 1953 and then were part of the conspiracy of 1954 in Champaign-Urbana that did much to uplift eastern football, not to mention the status of Penn State.

Three Of The Biggest Games

Rip Engle had a lot on his mind as he traveled to Champaign-Urbana, Illinois, for the opener of the 1954 football season. Not only was he thinking about meeting one of the strongest teams in the country, he was also worried about his own team.

Illinois was a known quantity with a collection of runners that purportedly eclipsed the strength of the legendary Red Grange powerhouses. Penn State had some fine players, too, but was in a tenuous stage of transformation. The loss of quarterback Tony Rados forced the Nittany Lions' game to change from a pass-oriented offense to an unproven running attack.

Of course, halfback Lenny Moore had displayed prowess in his sophomore year, but Engle's team in 1952 only rushed for a total of 1,661 yards—hardly a staggering figure when compared to the country's top balanced teams.

"It was plain when we lost Rados that we no longer had the passer to do what we did in 1952 and 1953," said Engle, talking about a quarterback who had broken just about every record in the Penn State books in his senior year as the Nittany Lions averaged 132 yards a game through the air.

So now it was Moore that Engle would build around. And the flashy Penn State junior would be assisted by Ron Younker and Billy Kane, a pair of strong inside runners.

En route to Champaign-Urbana, Engle also had his mind on some other runners—those of Illinois. Billed as the "nation's fastest backfield," it included J. C. Caroline, Mickey Bates, and

214

Abe Woodson. Caroline, incidentally, had broken all of Grange's running marks and was a full-fledged star as a sophomore in 1953.

Engle had to be more discouraged when he read the pre-season rankings and found Illinois voted No. 1 in the country. The Big Ten club had gone to the Rose Bowl the year before and was picked to repeat as conference champion.

It looked to Engle, and the "experts" as well, that Penn State did not belong in the ball game.

"Nobody gave us a chance," said Engle.

Memorial Stadium filled to 54,000 fans—the largest opening crowd in Illinois history. They were 54,000 noisy fans, too, because Illinois scored the first touchdown of the game. But an upset was in the making, perhaps the biggest of the 1954 college football season, and the participants knew it as Penn State walked off the field at halftime with a 14-6 lead.

The Illini got back on their feet again in the third period, drawing raves from their massive audience with quarterback Em Lindbeck's best pass of the day—a 36-yarder to Charley Butler. Several plays later Woodson ran the final 17 for an Illinois touchdown, although Penn State maintained a 14-12 lead when the Illinois PAT attempt failed.

Penn State wrapped it up in the fourth quarter on a long drive started on Moore's pass interception. The Nittany Lions marched to the Illinois five-yard line with time-consuming running plays, and that was where the game ended.

When Engle returned to a tumultuous welcome at Penn State, he called the victory "the most satisfying of my career." It was certainly one of the most important, for it gave eastern football a push in an era when it was considered unimposing.

"How did you stop Caroline?" was the question most asked of Engle.

Actually, the Nittany Lions did not stop Caroline altogether. He gained 116 yards. But Moore was a better runner that day with 137, and the next top two Penn State runners outclassed Illinois' fine backfield. Don Bailey had 76 yards and Bill Straub, 45. All Woodson and Bates could do was 36 yards combined!

Roosevelt Grier, Penn State's marvelous tackle, got a lion's share of the glory too.

"You could spot his huge frame making tackles on both sides

of the center," wrote the Penn State *Alumni News*. "Rosey did miss a few tackles, but it wasn't altogether his fault. The blame must be assigned to Earl Shumaker, junior guard from Beaver Falls, who played a tremendous game."

"That Shumaker sure chased me out of a lot of tackles," said a grinning Grier.

There were other victories in the Nittany Lions' 7-2 season that year, although none as significant. Moore was always the significant element, though. In a 35-13 success over Penn, the Nittany Lions' first nationally televised game, Moore shed six players on a 60-yard touchdown run. The week after, he made a 57-yard TD run in a 39-7 victory over Holy Cross, eluding five distinct tacklers on that jaunt.

"Maybe Lennie doesn't like to be tackled," kidded teammate Jesse Arnelle.

Penn State's new-found running power was dramatized against Penn and Holy Cross, when the Nittany Lions made 383 yards and 405, respectively, on the ground. In 1953 they had averaged 184.5 yards a game, and in 1954 the average was about 100 yards higher.

Moore went over 1,000 yards in 1954, and while slumping off the next season he established his highest single-game mark with 179 against Rutgers and battled Syracuse's Jimmy Brown in one of the most memorable running duels ever seen at Beaver Field.

A crowd of 30,434 witnessed a 21-20 victory for Penn State, another highlight of the early Engle era.

"It was, undoubtedly, one of our biggest upsets," said Engle. "We finished the season with a 5-4 mark that year, and we weren't really a good team. We did have Moore and Milt Plum in the backfield, but our line was one of the lightest in major college football, and we were playing a good Syracuse team which featured Brown, who was running over and around most everyone.

"The last quarter began with Penn State trailing, but then we caught fire. Moore made some great runs, Plum's passing started to click, and the whole team was inspired. Our defense man-handled Brown in key situations, and our fullback, Bill Straub, made yardage when it seemed impossible. It was one of the most thrilling and gratifying victories in Penn State history."

216

Brown gained 159 yards on 20 carries, scored three touch-downs, and kicked two extra points. Moore amassed 146 yards on 22 carries, scored a touchdown, and set up the winning score with those dynamic runs during an 80-yard drive in the final quarter.

"It's difficult to compare Brown with Moore," said the *Alumni News* after the tense game. "He lacks Lenny's great speed and deception as a runner. Brown just runs over you, and the boys say it really hurts when you grab hold."

Plum gained "great stature" in the Syracuse victory, said Engle. And, of course, Moore got the usual applause from his coach. "Moore was tremendous," Engle later recalled. "He never in three years equalled his performance against Syracuse."

After Moore's departure, Engle recorded his third big victory in three seasons, a 7-6 decision over Ohio State in 1956. To-gether with the victories over Illinois and Syracuse, these must rank as Engle's biggest accomplishments in his embryonic years at Penn State.

"The Buckeyes were undefeated at the time and had one of their longest victory strings going for them" said Engle. "They had Jim Parker, one of the best running guards in football, and he was quoted in the papers as saying that Ohio State would show the 'invaders from the East' just how good Big Ten foot-ball really was. The next day it became obvious the East could play good football, too.

"The ball see-sawed between the 20-yard lines until the fourth quarter when Milt Plum punted 72 yards out of bounds on the Ohio State three-yard line. We held, got the return punt at about their 45, and knew that this was our last chance. The drive that followed, well, I've never seen one so free of mechan-ical or mental errors. Plum threw at the right time, and Billy Kane, Ray Alberigi, and Bruce Gilmore ran as never before.

"The line moved some awfully big people, including the 250-pound Parker, and Gilmore scored after a Plum-to-Kane pass put us on their one-foot line. Plum kicked the all-important point. With less than four minutes to play, Ohio State came alive and scored, but they missed the vital extra point, and the 7-6 score held up.

"Our captain, Sam Valentine, had his greatest day as a line-backer in that game. Maybe it was because Sam had wanted to

"Too small" to play for Ohio State, Sam Valentine helped the Nittany Lions upset the Buckeyes in 1956.

play for Ohio State but was told he was too small. Anyway, Sam and his teammates put 83,000 people in Buckeye Stadium into a state of shock that day. Ten minutes after the game, they were still sitting frozen in their seats."

The victory was especially sweet since Penn State players had read disparaging remarks about themselves in the local newspapers. The Ohio State *Journal* called them "the beasts from the East" in one story. "They are an intruder on the Big Ten schedule," said the *Columbus Dispatch.*

Perhaps Ohio State Coach Woody Hayes was a bit too smug, too. While putting his players through their setting-up exercises before the game, they actually ran their game plays in a dummy scrimmage and even set up their defenses. Somebody in the press box remarked, "He's running through the plays he's planning for Wisconsin next week." This swaggering nonchalance might have been true, but it was also helpful to Penn State. A Nittany Lions' coach picked up a play that the Buckeyes had not previously used during the year, and it came in as a handy observation when it was later tried against Penn State in the game.

"That Ohio State game stands out as my greatest memory at Penn State," said Plum. "We were underdogs by four touchdowns, and everyone in Columbus thought we were coming in to just sell popcorn. But we put out 110 percent, and it was the best feeling of winning I've ever had."

Most of the Penn State team obviously felt that way, and that giddy feeling carried over to the next week's game with West Virginia. During the game the public address announcer reported that Ohio State had an early lead over Wisconsin, and a Penn State player interrupted Plum's huddle to ask if they had heard the news.

Valentine, Penn State's all-America guard, reacted sharply to the interruption, however.

"Listen, men, this is the West Virginia game, and we don't have it won yet. Let's forget that Ohio State game."

They beat West Virginia 16-6.

Who's Got The Tee?

With only seconds left in the first half of the 1959 Liberty Bowl game, the people on the Penn State bench were in a state of panic. The Nittany Lions had taken over the ball on the Alabama 22-yard line and had a good opportunity to score the first points of the tough defensive battle.

However, the kicking tee that was to be used for a crucial play was missing. After Alabama had punted into the wind and the ball bounced back and was downed on the Crimson Tide 22, Penn State Coach Rip Engle said to his players:

"Run two plays, and on the second play use the fake field goal."

With 55 seconds remaining in the half, Penn State used a swing pass on the first play. It netted four yards to the Alabama 18. Now time was running out, and the Nittany Lions could not stop the clock because they had used their last timeout only moments before.

At this point Engle and his assistants started running like madmen up and down the sidelines, shouting for the tee that would be used in the strategic fake field goal play. It was not found easily, however.

"Where's the tee?" yelled a nervous Engle. "Who's got it? Where is it?"

Earl Bruce, one of Engle's assistants, took up the chant: "Who's got the tee?"

As Engle ran one way and Bruce the other, another assistant, Sevor Toretti, began to scramble around, too.

"Tee, tee, who's got the tee?" he shouted.

The tee was finally found, but it was too late. Engle and his assistants no sooner had it in their possession when they looked up to see the ball being snapped on the field. The play was underway without the tee.

Quarterback Galen Hall had set up the play without going into a huddle. Hall knelt down and took the snap from center while Sam Stellatella presumably waited to kick.

Agitation on the Penn State sidelines during combat. White-haired Rip Engle, notes in hand, always looked the most worried.

221

Hall jumped up, rolled to his right, and threw a screen pass to Roger Kochman. Following a half-dozen blockers, the halfback took the ball across the goal line for the only score as Penn State won the first Liberty Bowl game, 7-0.

Engle later recalled the crucial incident in Philadelphia that provided him with an important victory.

"It's little things like that missing kicking tee that can cost you a game," he said. "Without a tee down, Alabama might have caught on that it was a fake kick play. The tee was supposed to be on the bench, but where it was I don't know. It sure had me worried. We put that play in the system just a few days before the game."

If Engle was concerned about small details, you could not blame him. He had seen too many games turn on technicalities. The most notable was a 13-9 loss to Syracuse in 1956 that became a cause celebre because of a bizarre illegal substitution penalty against Penn State.

Late in the game Syracuse was in an obvious punting situation deep in its territory when quarterback Milt Plum went to the sidelines to discuss strategy with Engle. Upon returning to the field Syracuse coaches immediately protested Plum's presence. Under the rules a player who started a quarter could reenter the game only once that quarter, and Syracuse claimed that Plum had already used his eligibility. Although perhaps a technicality, the referees sided with Syracuse and ruled that Plum's short visit to the sidelines was tantamount to a substitution.

While Penn State coaches hollered their displeasure, the referees stepped off a 15-yard penalty that allowed Syracuse to retain possession of the ball instead of turning it over to the Nittany Lions in good field position. What is worse, Plum was thrown out of the game.

"I was thrown out of the game falsely," said Plum, "and to this day I swear I could have gone in there and maybe won the game for us."

Ridge Riley, in his weekly football letter in the *Alumni News*, reported after the controversial decision: "Game movies later proved we were right. But it didn't do us any good. The worst thing is that Milt really might have won it by the way he was playing."

In the last two minutes of the first half, Plum had driven the Nittany Lions 66 yards and kicked a 29-yard field goal for a 9-6 halftime lead over the Orangemen.

Engle had a hard time beating Syracuse in those days, anyway, and could have used some good breaks. From 1956 to 1960, Syracuse won four of five games, including a crucial 20-18 triumph in 1957 that eventually led to the national championship.

Both teams were ranked high in the wire service polls, but after the close Syracuse victory the Orangemen moved up higher and Penn State dropped right out of the Top Ten. Engle had no use for polls after that.

"If a two-point loss to one of the best teams in the country dropped you out of the Top Ten, then the polls aren't a fair judge of college football teams," he said.

Penn State was obviously one of the best teams in the country, too, and the reason was a daring young man named Richie Lucas. Because of his flare for the unusual, the Nittany Lions' quarterback was nicknamed "Riverboat Richie" by sports writers. The connotation of a Mississippi riverboat gambler was clear. He was Engle's all-time favorite.

Once asked if Lucas exceeded even the greatness of running star Lenny Moore, Engle replied: "Lucas was the greatest of the two. He was an all-around player...good passer, good runner, good defensively. Moore was a great offensive back, probably greater than Lucas in that department."

Engle revered Lucas for his "gambling ability...he likes to take chances. He was dangerous at all times."

A stock photograph of Lucas issued by the Penn State sports information office showed the flashy quarterback dressed in a costume like the traditional riverboat gambler—sleeves pinched up by garters, a hat swaggeringly cocked to one side, and a deck of cards in hand.

It was easy to see why he got that image. He was always the guy with a sleeve full of aces. He even made Engle nervous, sometimes.

Lucas gained his reputation early when, as a sophomore, he pulled off an unorthodox play against West Virginia. Throughout the early stages of the game the big West Virginia linemen had been putting a strong rush on Penn State's punters. Lucas

223

The guy with a sleeve full of aces—gambling Richie Lucas.

turned the situation in Penn State's favor late in the first half. On fourth down with five yards to go Lucas dropped back as if to punt, but kept the ball and raced 25 yards for a first down. The play started a touchdown drive, and Penn State went on to score a 27-6 victory.

The thing was, Engle had ordered Lucas to punt on that particular play. Actually, Lucas often disregarded orders from the bench. Whenever Engle sent in a play to "Riverboat Richie," he was not sure it would be carried out. Said Lucas, matter-of-factly: "When he sends in a play, I treat it as a suggestion."

"We knew we had a gambler on our hands, a real good one," said Engle. "What we didn't know, however, was that he had so many qualifications for gambling—the nerve, the timing, the finesse, the savoir faire. He looked like a choir boy, but had murder in his heart when he played football."

Except for an accident, Lucas almost did not go to Penn State. During his senior year at Glassport (Pennsylvania) High School, Engle and his staff were viewing a film between Lucas' team and one from Bethel High School because they wanted to scout Bethel quarterback Jerry Eisaman. But as the film progressed, Eisaman was constantly being upstaged by a Glassport defensive player who was making most of the tackles, intercepting passes, and generally stealing the show.

"What's that kid's name?" Engle asked.

"It's Lucas—Richie Lucas," said backfield coach Joe Paterno.

"Let's run the film over again and see what he does on defense," said Engle.

Engle was so impressed that he gave up the hunt for Eisaman and instead induced Lucas to come to Penn State. Eisaman, as a matter of fact, wound up at Kentucky.

Lucas was a prize catch for the Nittany Lions. From 1957 through 1959 he became one of the most efficient quarterbacks ever at Penn State, establishing school records in his time for total offense in a career (2,431 yards) and total offense in one year (1,238 yards in 1959). His accomplishments, which also included defensive heroics, earned him first-team recognition on just about every all-America team.

The Lucas-led teams played the traditional Penn State opponents like Syracuse, Pitt, Penn, and West Virginia and also new teams that began sprinkling the schedule as part of a school policy to go national. In 1957, when the Nittany Lions had a 6-3 record, they played Vanderbilt and Marquette for the first time. In 1958 they won six games, including one over newcomer Furman. And in 1959 Penn State met Missouri and VMI for the first time and made them victims during an 8-2 record, the best under Engle to that point.

The Liberty Bowl victory over Alabama that year, fashioned despite an injury to Lucas, gave the eastern football establishment a much-needed shot in the arm. If the balance of power was in the Midwest, Southeast and Southwest, as some people claimed, you could not tell it by Penn State.

"I've insisted for many years that eastern football is the equal of many sections of the country, including the so-called hotbeds in the Midwest, Southeast and Southwest, and is better than most sections," said Engle. "Eastern teams have just as much imagination, hit harder than most, block and tackle with the best of them and have the records to prove it."

His reasoning appeared wholly logical after Penn State shut out powerful Alabama before a crowd of 36,211 at Municipal Stadium in the inaugural Liberty Bowl game.

"We just got a good ol' thrashing," said Alabama Coach Paul 'Bear' Bryant. "We were fortunate not to be beaten by four or five touchdowns. They out-hit, out-blocked, out-smarted, and out-coached us."

The incident involving the lost kicking tee was only one of the dramatic moments on the Penn State side of the field. From the moment assistant coach Sevor Toretti stuck his head in the Penn State dressing room and told the players, "Let's show them how to play eastern football," strategic wheels turned and nerves tightened.

Toretti and Paterno plotted strategy from high above in the stands and relayed information about the game to the Penn State bench. Skip Finkleston, a player sitting out the season with an injury, manned the bench phone and relayed information to Engle.

"That was a wedge play, coach," Finkleston said in answer to a question by Engle.

"Let me have the phone a minute," said the coach. He talked for a while and nodded in agreement on a suggestion made by

Toretti and Paterno.

Engle then became infuriated with a Penn State mistake on the field.

"Stay onside," he berated a player who drew a five-yard penalty for jumping the gun on a play. "Find out who that was. Never mind. Never mind."

Walt Sobczak was shaken up on a play a little while later, and Engle wanted a replacement. "Let's go (Pat) Botula. Get in there."

As Sobczak gingerly walked off the field, Engle asked him: "You okay?"

"Yup," said Sobczak.

Alabama tried a pass, and the ball sailed over Engle's head as the Penn State coach talked on the phone. He chuckled and waved across the field to Bryant as if to say, "You almost hit me with that one."

"Watch the quick kick," screamed one of Engle's assistants to the Penn State secondary.

Then, as Alabama kicked a beauty to the Penn State three-yard line, he moaned: "Oh, no."

Yells of encouragement came from the Penn State bench: "Let's go, gang...come on Big Blue...stuff it down their throats."

Lucas ran the ball out to the Penn State 27.

"Great call," said Finkleston. "That was the 26 inside belly keep."

A kicking situation presented itself in a few minutes, and Engle called for punter Dick Pae. But Pae was having his shoulder pads repaired, and so Engle turned the other way and yelled: "Lucas. Let's go!"

Penn State was in possession as the quarter drew to a close, and Engle yelled "The Army Look" to Lucas. He was instructing his quarterback to pass, using code words.

Lucas faded to pass, but slipped. Later, as the second quarter started, he appeared hurt. Lucas came off the field and complained about his hip.

"Lucas is hurt," was the word around the bench.

"That's the way to hit in there," yelled Earl Bruce, applauding Bill Popp and Bud Kohlhaas after the two linemen had just tackled an Alabama runner.

Penn State forced Alabama to retreat by bullying the Crimson Tide backfield.

"That's the way, gang," shouted Engle. "Make 'em punt."

Penn State took a 7-0 lead into the dressing room at halftime on the dazzling fake field goal play late in the second quarter. Engle was despondent, however, when he came out of the dressing room to talk to a writer.

"Lucas can't get into the second half," Engle said, shaking his head. "What a break! He injured the bone at the top of his left hip. He's finished for the game."

As the second half started, Lucas sat on the bench wrapped in a windbreaker and blanket to shield him from the 40-degree temperature and 20 mile per hour wind. He had been given a sedative for the pain.

He tried to loosen up twice during the second half, insisting he could play.

"I can run the team," he said, "but I can't pass."

Later Lucas yelled words of encouragement to his replacement, Galen Hall: "Use your time, Butch."

When it appeared that Penn State had the game wrapped up, officials called a timeout on their own. It made Engle testy.

"What are you calling time out for?" Engle cracked. "You want to get another commercial on television?"

With only a few seconds left, and Penn State deep in Alabama territory, some fans rushed onto the field at the other end and began tearing down a goal post.

"Wish they wouldn't do it," said an assistant coach. "That's bad luck."

In the dressing room Engle made a little speech after the entire team had gathered.

"Fellows, everyone won this game. Everyone. Thirty years from now, you'll look back on this as a great day. You'll be proud. God bless you."

Cold Duck
And Other Delights

Conditions for the 1960 Liberty Bowl game were far less than perfect. Fourteen inches of snow had dropped recently, and it sprinkled again the day before the game. Temperatures were in the low 30s, and winds cut through Philadelphia's Municipal Stadium at 25 miles per hour.

Even Oregon Coach Len Casanova expressed concern about the weather. "Oregon never has played on a field even encircled by snow," he said, cautiously eyeing the huge drifts rimming the field.

Both Oregon and Penn State had to show up, of course; they had no choice. A crowd of 16,624 did brave the elements at the 100,000-seat stadium, and not only were they frozen, they were also bored.

"I figured that we'd win, but the score was more one-sided than we had a right to expect," said Penn State Coach Rip Engle after his team embarrassed the Oregon Ducks 41-12 on December 17, 1960, for its second straight Liberty Bowl victory.

If the 1960 Liberty Bowl was a financial disaster for the organizers and participants, it was certainly an artistic success for Penn State. Engle's game plan worked to perfection.

Penn State coaches had said before the game that the Nittany Lions would "try to run at 'em.

"They're a fluid defensive team, and we aim to keep pressure on them with our two units," said assistant coach Sevor Toretti.

Penn State did just that and finally overwhelmed the Ducks

with depth. It took the Nittany Lions a while to get warmed up, though. They fell behind 6-0 in the first quarter before Engle's assistants in the stands starting spotting Oregon weaknesses.

"A hook pass should work," one of the scouts said over the telephone to the bench.

Quarterback Dick Hoak set up the first touchdown with a pass to Henry Oppermann. Don Jonas dove over from the one, and Penn State had a 7-6 lead in the second quarter.

"T-power-right play off guard," instructed the scouts in the stands, and Al Gursky went off tackle from two yards out for another Penn State score in the period.

Joe Paterno, Dan Radakovich, Frank Patrick, and Toretti were the phone men who played a key part in Penn State's impressive victory that day. At halftime Penn State had a 21-6 lead but still needed some football lessons. Paterno provided them in the dressing room, explaining that the Nittany Lions had shown some defensive weaknesses. He pointed out how they might take more advantage of the Oregon defense, too.

When Oregon cut the Penn State lead to 21-12 in the third quarter and it looked as if the Nittany Lions were in a slump, Paterno came down from the stands to inspire the team as a holler guy.

"Come on, boys, this is it," he yelled at the seniors. "You'll never play college ball again."

Paterno's screaming built up enthusiasm on the bench, and Hoak's playing gave Penn State inspiration on the field. The senior quarterback set up two touchdowns with interceptions on Oregon star Dave Grosz as Penn State scored three times in the final period to win going away. In all, Hoak had quite a day for himself. He received the Most Valuable Player Trophy by directing five of the six touchdowns. He scored twice himself on rollouts and passed 33 yards to Dick Pae for the final touchdown.

"I guess," said Hoak, "that was about as good a day as I've ever had."

Hoak and Galen Hall shared the quarterback duties under Engle's unique system of two starting teams—one, the regulars, and the other, the "Reddies." There was no class system here, though, since either unit was considered a "first" team.

It had been a typical Engle team that year—slow starting and fast finishing. The Nittany Lions lost three of their first five games and then won five in a row, including the Liberty Bowl.

The 1960 opener, a 20-0 victory over Boston University, was a landmark game for Penn State because it was played in the Nittany Lions' new Beaver Stadium. Old Beaver Field, named for General James A. Beaver, a former governor of Pennsylvania and school trustee, had been relocated from its site on Center Campus to a more spacious location.

When Beaver Field was dismantled after the 1959 season, it closed out a successful record for Penn State of 184 victories, 34 defeats, and 11 ties on the original football field. Workmen moved the stadium in 700 pieces one mile to the new East Campus location and reassembled the old seats beneath a new steel superstructure. The seating capacity was more than 50 percent larger than the original field, jumping to 46,284. The new stadium afforded fans a good view of the field, and the new location also gave fans a pleasant view of the various mountain ranges that surround the campus.

"It sounded like an unbelievable task, just cutting that steel in sections and moving it over there," says Ed Czekaj, Penn State's athletic director. "The new Beaver Stadium was built backwards—they started from the top and worked down. They had to do it that way so they wouldn't lose any time."

The Monday morning after Penn State played Holy Cross in 1959 in the last game on old Beaver Field, contractors moved in to start the ball rolling. By fall they had the stadium finished and ready for the game with Boston U. on September 17, 1960.

The new stadium symbolically opened a gaudy new era in Penn State football history. No matter what had happened before, the 1960s embraced the most glamorous years of popularity and artistic and financial success.

New heroes appeared such as Bob Mitinger and Dave Robinson, among the best pair of ends on any one team in the country. Mitinger had established himself a couple of years before Robinson came into his own in 1961. Both were all-Americas, Mitinger in 1961 and Robinson in 1962. Both were over 6-foot-2, about 220 pounds.

Mitinger, especially, was one of Engle's all-time favorites for his "strength, quickness, and aggressiveness."

"He was mentally tough and possessed a great second effort," recalled Engle. "He was possibly better on defense but also was an exceptional blocker and adequate pass receiver. He'd be on any coach's all-time team."

Mitinger reacted well to Engle's tutelage. He had a warm feeling for the coach and responded accordingly on a playing field.

"I remember Engle most in his blue bermuda shorts and pink sailor's hat," says Mitinger. "He wore tennis shoes with no socks. That's the one picture I always have of him. He never swore. Whenever you'd make a mistake, Engle would put his arm around you and say, 'God love you, son. Surely you can give a little better effort than that.' "

A 27-16 victory over Army and 21-15 loss to Syracuse in 1960 were among Mitinger's memories, one good and the other bad.

"I drank beer for the first time after beating Army that year, it was such a great victory for us," Mitinger recalls.

At Syracuse, Mitinger had one of his best days in a losing cause. But, he recalls, it was a day when he "couldn't pick up a fumble and walk into the end zone...I kicked the ball about 10 or 15 yards."

"It must have been about 100 degrees in Syracuse that day and I played 59 minutes," says Mitinger. "We should have won that game. We had the ball on the two-yard line, and officials wouldn't let us call time out when quarterback Galen Hall lost his shoe. Time just ran out on us."

In a game against Illinois, Mitinger continually plagued Illini quarterback Johnny Easterbrook. Asked how he enjoyed spending the afternoon with Mitinger, Easterbrook responded: "Every time I looked up that big number 86 was bearing down on me. I couldn't seem to shake him. He's a great end."

In 1961 Mitinger and Robinson were key elements in a 7-3 season that earned the Nittany Lions a trip to the Gator Bowl in Jacksonville, Florida, against Georgia Tech.

Robinson was a little apprehensive about being the first black man to play in the Gator Bowl, and legend has it that when the Penn State plane landed in Florida he stepped off wearing dark glasses.

When he saw Robinson, Engle said: "Hey, Dave, what are you, a hot dog or something, wearing dark glasses?"

232

"No, coach," Robinson was supposed to have responded, "but when I travel in the South, I travel incognito."

If the story was half-true, it was a lot funnier than the events that followed. Joe Paterno, who was an assistant coach then, remembers the situation.

"When we wanted to eat dinner at the airport restaurant, they would not serve Dave because he was Negro," recalls Paterno. "The whole squad walked out. It was their decision. It just shows you how close we were."

The situation was faintly reminiscent of the Cotton Bowl in Dallas in 1948 when the Nittany Lions were forced to live in a naval base several miles outside of town because of blacks on the team. For the 1961 Gator Bowl the Nittany Lions had to stay in St. Augustine because no hotels in Jacksonville would let in Robinson.

Things appeared to get progressively worse for the Nittany Lions. One day they showed up to tour the Gator Bowl and found it was locked. A caretaker had to be flushed out to open the place. They also were scheduled to practice on the Gator Bowl field but discovered that the Georgia Tech band was rehearsing there. Engle's team had to work out in an adjacent parking lot.

Engle kept missing appointments for television interviews, too. "I guess these people down here are going to think I'm an awful cad," he said. "But I don't mean to miss these television things on purpose, and I'm not the shy type. I just get so wrapped up in other things, I don't remember to show up."

As usual Penn State was not treated too kindly by the foreign press. Writers from Atlanta, home of Georgia Tech, wondered what the Nittany Lions were doing in the Gator Bowl in the first place. The Atlanta writers believed that the intersectional aspect of the game was a concession to national television and pointed out that perhaps Maryland or Miami would have been better choices. Both beat Penn State during the season.

As the stadium filled to 50,202 spectators, the fates seemed to further conspire against Penn State. Georgia Tech won the opening toss, and a statistician for the Engineers reported in the press box that his team had never lost a bowl game after winning the toss.

After getting possession of the ball, the Nittany Lions had

immediate problems. Galen Hall called for a screen pass, but Georgia Tech tackle Ed Griffin charged through before the Penn State quarterback could set himself. Hall was chased clear back to the end zone, where he intentionally threw the ball away. The officials invoked the relatively obscure rule of intentional grounding and awarded Georgia Tech with a safety and a 2-0 lead.

"We had called a screen play along the sideline," said Hall, "but Bob Mitinger (the intended receiver) couldn't fool the Tech left end who tailed him out. We had expected him to crash. I was afraid of an interception, and I didn't want to be tackled in the end zone. I knew what THAT was. So I threw out of bounds over everyone's head. I didn't know anything about the safety rule."

Joe Auer, a regular only because Chick Graning was hurt, gave Georgia Tech a 9-0 lead on a 68-yard touchdown run in the second quarter.

"Coach Bobby Dodd (of Georgia Tech) had a great record in bowl games," said Engle, "and it surely looked like they were ready for this one."

Late in the second quarter, however, the flow of the game made a dramatic turn. Hall, who was near-sighted and claimed, "I just can't see very far," saw far enough to complete four of five passes on a 78-yard touchdown drive. He threw a 22-yarder to Dave Robinson and the last one for a touchdown, a 13-yard rollout pass to the left to Al Gursky. Just before intermission Hall hit Roger Kochman with a 27-yard TD pass for a 14-9 Penn State lead. It was clearly the play of the day, for Kochman faked the Georgia Tech defender into leaping for the ball too soon and then ran into the far corner of the end zone to make an over-the-head catch.

"It wasn't a very good pass," Hall apologized to Kochman.

"No," replied the halfback with a grin, "I didn't see it until it hit my hands."

Junior Powell had a little easier time with the next touchdown pass by Hall, this one in the third quarter. The receiver was wide open on the 10-yard line and started to dance a jig even before he went into the end zone. The play covered 35 yards and gave Penn State a 20-9 lead after a two-point conversion attempt was missed.

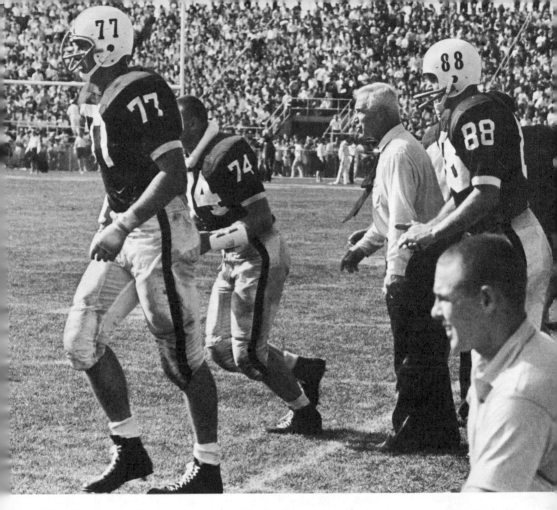

Rip Engle sends in players with instructions during a tense moment.

Georgia Tech got back into the game with a fourth-quarter touchdown but made too many mistakes after that and faded. Penn State took advantage of those mistakes to score a field goal and a touchdown at the end and turn a respectable game into a near-rout, 30-15.

"It appeared to me like those old Penn State boys were just awaitin' their turn with the dice," said a Jacksonville native.

The losing coach summed it up with more sophistication.

"We never did stop them," said Dodd. "It was not the kind of plays they used but the way they executed them."

"A Most Depressing Loss"

"I always attributed the loss in the 1962 Gator Bowl to the fact that nobody cared about winning it," says Roger Kochman. "We had so many guys eligible for the pros that nobody had his mind on the game. We were getting hustled quite vehemently by the professional teams."

Kochman was among three Penn State players who signed professional contracts immediately after the 17-7 loss to Florida. The halfback signed with the Buffalo Bills while end Dave Robinson signed with the Green Bay Packers and tackle Chuck Sieminski with the San Francisco 49ers.

Kochman himself exemplified Penn State's lackadaisical play that day with a crucial fumble while running for a big gain.

"I pulled a trick I'd been taught not to do all my life—switch the ball from arm to arm while in motion," he says. "Why did I do it? I'd like you to tell me."

In their last six games of the regular season, Penn State lost the ball only three times on fumbles. They lost the ball three times on fumbles in the Florida game alone. The first two, incidentally, led directly to Florida scores.

The Nittany Lions only had eight passes intercepted all season. Against Florida a pass interception led to the Gators' clinching touchdown in the final period.

A ball control team all year, Penn State kept possession for only 19 minutes during the entire game and for only four plays in the fourth quarter. The Nittany Lions ran a meager total of 52 plays from scrimmage.

"Personally we've had our fill of bowl games for a few years," the Penn State *Alumni News* said after the disappointing showing. "We are convinced that no team should play in any bowl unless the players are completely in favor of the venture and willing to make all the necessary sacrifices, if not for their own benefit, then for the benefit of the university and the sport which has made their education possible."

The winners of the Lambert Trophy had plainly been beaten by their own lethargy. The fact that Penn State was officially proclaimed champion of the East for the second straight year only fired up Florida more. The Gators had a mediocre 6-4 record, in comparison to Penn State's flashier 9-1 mark, and received a bid only after the bowl committee had given strong consideration to Georgia Tech, Miami, and Duke.

By the same token Penn State players appeared to be unhappy that they were not going to a bowl with more stature, such as the Orange, Sugar, or Cotton.

An editorial in a Florida newspaper entitled, "Are Nittany Lions Sulking?" commented "word is out that Penn State's Nittany Lions, angry at having been overlooked by other bowl committees, are regarding their December 29 Gator Bowl date with the Florida Gators as 'just another stop along the road' and haven't been practicing regularly."

Southern newspapers reported that Penn State players were disturbed about not being home for Christmas. However, the papers pointed out, the Florida players had given up THEIR holidays for extra practice.

The scene was dramatically punctuated when Florida players raced onto the field with newly-painted Confederate flags on their helmets. It was obvious that they meant to prove something—and did.

"There has never been a more clear-cut demonstration of the football truism that victory goes to the team who wants it most," said the *Alumni News*.

Earlier in the season it had been a different story. Penn State players had not taken a game so lightly. The Nittany Lions were only beaten by Army, and Kochman remembers it as "the most depressing game of my career."

"We didn't adapt too well to Army," says Kochman, recalling

Roger Kochman (No. 46) drives through the snow against Maryland with Al Gursky blocking. The Nittany Lions beat the Terps 23-7 in the 1962 game.

the 9-6 loss. "We always had a history of preparing a good game plan, and we came out to blow them off the field with a running attack. We had great size advantage.

"Well, Army came out with a nine-man line and played it the entire game. We still stayed with the running game, and it was suicidal just trying to batter them. It's hard to gain yardage in a situation like that. We threw a couple of passes, but not many."

One of the few passes that Pete Liske threw that day was dropped in the end zone by Dick Anderson. On another play Bill Coates completed a touchdown pass to Bill Bowes, but it was nullified by a penalty.

The Nittany Lions, who had averaged 27 points a game that season against the other nine teams, could not even score a touchdown against Army. It was an irritating afternoon in more ways than one at Michie Stadium. Not only did the Nittany Lions have to put up with Army's defensive wonders, called the "Chinese Bandits," but also the Cadet cheering section whose noise was magnified by electrical amplification.

"When the voice noises are continued while the visiting team calls its signals, we think it's just plain discourteous," wrote the *Alumni News*. "This type of sportsmanship has bothered our teams in the past (West Virginia and Syracuse have also protested), but apparently quarterback Liske was able to live with it.

"Late in the game when our team was directly in front of the Army stands quarterback Coates did appeal to an official, who appealed to Army Coach Paul Dietzel, who appealed to the Army cheerleaders. Quiet was maintained—for about two plays."

The Army cheerleaders, incidentally, had signs reading "Shhh!" which they displayed when their Cadets were on offense.

Two field goals by Coates were the only scores registered by Penn State. Army had a field goal in the first quarter by Dick Heydt and the winning touchdown in the last quarter on a pass from Cammy Lewis to Dick Peterson.

Kochman, among other Penn State players, had a sub-par game. His rushing total was only 42 yards, a figure he sometimes exceeded by halftime.

"Losing to Army was my most disappointing moment at Penn State," says Kochman, "it was a game we should have won."

Kochman had other moments of distress, mostly of physical pain, not mental. He suffered so many injuries in his college and professional career that he eventually wound up crippled. Before he was forced to leave the game he loved, he underwent enough agony for a couple of lifetimes.

"He is a living example of courage and the many other qualities so necessary to be a winner," says Penn State Coach Rip Engle.

Kochman played in 1962 despite a lot of injuries and still managed to lead the team in rushing and scoring and was third in receiving. He made all-America status in his senior year while making Penn State a power.

With the aid of Kochman, Robinson, and Sieminski, and young faces like Liske and lineman Glenn Ressler, a couple of future pros, the Nittany Lions defeated Navy 41-7, Air Force 20-6, and Rice 18-7 before the Army loss. Afterwards they beat Syracuse 20-19, California 23-21, Maryland 23-7, West Virginia 34-6, Holy Cross 48-20, and Pitt 16-0.

"I look back on my career at Penn State and remember that we were always well schooled in fundamentals," says Kochman. "That was one of the reasons that we had a certain degree of success. We didn't care about rankings or winning the Lambert Trophy, either. We just were concerned about playing winning football."

Kochman, whose best year was 1961 when he rushed for 666 yards despite missing most of three games with an injury, rarely carried the ball more than 12 to 15 times a game. He would have wanted more opportunities to run, but accepted it as the Penn State style.

"I don't think I carried the ball enough," Kochman says, "but I wasn't displeased because we were winning. I was a very good blocker who made the offense go. Most teams keyed on me."

Kochman's name is in the Penn State record books because of his 100-yard kickoff return against Syracuse in 1959. The longest kickoff return in Nittany Lions' history was made out of "fear," Kochman says.

"I looked up the middle of the field and saw five Syracuse players coming at me. I made the best 90-degree cut of my life.

It was basically a self-preservation move."

The word "fear" seems incongruent with Kochman's character. Engle would have taken 40 like him.

"He was an outstanding halfback," says Engle. "His blocking was superb, his running more than adequate, and his pass receiving out of this world at times. Every play, Kochman gave 100 percent. He was truly an all-American in his senior year."

Goodbye, Columbus

A Penn State alumnus approached Woody Hayes in a Columbus, Ohio, restaurant one day and asked him for a favor.

"Would you sign a pledge that you'll never try to beat Penn State?" the alumnus said tongue-in-cheek to the Ohio State football coach.

Good-naturedly, Hayes went along with the jest and wrote a pledge: "I promise not to beat Penn State. Signed, Woody Hayes."

Actually, what he meant to say was that he could not beat Penn State.

For all his successes in the football world, the ultra-successful Hayes undeniably had his problems with the Nittany Lions. Continuing a winning tradition over the Buckeyes that started in 1912, Penn State beat Hayes-coached powerhouses in 1956, 1963, and 1964.

Penn State players could not explain it—they could only enjoy it.

"The games I played against Ohio State were the most exciting of my career," recalls Glenn Ressler, "because Ohio State was the best team we played."

Ressler, one of the best interior linemen in the country, was a factor in Penn State's 10-7 triumph over Ohio State in 1963.

"Ressler made 14 tackles without assistance, and most of them came in the second half when we won the game," says Penn State Coach Rip Engle. "He simply discouraged the Ohio State offense and did a fine job of blocking when we had the ball."

Ohio State literally came at Penn State in numbers that day. Some 80,000 Buckeye rooters roared their approval when their huge squad of 77 came on the field to start the game.

"It just didn't seem fair—all that power," observed a Penn State fan.

Matt Snell exemplified the Ohio State power with runs through the Penn State line, especially over the tackle spots which were depleted by injuries. The Buckeyes drove from the Penn State 46 in the second period, with Snell and Paul Warfield moving most of the yards on the ground. Warfield went over from close range, and the Buckeyes had a 7-0 lead at the half, the first time they had ever led Penn State.

The Nittany Lions tied the score on a touchdown drive from their 39-yard line in the third period. Quarterback Pete Liske, having one of the best games of his career, bootlegged to his right and fired a TD pass to Bill Bowes from the two.

"Liske was as good at faking the ball as anyone," says Ressler. "Even the television cameras had trouble keeping up with the Penn State ball carriers. The cameramen didn't know where the ball was."

Liske was so adept at ball-handling trickery that he even fooled his own teammates on one occasion during the touchdown drive. The Nittany Lions had an extra blocker downfield on a pass play and were penalized 15 yards for an "illegal receiver." It momentarily set the ball back from Ohio State's 36-yard line.

While Liske worked magically on offense, Ressler led the defense that held Ohio State backs to but 30 yards rushing in the second half. Liske moved the team for the winning score later in the third period. Starting on the 50-yard line, Gary Klingensmith made a first down in two rushes. Liske passed to Ed Stuckrath on the 28. Liske threw a hook pass to Dick Anderson on the 11. After a pass went awry and Liske was thrown for a five-yard loss, Stuckrath ran the draw play to the six, and on the fourth down, Ron Coates kicked a field goal from the 13.

"Our teams of that day were more defense-oriented than anything," recalls Ressler, an all-America who later starred in the National Football League with the Baltimore Colts. "We

Lineman Glenn Ressler made several all-America teams in 1964.

just seemed to score enough to win."

The Ohio State victory was the most glamorous in a 7-3 season that also included a 17-14 thriller over UCLA. The notable successes, however, did not insure a Lambert Trophy for the Nittany Lions because they lost to Army, Syracuse, and Pitt that year. Penn State would have to wait until 1964, the season Engle called his most memorable, to secure the trophy that was emblematic of the eastern major college football champion.

The Nittany Lions won the trophy for the fourth time in history in 1964 with a team that started raggedly and ended with a flourish of five straight victories, including a 27-0 humiliation of Hayes' proud, unbeaten Buckeyes.

"A football team has never played a perfect game, but at Ohio State in 1964 our team came as close to it as I've ever seen," said Engle.

Ohio State entered the game as the second-ranked team in the country after victories over Southern Methodist, Indiana, Illinois, Southern California, Wisconsin, and Iowa. Penn State had a poor 3-4 record and was rated a 21-point underdog.

"The situation did look pretty bad for us," recalls Engle.

Before the game Joe Paterno, then an associate coach, attempted to loosen up the Nittany Lions in the dressing room. "How are you going to feel out there before 85,000 people?" he said to Mike Irwin, a sophomore defensive back from Altoona, Pennsylvania. "That's more than you have in your home town."

Paterno kept his sense of humor despite a rough year. He had been openly criticized for his choice of Gary Wydman as the Penn State quarterback, but stubbornly stuck to his man throughout early-season mistakes that cost four games.

Against Ohio State on November 7, 1964, however, Paterno looked like a genius because Wydman looked like a quarterback. Wydman drove Penn State for touchdowns in each of the first three quarters, scoring once himself on a run before he handed the ball over to the reserves at the end.

The Buckeyes were thoroughly outclassed that day. They did not get their initial first down until late in the third quarter and amassed just five first downs overall. In addition Penn State's rugged defense, led by Ressler, held Ohio State to 33 yards on the ground and 30 in the air while inducing two fumbles and two interceptions.

"Even though the Buckeyes had not been able to mount an offense, or even make a first down, the 84,000 (actually 84,279) in the stadium expected the dike to break at any moment," says Engle. "We coaches were wondering if we could keep it up, too, and it wasn't until the middle of the fourth quarter when we scored our fourth touchdown that we realized it might be a victory for us.

"I remember being quite apprehensive when we missed the extra point after our last touchdown. But I finally realized that a great group of Penn State players was maturing into what I believe to have been the finest team we ever had. The game was picked as the 'Upset of the Year' and will always be a high spot in my hall of memories."

Hayes would not forget it for a while, either.

"Rip Engle may have a 4-4 team, but we didn't play that team today," he said.

After the dramatic victory over Ohio State, Engle's "most memorable team" closed out the season by beating Houston and Pitt.

"This team had courage, heart, desire, and a great willingness to give of themselves," Engle says. "We struggled hard early in the year, and when the season was at the halfway point we had only one victory and four losses to show for our efforts. One more loss and a 26-year record of winning seasons would go out the window.

"Remaining on the schedule were West Virginia, a team which had beaten Syracuse, which in turn had beaten us; Ohio State, unbeaten and ranked No. 2 in the country; a good Maryland team; a quick, young Houston club which we had to play in muggy Rice Stadium; and Pitt, which had come so close to upsetting mighty Notre Dame (17-15).

"With these prospects I started receiving calls from sports writers asking how it felt to have our first losing season, and I searched for reasons and alibis. I never could admit to them—or myself—the possibility that we'd have a losing year. For some reason something happened—something I believe in strongly but cannot explain. Anyway, from mid-season on we were a great football team, and I received my biggest thrill and greatest satisfaction through those five Saturday afternoons. The team grew stronger, day by day, game by game, and when we upset Ohio State we thought we could avoid that losing season."

After his season of greatest satisfaction, Engle went through a year of discontent. The Nittany Lions had their first non-winning record under the silver-haired coach with a 5-5 mark in 1965.

And Engle, who had been thinking about retiring since 1962, made it official after his 16th year at Penn State.

Time Out: Joe Paterno

Joe Paterno kept his date, as promised. He sidestepped a crowd with the flare of his quarterbacking days at Brown and ducked into a booth in the rear of the noisy Nittany Lion Inn.

The famous Penn State football coach parked his umbrella underneath the table and ordered.

"Black coffee," he said, and the waitress nodded her head.

It was fitting that an interview with Paterno should take place at the Nittany Lion Inn, a traditional campus meeting place. Amid the clatter of plates and accompanying background of loud talking, Paterno discussed the Penn State football philosophy.

"We coach good, tough, aggressive football here," he said, sipping his coffee. "When you knock a guy down, you pick him up. There's no meanness involved in the thing, see?"

Paterno made the comment in response to a question about violence in football. Paterno, a tough man with the soul of a poet, saw no violence from his side of the field.

"We never talk about hurting people," Paterno said. "It's a question of playing within the rules and competing in a very physical sport. Sometimes when people see these kids going after each other, they think 'Wow!' To people who haven't been involved in the tackling and blocking, it really looks a lot more violent than it is.

"More emphasis is being placed these days on the things players do in the way of volunteers to fight drug abuse, that kind of thing. Men who like to play tough football go out there after each other, but they're usually quiet, warm, sensitive human beings with interests in other areas."

Paterno himself would be classified in that group. He teaches tough football but is a warm, sensitive human being with interests in other areas.

When Paterno was a football player at Brown in the late 1940s, he was an English Literature major, very much interested in the arts. He would have liked to be a writer at one time. He almost was a lawyer. But he wound up as a football coach because of one man—Rip Engle.

Engle had accepted the head coaching job at Penn State for the 1950 season and asked Paterno to go along with him as assistant. Engle needed Paterno's help in converting Penn State from a Single Wing team to a Wing-T.

"I decided to go along just to broaden my experience before entering law school,". Paterno recalls. "But I grew to love Penn State so much that after two or three years with Rip, I dreamed about nothing other than becoming head coach."

The transition to country living was quite an adjustment for a city slicker like Paterno, who lived in Brooklyn all his life. It was doubly hard for a boy fresh out of college, which Paterno was. It did not make it any easier, either, that Paterno had an explosive temper and never backed down on arguments with older members of the coaching staff.

As coach in charge of the quarterbacks, Paterno eventually achieved national recognition for his development of players like Richie Lucas, Milt Plum, Al Jacks, Tony Rados, Dick Hoak, Galen Hall, and Pete Liske.

Paterno was always Engle's golden boy and, naturally, was his choice as coach when Engle retired after the 1965 season.

"I knew that Joe would become an outstanding coach," Engle said in later years. "I knew even when I came here that he had a keen football mind. His leadership and competitive attitude made him a fine quarterback, and when I came to Penn State in 1950 he was the one person I brought along even though he had just graduated from college. I was aware even then of his potential as a fine coach."

A sports writer once said of Paterno, the player: "He can't run and he can't pass. All he can do is think—and win!"

The same might be said of Paterno, the coach. He is re-

Penn State Coach Joe Paterno: "We coach good, tough, aggressive football here."

nowned as a gridiron gambler, never afraid to take chances or try innovations.

"I think that's the way life is," he says. "I think you've got to go after things, and you've got to take a chance. You've got to gamble, and when something appears to be right to you you've got to take a chance and not be afraid to lose."

This wide-open philosophy was dramatized in the Orange Bowl game with Kansas on January 1, 1969, when Paterno went for a risky, two-point conversion attempt instead of the safer extra-point kick after a touchdown. The result was a 15-14 Penn State victory.

Of course that gambling instinct of his has backfired on occasion, but Paterno takes it as part of life.

"I've always preached to my boys that there's one thing I want you to do and this is don't ever be afraid to lose," says Paterno. "If you're afraid to lose, you don't have a chance of winning."

Paterno, the 14th coach in the 80th consecutive year of Penn State football, began his career rather inauspiciously with a 5-5

An exuberant Joe Paterno signals "touchdown" as the Nittany Lions score.

record in 1966. He went up like a shooting star after that, though.

Under Paterno's direction in the next six years, the Nittany Lions lost only eight games while reaching the giddiest football heights in Penn State history. Paterno's seven-year record of 63-13-1 puts him at the top of the country's "winningest" major college football coaches with at least five years experience.

From 1967 through 1972 the Nittany Lions finished in the wire service polls' Top Ten five times, went to five bowl games, and had two unbeaten, untied seasons. At one point Penn State played 31 games without a defeat, one of the longest streaks in college football history.

During this time Paterno not only challenged opponents, he challenged presidents. The Penn State coach became a celebrity when he publicly disputed President Richard Nixon's football faux pas in the 1969 season. After Texas had whipped Arkansas in a battle of unbeatens, the president proclaimed the Longhorns the national champion with a "No. 1" plaque. The plaque was presented to Texas Coach Darrell Royal on national television, before millions of viewers.

This action, naturally, drew sour reaction from Penn State and Paterno. And when the president attempted to placate Paterno with a plaque for the "nation's longest unbeaten streak," the Penn State coach refused the award. The Nittany Lions finished No. 2 in the Associated Press and United Press International polls that year, but in Paterno's mind they finished first after they beat Missouri 10-3 in the Orange Bowl.

Paterno received awards that he did not refuse, however. He was named National Coach of the Year in 1968, when undefeated Penn State won 11 games, including the aforementioned dramatic victory over Kansas in the Orange Bowl. Paterno has been named Eastern Coach of the Year three times and has also received the Pennsylvania Award for Excellence in Athletics, joining people like baseball stars Stan Musial and Robin Roberts and golfer Arnold Palmer.

Paterno became even more of a campus hero when he turned down big money to join the pros. In 1969 he refused "a very attractive offer" to join the Pittsburgh Steelers. It was said to be a yearly salary in the neighborhood of $70,000, about $50,000 more than he made at Penn State. In 1973 he decided to remain in college coaching despite an offer from the New England Patriots that would have meant lifetime security. That contract was supposed to be about $1.25 million over five years.

"I realized that I wouldn't be happy just being a football coach in which winning and losing was everything " says Paterno, explaining his decision. "When I analyzed the situation, I realized that I'd always wanted to work in a college atmosphere where the administration allowed me to be more than just a football coach. And that's what Penn State has allowed me to do.

"The fact that I'm just not a football coach and a businessman is because of Penn State's approach to athletics within the entire framework of the university. I have an opportunity to work with young people and have an influence on their lives. I think that was an overriding factor in my decision—the fact that it is such a healthy atmosphere."

Paterno calls himself a "cornball" and an "idealist."

"Some people may think I'm nuts for turning down such an offer," says the dark-haired Paterno, his smile ever-ready. "But I think there is more to life than money. I don't want to restrict myself to football."

This is the liberal approach he brings to football players at Penn State, something he calls the "Grand Experiment."

"We want our players to enjoy football," he says. "But we also want them to enjoy college. We want them to learn about art and literature and music and all the other things college has to offer. College should be a great time. It is the only time a person is really free. We don't want them just tied to a football program."

For that reason Paterno has insisted that there be no athletic dorms at Penn State. Saturday's heroes live among other students on the sprawling campus and get a liberal diet of university life. And, as a result, most of the athletes graduate. That is important to Paterno.

"I don't think you'll find many football coaches like him," says a friend. "Joe's very interested in the arts and probably knows almost as much about our English department as the people in the department. He's very interested in what goes on outside the athletic sphere. I doubt if the majority of football coaches can tell you where their English department is, much less what's in it."

Paterno works at home to the tune of classical music.

"You don't find too many coaches who draw their football plays to Beethoven," says the friend. "But this helps him relax."

Despite all this intellectual stimulation, football is Paterno's No. 1 passion. Make no mistake about it. He has expressed a desire to make Penn State a national champion, one of the few honors that has eluded him.

"I enjoy the day-in, day-out work with young men," he says. "You work with them, they have confidence in you and you in them, and all of a sudden on a Saturday afternoon you look up and there are 40,000 people.

"Then the whistle blows and you're in the middle of things. It's great excitement—a great feeling of pride when the players and the coaches get the job done. Of course you're frustrated when you don't, but this, too, is exciting."

Paterno's loyalty to Penn State is a mutual affair. Even if some of his players have not adored him, they have respected him.

"Joe's tough," says Charlie Pittman, a star halfback of the late 1960s. "He wants you to put out. He has hard practices and tough discipline on and off the field. He dictates the whole show, and he's driving you so hard you don't want to lose.

"Some coaches try to get you to love and respect them so you'll do anything for them. Joe's not loved, but he's respected because of the type of person he is. He's really tough, and he's intelligent. You're afraid not to respect him."

Paterno has had his critics, too. Neal Smith, an all-America safety in 1969, was one of the most outspoken against the young coach. He claimed that Paterno's image was phony, that he cared more about winning football games than getting an education for the athletes.

"Personally, I think he will go to the pros eventually," says Smith. "I feel that the opportunity with New England was not what he was looking for. I'm sure that if he could do the same thing with a pro team that he did at Penn State, he'd leave the university. New England was a loser. Paterno wants a winner."

By the same token Smith respects Paterno as a coach.

"I admired him when I played for him," says Smith. "I think he's a great football coach. As a football mind, he's the best in the country."

Halfback Bob Campbell, star of one of Paterno's Orange Bowl victories, scored the coach's disciplinary tactics.

"I'm a free spirit," says Campbell, but he stayed—and won—with Paterno.

The controversial Paterno was chastised in print when he closed his first pre-season practice to the public in 1966. He was barraged by crank calls the day after Penn State's 31-game undefeated string was broken by Colorado in 1970. He has had people mad at him at times for his outspoken statements. He had had it all, good and bad, and decided to stick with his noble "Grand Experiment."

"So many people have asked us what kind of an offer Penn State made to Paterno to get him to stay," says a school official. "Did you have to buy him a car? This kind of thing. No, the answer is that Paterno just has a commitment to education and to young people. If you turn down the kind of money that the New England Patriots offered, you must really have a commitment to your beliefs."

But For One Yard . . .

"After coaching all these years, I should have been able to come up with a play for just one yard," said a disconsolate Earle Edwards.

Because North Carolina State could not move the football one yard on a crucial play, the 1967 season was somewhat of a failure for the Wolfpack—and something of a success for Penn State.

The play came in the closing seconds of one of the most dramatic games contested at Beaver Stadium. Penn State stopped a North Carolina State drive on the one-yard line and pulled off a major 13-8 upset.

"It was an off-tackle play, one that they had been using all day," remembers Penn State linebacker Denny Onkotz, who was in on the game-saving tackle. "You didn't have to be too smart to guess that they would use it again."

Losing 13-6 in the last five minutes, the Wolfpack moved downfield behind quarterback Jim Donnan. With 2:51 left, a holding penalty put the ball on the Penn State 20-yard line. Three plays later they were inside the 10. Fullback Bobby Hall picked up six yards around right end to the three, stopping the clock with 51 seconds remaining by running out of bounds.

By this time most of the crowd of 47,000 was on its feet.

Hall bucked a couple of yards to the one, and there were 40 seconds left when Donnan called time out to talk over strategy with Edwards.

"Let's give it to Tony on a smash over the middle," Donnan

said, referring to halfback Tony Barchuk who had been a work-horse. "We might as well go back to the play that's done the job all day."

"I was thinking more of a quick pitchout, something to surprise them and get outside," Edwards said later. "But when the boys really want to do a certain thing they often execute it better than a play you give them."

Onkotz says he was watching for Barchuk as the Wolfpack players lined up.

"My first responsibility was to be opposite the flanker," said Onkotz. "But as soon as I saw their linemen block toward the inside, I rushed over to the middle."

The crowd roared continuously as Dannon faked a handoff to fullback Settle Dockery and handed off to Barchuk. The Penn State defense jammed up the middle. Middle guard Jim Kates hit Barchuk high, and Onkotz hit him low. They stopped him without a gain, and the crowd noise reached new levels.

The Nittany Lions took over the ball. Four plays later punter Tom Cherry intentionally took a safety rather than risk kicking to elusive Freddie Combs, and North Carolina State had lost its last chance to pull out the game.

The excitement of those last five minutes seemingly left the hometown fans limp. They were reluctant to depart the stadium and milled around on the field long after the game was over. The moment after Penn State had stopped North Carolina State on the one-yard line, some of the fans attempted to tear down a concrete-based goal post but had no success.

Coach Joe Paterno, jubilant over the biggest victory of his young career, was carried from the field by his players. Someone grabbed a red and white North Carolina State banner which said, "Beat the Pussy Cats," and made off with it. Other Penn Staters snatched Confederate flags from the southern visitors and disappeared under the stands.

It was a mad scene, one befitting a big victory. The Wolfpack had not only lost their prestige but also an undefeated season and a probable bid to the Sugar Bowl. They had come into Penn State with an eight-game winning streak, No. 3 ranking in the nation, and a cautious coach.

"This is certainly one of the biggest challenges of our season," said Edwards, a former assistant coach at Penn State who had left hastily eighteen years before after losing a battle for the head coaching job.

Claude Gibson, Edwards' assistant who scouted Penn State, noted, "They have so many good athletes that they have kept improving, despite injuries that would have killed our team. And Ted Kwalick, their tight end, may be the best in the country."

"We have a much better club than people give us credit for," said quarterback Tom Sherman after the game (Penn State was not ranked). "Our defense is especially terrific. Today our offense did not have one of its better days, but you saw how the defense won the game for us."

Onkotz was asked if he felt Penn State deserved a bowl bid.

"All we were thinking about today was that the guys we were playing were supposed to be a Sugar Bowl team," he replied.

As it turned out Penn State did get a bowl bid. The Nittany Lions were invited to the Gator Bowl, largely on the strength of the North Carolina State success. They had beaten some other good teams in 1967, including Miami and Syracuse, and suffered a two-point loss to mighty UCLA and a one-point loss to Navy in an 8-2 season.

The defense was largely responsible for that record, although the offense could score points with Sherman, Kwalick, and receiver Jack Curry. Paterno was blessed with some excellent sophomores on defense including Onkotz, Jim Kates, and Steve Smear, and this group would help make Penn State a national power in coming years.

When Paterno first took over as head coach in 1966, he had no such talent, and Penn State was just another team. The Nittany Lions finished with a mediocre 5-5 record and—in fact—had to defeat Pitt in the last game to make a .500 season.

One of the rare moments of excitement on campus in Paterno's first year came when the Nittany Lions' statue got painted by Syracuse students; that is the kind of year it was.

The statue, a gift from well-known sculptor Heinz Warneke in the 1940s, had been a proud symbol of Penn State athletics for years. The lion stood in front of Recreation Hall on Center Campus, its head tilted to one side and crouched as if ready to spring. The athletic symbol, chosen by the student body in 1906, is a beast once said to have roamed the mountains in central Pennsylvania.

Because of its meaning to Penn State, the statue was usually the target of mischievous visiting students in town for football games. A band of Army cadets once attempted to steal it, and eventually Penn State students had to set up guards for the coveted statue on football weekends.

By 1966 activity around the statue had slackened somewhat, and there were no guards when Syracuse came to town. Without protection the attractive white-stone lion was an easy prey for attackers. And the "enemy" took advantage of the situation. In a sneak attack at night three Syracuse students washed the

The crowd lingers after the game, seemingly to savor Penn State's 13-8 upset of North Carolina State in 1967.

proud figure in gaudy orange paint from head to toe. By morning, the freshly-painted lion was the talk of the shocked campus. The vandals were found and had to suffer the consequences. While spending the weekend in jail, they missed seeing Syracuse beat Penn State 12-10 that Saturday.

A loss to Georgia Tech followed, and Paterno wondered whether he was in the right profession. These thoughts became ever more present in his mind when Penn State opened the 1967 season by suffering a 23-22 defeat from Navy. The Nittany Lions' dapper young coach confessed concern over his future in college football. But then positive things began to happen.

The Nittany Lions had started the 1967 season with a predominately senior team, but some injuries forced the use of sophomores. By the time the season was in full swing 10 sophomores were in the starting lineup. The best of these were halfback Charlie Pittman, fullback Don Abbey, and Onkotz. They blended with three good upperclassmen, Sherman, Curry, and Kwalick, to establish the Nittany Lions as a palpable threat in the college football world.

Penn State defeated Miami 17-8 in the second game of the season and then lost by only 17-15 to a UCLA team considered one of the best in the country. That, incidentally, was the last time the Nittany Lions lost for 31 games. The dramatic upset over North Carolina State was later included in a season that also showed victories over Boston College, West Virginia, Syracuse, Maryland, Ohio University, and Pitt. The record earned the Nittany Lions their third visit to the Gator Bowl in seven years.

"This could be the best bowl game of them all," said Paterno, a bit more chipper by this time than he was at the beginning of the season. "We don't feel we can stop Florida State, and we don't believe they can stop us. Who knows, the final score might be 42-41?"

It was actually 17-17, but the tie was not really like kissing your sister, as the expression goes. The result was probably just as satisfying for both sides.

Paterno went into the game with his usual complex about eastern football. He had been bothered by the perennial remarks about the caliber of play in his section of the country.

"We'd like to use the Gator Bowl to show the country that the East still plays a great brand of football, contrary to what people think," said Paterno.

It was an interesting matchup of regional powers—Florida State's high-powered offense with quarterback Kim Hammond and flanker Ron Sellers vs. Penn State's strong defensive club. Certainly the personalities were interesting. Kwalick was ringleader of a group of Penn State players who shaved their heads "for identity." And Florida State had a superstitious halfback, Larry Green, who had students in the school band feed him peanut butter for luck on nights before games.

Preparing for one of the best passing combinations in the country, Paterno made some drastic changes in his defensive alignment during practice at Daytona Beach, some 90 miles

Florida State quarterback Kim Hammond dives over for a touchdown against Penn State in the 1967 Gator Bowl. Penn State defenders include Jim Kates (No. 55) and Pete Johnson (No. 40). The teams tied 17-17.

Florida State's Ron Sellers (No. 34) scores a touchdown in the 1967 Gator Bowl game which resulted in a 17-17 tie. Penn State defenders include Tim Montgomery (No. 12), Jim Kates (No. 55), and Denny Onkotz (No. 35).

from the Gator Bowl site in Jacksonville. Kates was moved to middle guard, Neal Smith to rover back, and Wally Cirafesi joined Tim Montgomery and Bob Capretto in the deep secondary. The idea was to give the Nittany Lions more speed and quickness to cope with Florida State's great passing game.

As it turned out Florida State completed 37 passes against Penn State. But Smith made an interception of one Hammond pass that led to a Penn State touchdown. And Capretto saved a loss by deflecting a Hammond-to-Sellers pass in the end zone with less than a minute to play. Despite the unusually large amount of successful passes by Hammond, Florida State was not able to score until late in the third period.

Pittman, who had averaged about five yards a carry during the regular season, set up a Penn State field goal with his running in the first quarter. Sherman kicked it from the 17-yard line. In the second quarter Sherman threw touchdown passes to Curry and Kwalick, and Penn State had a 17-0 lead at the half. Pittman, who gained 127 yards in the game, set up the Nittany Lions' second touchdown with some spectacular broken-field running.

In the third quarter Penn State had an opportunity to insure a victory but lost it on one of Paterno's well-known gambles.

The ball was on the Florida State 15-yard line, fourth down and six inches to go. Instead of going for an almost-sure field goal, Paterno elected to go for the first down. Sherman tried to sneak the half foot but did not make it.

"The play was piled up, but I looked down and the ball was more than a foot past the line," said Sherman. "Someone caught the seat of my pants and pulled me back. Then the official came in, grabbed the ball, and spotted it where I ended up after they finished pulling me back. As far as I'm concerned we made that first down."

"I take full responsibility for that fourth-down call," said Paterno after the game. "I tried to convince our players between halves that we should be aggressive and daring and fight against a tendency to go conservative with a good lead. We nearly lost to North Carolina State and Syracuse that way. Now, when I knew the boys wanted to go for that first down, I wasn't going to stop them. I'd call it that way again."

Hammond then guided Florida State to two touchdowns in the third period, one on a pass to Sellers and the other on a one-yard quarterback sneak. With 15 seconds remaining in the game, Florida State had the ball with fourth down on the Penn State eight and decided to go for the tying field goal instead of a possible game-winning touchdown. The conservative decision was Bill Peterson's, the Florida State coach.

"There was no question in my mind," said Peterson. "Our boys had made a tremendous comeback. Penn State had showed how tough they could be in there. I think we did the right thing."

If the tie was a moral victory for Peterson, it was also for Paterno.

"It was natural for many of our fans to be disgruntled with a tie," said Paterno, "but I want to emphasize how well everyone played and how hard we all worked to win. We played a really great team, a team whose passing we didn't think we could stop.

"I was disturbed early in the season when so many of our people seemed satisfied because we lost to UCLA by only two points. Now, when I hear our fans aren't pleased with a tie against a team as good as Florida State—that's fine. We've come a long way."

It was nowhere, however, like where they were going.

The Rover Boys

Whenever Penn State stopped an opponents' running play in 1968, chances were good that the public address announcer would say: "Tackle by Reid." Or, "Tackle by Smear." Or, "Tackle by Reid AND Smear."

Mike Reid and Steve Smear were two brutes credited with 108 tackles and 62 assists that year, not to mention two blocked kicks, four fumble recoveries, and countless pass rushes that led to either interceptions or incompletions.

Coach Joe Paterno had been saying it all along, and Miami Coach Charlie Tate also said it positively after watching the two line stars up close.

"They're the best pair of defensive tackles we have ever faced," said Tate after losing a 22-7 decision to Penn State that season.

Reid and Smear were two of the reasons that Penn State's proud defensive unit had come of age that year and helped mold a brilliant 10-0 season.

In the victory over Miami, Reid and Smear rushed Tate's quarterback, David Olivo, into two interceptions, forced him to fumble twice, and helped throw him for 31 yards in losses.

In a 21-6 success over UCLA, the Reid-Smear combo tossed quarterback Jim Nader for a total of 43 yards in losses. When Penn State beat Navy 31-6, Reid and Smear hurried Middie quarterback Mike McNallen into five interceptions and threw him for 38 yards in losses. The brutish pair held Mike Sherwood of West Virginia to minus four yards rushing in Penn State's

31-20 victory and stopped Kansas State's Bill Nossek for minus 19 as Penn State won that one 25-9.

"With those two in the middle, we know we can do a lot of other things with our other people on defense, because we know Reid and Smear will hold up their end of the assignment," said Paterno. "They're both great leaders, and they're both giving us some of the finest tackle play we've ever had."

With Reid returning from an injury that forced him to sit out the 1967 season, Penn State's defense was awesome, indeed. It included people like Denny Onkotz, whom Paterno called "one of the greatest linebackers Penn State has ever had," and Jim

Penn State defenders close in on Miami quarterback David Olivo. The Nittany Lions won this 1968 battle, 22-7.

Kates, Pete Johnson, Paul Johnson, Neal Smith, Mike Smith, John Ebersole, Jack Ham, and Gary Hull.

The Smiths and the Johnsons, not any of them related by blood lines, were a family nevertheless. The four players were part of a fluid "Rover Boy" defensive unit that intercepted 25 passes and recovered 17 fumbles in 1968. Safety Neal Smith led the Nittany Lions in interceptions that year with 8. Mike Smith and the two Johnsons, also defensive backfield players, each had 3 interceptions.

Paterno's smart players had no trouble carrying out his innovative 4-4-3 defensive setup. It was something that a coach dreamt about—a plan on paper that was carried to perfection on a football field. It meant, quite simply, that Penn State's defense used four men on the line, four directly behind them as linebackers, and three defensive backs. The plan gave the Nittany Lions one of the most mobile defenses in the country and gave their opponents nothing but fits.

Along with this magnificent defense, Penn State also had a fine group of offensive players including quarterback Charlie Burkhart, halfbacks Charlie Pittman and Bob Campbell, end Ted Kwalick, tackles John Kulka and Dave Bradley, guards Tom Jackson and Charlie Zapiec, and center Warren Koegel. This historic team, the first Nittany Lions' squad to win 10 games in a season, produced two all-Americas in 1968—Kwalick and Onkotz. Reid, Pittman, Neal Smith, and Onkotz made all-America status in 1969, and Ham was an all-America linebacker in 1970.

"It was quite a thrill to play for a team like this in my first year as a starter," said Burkhart, one of several sophomores in the lineup. "I don't think I really ever had much time to think of the pressure of quarterbacking a history-making team, because I was so excited about the opportunity of just playing."

Pressure obviously did not mean much to Burkhart. It seemed he always came up with a big play when the Nittany Lions needed it most. In the UCLA game he threw a 76-yard touchdown pass to fullback Tom Cherry to give Penn State a 14-6 lead. Against Syracuse he dropped back to pass and found his primary receiver covered—so he connected on a 26-yard scoring toss to split end Leon Angevine.

Two Penn State all-Americas—Ted Kwalick (left) and Denny Onkotz.

"The first few games that year I was seeing a lot of different defenses for the first time while still learning our pass patterns," said Burkhart. "But as the season went on, I started feeling a lot more confident, especially in my ball handling."

Burkhart completed 87 of 177 passes for 1,170 yards and six touchdowns and only threw seven interceptions all year. At one point he went through five games without an interception. Pittman rushed for 950 yards that season and scored a team-record 14 touchdowns. Kwalick caught 31 passes for 403 yards, an average of 13 yards a catch. This heady offensive play, combined with one of the best defenses in the nation, helped Penn State beat Navy, Kansas State, West Virginia, UCLA, Boston College, Army, Miami, Maryland, Pitt, and Syracuse.

The undefeated streak over two years was now 18 games but was not fashioned easily. The Nittany Lions broke away from UCLA in the second half despite the loss of injured key players. They came from behind to beat West Virginia. And they had an awfully tough time with Army, cinching the game 28-24 when Kwalick picked up a loose onside kick in the closing minutes and ran 53 yards for a touchdown.

If the phrase "team effort" was overworked, it was nevertheless appropriate for Penn State's fine 1968 squad. Such people as Bradley and Kulka, who got little notice in the headlines, were singled out by offensive line coach Joe McMullen.

"You only notice those tackles when they miss a block," said McMullen. "When Burkhart gets up from underneath a pile of the wrong-colored jerseys or Campbell or Pittman get smeared for a loss, then people take notice. But when they do their job, no one notices and they don't get many thanks."

Pittman noticed, however, if the average fan did not.

"Before each game I sat down and talked with Kulka and Bradley and let them know that I was aware of what they were doing and that I was thankful," says Pittman. "Our best play that year was off-tackle on Bradley's side. When I heard that one called in the huddle, I just knew there was going to be a hole there. Kulka did most of the trap blocking on my trap plays. That was one of my favorites. If he didn't do the job, I would have gotten clobbered."

As a result of their remarkable year, the Nittany Lions were invited to the Orange Bowl to meet Kansas. Even Paterno, renowned for his unexpected gambles, could not envision what would happen in that game.

Twelve Angry Men

Pepper Rodgers did public somersaults on a football field and sometimes sang "Jingle Bells" on his television program. His flights of fancy seemed appropriate for the Kansas style, which usually included gambles like quick kicks and deep passes on third and one. Here was flamboyance to match Penn State's Joe Paterno.

"If I had to make a guess, I'd say this might turn into a wild game," the Kansas coach said before his 1969 Orange Bowl battle with the Nittany Lions.

It was Penn State's rough defensive crew against Kansas' "Rip City Boys," a name Rodgers applied to his big backs. Quarterback Bobby Douglass, a left-handed thrower, ran the attack with able assistance from fullback John Riggins, tailback Dan Shanklin, and ends George McGowan and John Mosier. This bunch had helped average 38 points and 442 yards total offense a game during the Jayhawks' 9-1 season. The Big Eight team, given a slight edge in offense, was also a larger defensive team although not as accomplished as the Nittany Lions in that department.

"Our defense has a knack for coming up with the big play," said Paterno, pointing out that Penn State had allowed less than 11 points a game to opponents in 1968. "They like to exploit a situation."

The Penn State offense was not to be taken lightly, either, said Paterno: "I imagine we'll be freewheeling it against Kansas."

Penn State was ranked No. 3 in the country in the wire service polls, and Kansas was No. 6 and their stature justified all the attending hoopla and interest in such a match. A crowd of 78,000 was in the Orange Bowl while millions more listened on radio or watched on TV.

The Orange Bowl hosts provided gaudy sidelights, such as a technicolor blimp, synthetic lightbulb snowflakes in the dark, and a bubbling mass of detergent suds to simulate snow. The crowd did not need any reminder of northern weather, though, since the temperature at game time was in the 60s, outrageously low for Miami.

The sideline theatrics, however, paled in comparison to the game itself.

Although the most intense drama was packaged into the last few minutes, it had been a good, sound football game between two well-matched teams. The Nittany Lions' offense appeared superior to the Jayhawks' defense in the first half, but still Penn State could only manage a 7-7 tie at intermission. The Nittany Lions scored the tying touchdown on a 47-yard drive capped by Charlie Pittman's 13-yard run up the middle.

The tenseness of the game was reflected in Paterno's actions. He paced up and down the sidelines throughout and complained when a roughing-the-kicker penalty was not called on Kansas following Penn State's successful extra-point kick.

"That's all right, coach, we made it," said a Penn State player.

"No, it's not all right," Paterno snapped back. "We've got 15 yards coming to us on this kickoff."

Early in the fourth quarter Kansas went ahead 14-7 as Shanklin returned a punt 47 yards and Riggins took it over on two short runs up the middle. It remained that way until there were less than two minutes to play and Kansas was forced to give up the ball. The Nittany Lions attempted to block the Jayhawks' punt with a play called the "10-Go Charge."

"It's a desperation play with 10 men trying to block the kick," Paterno explained afterwards.

Neal Smith partially blocked the ball with one hand, and the Kansas punt rolled dead on the 50-yard line with 1:20 remaining in the game. It was an obvious situation for short, sideline passes where Penn State could eat up chunks of yardage and

271

stop the clock by running out of bounds. Penn State did not do the obvious, though.

"Throw downfield for the left goal post," halfback Bob Campbell said to quarterback Charlie Burkhart. "I'll be there."

A second before he was knocked down Burkhart threw the ball where Campbell had suggested. The halfback made the catch behind a leaping Kansas defender, and the Nittany Lions had the ball on the three-yard line with a minute left.

On the sidelines Paterno then outlined the next three plays with Burkhart.

"Chuck was positively the coolest guy around," Paterno said. "He kept telling me, 'We'll win, coach. Don't worry.' It was great, but sometimes I wonder if he has quite enough talent to be all THAT cocky."

The first two running plays ordered by Paterno were stopped by the Jayhawks' goal-line defense. Burkhart was then supposed to use an exercise called 56 Scissors, a handoff to Pittman into the line. But the quarterback changed the play at the last second and "did something I've never done before, never even thought of before." He faked the ball to a surprised Pittman and bootlegged it around left end for a touchdown to cut the Kansas lead to 14-13.

Pittman, who had sliced through without the ball, was frightened for a moment "because I thought we had fumbled. Then I was tackled; then I saw Chuck score."

The first touchdown that Burkhart ever scored for Penn State could have been the most important, for it set up a play that became Orange Bowl legend. Anyone who knew Paterno had no doubts what he would do in the heat of the moment.

"If we couldn't win, we'd lose," Paterno said later, explaining the strategy to try for the more difficult two-point conversion rather than the safe extra-point kick.

The Nittany Lions appeared to have lost the gamble when Burkhart's conversion pass to Campbell was knocked down by a group of Kansas players. But a flag was down in the orange-colored end zone.

"I knew before the ball was ever snapped that I'd have to call a foul," said Foster Grose, one of the umpires in the team of five Orange Bowl officials.

Grose had noticed that Kansas was playing the last frantic

seconds with 12 men on the field instead of the legal 11.

"I had my hand on my marker when the play started," he said. "It was all very routine, the counting of the players I mean. I do it every play. My heart was thumping some, though."

Photographs later showed that the Jayhawks had used 12 men earlier, when they were making their goal line stand against the Nittany Lions. But apparently this faux pas had gone unnoticed in the intensity that surrounded the final 80 seconds. Through a misunderstanding, when the Jayhawks sent in their goal line defensive team, two players had gone in—but only one had come out. The infamous "twelfth man" was linebacker Rick Abernethy, the unfortunate who never felt a tap on his shoulder.

The penalty for "illegal procedure" was stepped off against Kansas, and Penn State had another chance. The Jayhawks called time out to reset their defense, and this gave Burkhart a chance to talk over strategy with Paterno. The coach decided that the conversion should be made with a quick pitchout to the right to Campbell. Burkhart resumed command of the team with the intention of making this play but could not start because of the crowd noise. He held up his hands for silence but got no response. He was granted permission for another huddle, and Paterno changed his mind on the play, sending in one that would give Campbell the ball on a handoff-sweep to the left. Penn State had to face "only" 11 defenders on this play, and Campbell took the ball in for the two-point conversion and a 15-14 victory. The result was an undefeated, untied season for Penn State and No. 2 ranking in the final polls.

"Let's just say that it was good show biz," Rodgers said afterward, somewhat sarcastically. "We turned what would have been a dull win for us into an exciting win for them."

Rodgers must have been kicking himself for earlier throwing away the game on a bad judgment call. In the fourth quarter he ordered his players to pass up an almost sure field goal on the Penn State five-yard line with fourth down and one yard to go for a first down. The try for the yard failed.

"Yeah, it was a lousy play, and I shouldn't have done it," Rodgers said. "So I was wrong. I wish I'd been right."

The Penn State dressing room was obviously more pleasant

273

than Kansas' gloomy atmosphere.

"You know," said Paterno, "there was enough glory in that game for both teams. No one should be ashamed. We were both great teams tonight."

For several days after the Orange Bowl game, stories about the "Twelfth Man" episode emanated from Lawrence, Kansas. A defensive coach for the Jayhawks was quoted as saying the extra man had been in the game for four plays, not one. A Kansas linebacker then insisted that it was impossible for the Jayhawks to have 12 men in the game. He said it was either

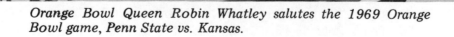

Orange Bowl Queen Robin Whatley salutes the 1969 Orange Bowl game, Penn State vs. Kansas.

11—or 13.

The outcome was not in doubt, though. Penn State had won its first Orange Bowl game and put to rest questions about the power of eastern football.

"I plan to have a barbecue of prime buffalo later this year," said Pennsylvania Governor Raymond Shafer, talking about a bet he won on the game.

Shafer had wagered with Kansas Governor Robert B. Docking—a white pine tree from Pennsylvania's forest against a Kansas buffalo.

The significance of the game is mirrored in Orange Bowl trinkets, placed prominently in the Penn State trophy room. A tan animal skin, hypothetically that of a buffalo, is stretched on a wall. "Penn State 15, Kansas 14" is emblazoned on the skin in bright blue. And to the left of the skin is a painting of a football team in white making a goal-line stand against one in blue. The defending team has seven men on the line and five in the back-field.

The President
And The Plaque

On December 9, 1969, President Richard Nixon addressed a football dinner in New York, and the significance of one telling remark was not lost at University Park, Pennsylvania, a couple of hundred miles to the west.

"I would like to say that now I think Penn State is among those who should be considered for the No. 1 spot," said the president.

Nixon was a few days too late with the statement, which apparently attempted to assuage hurt feelings.

The nation's "No. 1" sports fan appeared at the Waldorf Astoria Hotel in New York to receive the coveted gold medal award for his contributions to college football—but it was questionable what contributions he had made in the past week.

Nixon had taken it upon himself to name Texas the No. 1 team in the country, the first such presidential stamp of approval in college football history. The action triggered a cause celebre, with much indignation coming from Penn State. After all, Coach Joe Paterno and his Nittany Lions possessed the nation's longest undefeated streak and took umbrage to Nixon's decision.

Nixon just about admitted that he had stuck his foot in the presidential mouth. He told his Waldorf audience he was thinking of suggesting that some sort of college super bowl be played after the January 1 bowl games to decide a true national champion.

"But I was in deep enough already," said the president, "so I decided to skip it."

The controversy started when someone suggested to Nixon that it might be a good idea to present a "No. 1" plaque to the winner of the Texas-Arkansas game on December 6. The reasoning went like this: Both Texas and Arkansas were unbeaten and ranked higher than Penn State in the wire service polls. The game would be a publicity man's dream, on national television with millions watching. It was a natural spot for the nation's "No. 1" sports fan. Nixon could walk on camera in the winner's locker room and present the presidential plaque to the winning coach. Adding spice to the drama was an historic ingredient, football's 100th anniversary.

Penn State had finished its regular season on November 29 by routing North Carolina State 33-8 for its 29th straight game without a defeat. The Nittany Lions accepted a bid to play Missouri in the Orange Bowl, and Paterno, like any other interested football fan, settled down to watch the Texas-Arkansas battle on TV.

Texas Coach Darrell Royal went for broke, a la Paterno, with a daring two-point conversion that helped the Longhorns beat the Razorbacks 15-14. There, in the noisy, sweaty Texas locker room, the president of the United States handed Royal the "No. 1" plaque. Nixon, incidentally, then announced on national TV that he was presenting a plaque to Penn State for having the nation's longest unbeaten streak.

"Who needs it?" was the reaction from Paterno in so many words.

Paterno, obviously annoyed with the whole scene, issued a public statement that nicely told the president what he could do with such a plaque. The Penn State coach said that his players would be disappointed with nothing less than No. 1, if so deserving after the bowl games "which supposedly determine the final No. 1 team." Paterno suggested that the president was also doing a disservice to Penn State's Orange Bowl opponent, Missouri, who might very well be the best team in the country.

If the Nittany Lions were not officially No. 1, they certainly deserved serious consideration. Here was a team that went through a second straight undefeated season with one of the best defenses in modern college football history. In the opinion of one opposing coach, even Texas would not have scored

277

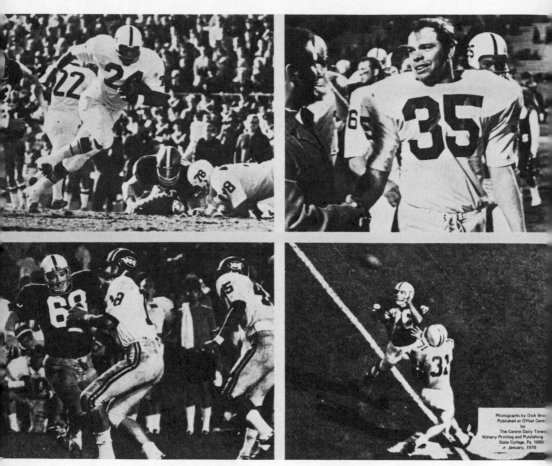

*Four stars of the fine 1969 Penn State team: Charlie Pittman
(upper left); Denny Onkotz (upper right); Mike Reid (lower
left); and Neal Smith (lower right).*

against that rugged bunch.

"Pride and poise," is the way Paterno sums up the 1969
squad.

"It was a combination of superior personnel, experience, and
fine young men with tremendous pride," says Paterno. "They
liked each other, played together well and enjoyed the game.
Everyone of them was unselfish. And that was the biggest thing
going for them. They were not concerned about who got the
credit."

The strong defense, basically intact since 1967, included
Mike Reid and Steve Smear at tackles; Denny Onkotz, Jim
Kates, Jack Ham and Mike Smith at linebackers; Neal Smith at

safety; John Ebersole and Gary Hull at defensive end; and Paul Johnson and newcomer George Landis at defensive halfbacks.

Their efforts helped the Nittany Lions set a new school record for fewest points allowed during a 10-game season. They gave up but 87, an average of 8.7 a game. In addition the defense scored 107 of Penn State's total 312 points with the help of twenty-four pass interceptions, nine fumble recoveries, and three blocked punts.

Colorado's Bob Anderson, the best running quarterback in the country, was among those who found the Penn State defense immovable. During the Nittany Lions' 27-3 victory before 51,342 fans at Beaver Stadium in the second game of the season, Anderson gained a paltry sum of four yards. He threw the ball twenty-six times, completed only eight, and was intercepted three times. He also fumbled once. And after the game, he looked as if he had been mugged in an alley.

"I think this was the greatest defensive unit I've ever played against," said Anderson. "I think Penn State would be a great team in our Big Eight conference, or any other conference for that matter. Our coaches told me I would have no more than three seconds to set up and throw. After that I could expect Reid or Smear on my back. That Reid is something. He nearly tore off my head once.

"What makes Penn State's defense so tough is they are so strong all the way down the line. The deployment of their linebackers bothered me. One of them always seemed to be right in the pass route. I've never had a day like this before. How do I like playing against Penn State? It's pretty discouraging."

The Penn State offense, if not as awe-inspiring as the defense, was also a competent group. Charlie Pittman gained 100 yards or more in three different games while Paterno used a shuttle system of six or seven running backs. Don Abbey and Franco Harris shared the job at fullback while the halfbacks included Pittman, Lydell Mitchell, Gary Deuel, and Fran Ganter. Pittman, Mitchell, Harris, and Greg Edmonds all were potential receivers for quarterback Charlie Burkhart.

"I think they were a group of players with character and quality," says Paterno, "I think that's why we were able to go undefeated again."

Penn State opened with victories over Navy, Colorado, Kansas State, and West Virginia before meeting Syracuse in the season's most controversial and exciting game. The Nittany Lions had taken their 23-game unbeaten streak into Syracuse's Archbold Stadium and looked like they were going to lose it when the Orangemen took a 14-0 lead at halftime.

"When we came in at halftime, behind by two touchdowns," says Smear, "Coach Paterno talked to us about pride. He said if we ever had it, we'd better show it now. He just told us that losing wouldn't be any disgrace, but the thing that would hurt him most would be if we went out and were out-played and out-hit. It looked bad. We couldn't get anything generated. Syracuse was really ready for us."

Syracuse held that imposing two-touchdown lead as late as the fourth quarter before Penn State rallied behind Burkhart.

"There was no tension, no emotion along the bench," said the quarterback. "We knew what we had to do. We had to play a lot more as a team because we were behind by two scores."

Within a span of three minutes and seventeen seconds, Penn State scored two touchdowns. With the help of an interference call on a pass that put the ball on the Syracuse four, the Nittany Lions recorded the first touchdown. Mitchell carried it over with 10 minutes to play, and Penn State made a two-point conversion to cut the Syracuse lead to 14-8. Incidentally, Penn State got two cracks at the conversion because of a Syracuse holding penalty on the first play.

Shortly thereafter Harris scored the tying touchdown, and Mike Reitz kicked the go-ahead extra point with 7:01 left. That was the game, but Paterno confessed afterwards that he had morbid apprehensions in the third quarter when Penn State could not score after recovering a fumble on the Syracuse 11.

"I wondered then if we had the stuff to do it," said the coach.

Scouts from the Orange and Sugar bowls witnessed the game, and there was no doubt in their minds that Penn State "had the stuff" to win.

"Penn State didn't show much offense, but they have to have something special to come off the floor like that in the fourth

Penn State's bull in a china shop: Steve Smear.

280

quarter," said one of the scouts.

Whatever it was that Penn State had, though, it did not impress the Syracuse coach, Ben Schwartzwalder. He complained bitterly that the Nittany Lions were given the game by bad officiating.

Leveling his attack at the officials during a New York Football Writers luncheon, Schwartzwalder said: "This was a case of 25 or more bad calls, and it was seemingly unending."

Schwartzwalder questioned the allegiance of the officials, among other things.

"First, my boys want to know why three of the officials who worked our Penn State game have to be from Pennsylvania, where they work, live and eat?

"Second, my boys asked me—and I don't know the answer—why the Penn State coaches are permitted to run up and down the field, screaming and cursing the officials without penalty? My boys said those coaches succeeded in effectively intimidating those officials. My boys asked me how come we don't protest anything.

"And they want to know why Stan Peffle, who lives in Philadelphia, kept calling holding calls on our boys when Penn State's No. 63 (tackle Tom Jackson) kept holding continuously and flagrantly without punishment?"

Paterno answered the charges in a more dignified manner.

"The only coaches on the field were myself and Jim O'Hora, so I guess it's us he's accusing," said the Penn State coach. "I don't even want to comment on accusations that we were swearing at officials. The ones to ask about that would be the officials. I don't even want to get into the rest of it. I've got to worry about getting ready for our next game. It's a shame Ben would resort to this kind of thing to discredit a great comeback victory for our kids."

After an intensive study of the Schwartzwalder complaint, the Eastern College Athletic Conference knocked it down. "There was no evidence of any laxity in officiating," said Asa Bushnell, commissioner of the E.C.A.C.

The Penn State undefeated string was thus preserved and continued with victories over Ohio University, Boston College, Maryland, Pitt, and North Carolina State. This performance cinched an Orange Bowl berth for the powerful Nittany Lions, who might have been No. 2 in the eyes of Texas but certainly No. 1 in Pennsylvania.

Pennsylvania Governor Raymond Shafer, a vociferous critic of President Nixon's controversial "No. 1" plaque, gave the Nittany Lions a pep talk during a student-alumni rally the morning of the Orange Bowl game.

"I don't want you to prove anything to anybody," Shafer told the team. "You don't have to prove you're No. 1 in the newspapers, to the fans, or even to the president. Just go out

The joy and pain of football is expressed as Governor Raymond Shafer of Pennsylvania gets traditional shower after Penn State's 10-3 victory over Missouri in the 1970 Orange Bowl (upper left), captains hold Orange Bowl trophy (lower left), and Penn State player rests from fierce competition and oppressive heat.

there and win this game for yourselves."

Despite playing most of the first half with blurred vision—he had lost one of his contact lenses—Burkhart led the Nittany Lions to a quick 10-0 lead. Burkhart, who completed 11 of 26 passes for 187 yards, connected on a 28-yard toss with Mitchell for a touchdown. The early lead turned out to be all the points that Penn State needed in a 10-3 victory.

"That's the best defensive team I've seen in 20 years of college football," said Missouri Coach Dan Devine. "It may not have been obvious at times, but our staff put more time and effort into this bowl game than any of our previous five bowl trips."

Devine added, "I can't see how anybody in the country can be any better than Penn State."

"Not even Texas?" he was asked.

"I might vote a tie," said Devine, diplomatically. "I certainly wouldn't vote Penn State No. 2."

After the game, Penn State's 30th straight without a defeat, Paterno was still ready to take on President Nixon.

"I put an awful lot of pressure on these kids by talking about their right to be rated No. 1 before the Orange Bowl game," said Paterno, who had just been put through the traditional shower soaking with Governor Shafer. "I don't like to keep pushing this thing. But I still think we have as much right to be No. 1 as Texas or anybody else. We beat a very good team in Missouri.

"We haven't been beaten in 30 games. Every challenge that we come up against, we overcome. We play the games and we win. People can say it's sour grapes. But why should I sit back and let the president of the United States say so-and-so is No. 1 when I've got 50 kids who've worked their tails off for me for three years. If I didn't argue for my team, I'd be a lousy coach.

"I don't really know if we're No. 1, but I think we have every right to be No. 1 until they start having national playoffs."

Penn State finished No. 2 in the final wire service polls that year. Texas was recognized as the official national champion after beating Notre Dame 21-17 in the Cotton Bowl.

"If we're not No. 1, we're at least No. 1A," quipped the irrepressible Burkhart.

284

The End Of The Streak

The first sign of bad luck was an appendicitis attack to Charlie Zapiec. Lydell Mitchell put both his hip and shoulder pads on wrong and left his football shoes behind.

Penn State rooters tried shooting confetti out of air pressure cans, but the wind worked against them. They were soon buried under an avalanche of green and pink confetti.

All that had to happen next was the end of the 31-game undefeated streak...and it happened.

"It had to come sooner or later," said Mitchell, Penn State's fine running back, after the Nittany Lions were beaten 41-13 by Colorado in the second game of the 1970 season.

The end of the unbeaten streak came at a most inopportune time, though. It happened while millions watched the Boulder, Colorado, affair on national television.

Only a week before, the Nittany Lions had extended their glamorous streak to 31 with a 55-7 rout of Navy. It gave rise to false hope, because Navy was a weak team. Penn State was definitely not as strong as it had been the two previous seasons. Gone was the heart of the solid defensive team that had gained the Nittany Lions their greatest recognition in history. New faces replaced the Reids, Onkotz, Smears, Smiths, and Johnsons. The situation became so critical that Coach Joe Paterno had to move Zapiec, a star offensive tackle, to line-backer.

Along with rebuilding the defense, Paterno had to replace quarterback Charlie Burkhart. He had a group of three to choose from—Mike Cooper, Bob Parsons, and John Hufnagle. Cooper, Burkhart's back-up man for two years, got the opening-day assignment and looked like a good choice after the Penn State rout over Navy.

The following week was a different story, however. The Nittany Lions had trouble even before their plane landed in Denver for the September 26 game with Colorado. Zapiec had severe stomach cramps on the flight, and it was discovered to be appendicitis. He was taken to a Denver hospital immediately upon arrival in the Rocky Mountain city.

Cooper, a hero in the Navy game, put the Nittany Lions into a hole right away against Colorado by throwing an interception. The Buffaloes continued to take advantage of Penn State mistakes to run up a 20-7 lead at the half and 34-7 at the end of three quarters.

"I didn't think about the streak when we were down 34-7," said Mitchell. "All I could think of was we had lost this game."

Indeed, they had.

"We just got whipped," said Paterno. "They were better prepared for us, and I just got out-coached. I didn't do a very good job today."

Colorado Coach Eddie Crowder's game plan worked as expected.

"We felt that our defense had to play a super game, and it did," said Crowder. "We were greatly impressed with their offense, and we knew we had to try to keep the ball away from them. I thought our offense did a good job in that respect. Of course they didn't have people in there like Reid and Onkotz on defense..."

Don Popplewell, the Colorado center, found Penn State gracious in defeat.

"Penn State has great people and great players," he said. "I felt honored to be on the same field with them. They were great sports. Even as bad as they must have felt after losing, every one of them I talked to had a nice word to say to me when we were coming off the field.

"I'm glad we were the team to stop their streak. But even though I'm the victor, I still feel sorry for them. I have the feeling that something great has gone by the wayside. But that streak is something which won't be forgotten."

Penn State's record-breaker—halfback Lydell Mitchell.

Paterno, who had always taught his players nobility, added a touch of class to the occasion by visiting the Colorado locker room after the game. He congratulated Crowder on the victory and wished him luck the rest of the season.

After Paterno had left the room, two Colorado linemen looked at each other in surprise.

"Can you believe that?" said one, incredulously. "Can you believe that after what just happened that he could come over here and say that?"

"That's why they win, man, that's why they win," said the other. "That's class."

The fallen heroes came home to a welcome befitting victors. Two buses carried the Nittany Lions from the airport to campus, escorted by two fire trucks with lights flashing. The players were escorted to Recreation Hall on Center Campus, where 2,000 people waited.

"I've never been prouder of a Penn State football team," Paterno told the crowd. "And I've never been prouder of our student body. I'm sure the players appreciate this."

The players arrived home amid chants of "Beat Wisconsin" and signs that said, "Beat The Badgers." However, the fans were in for a second straight disappointment. Penn State lost the following weekend, too, this time by a 29-16 score.

After a 28-3 victory over Boston College, Penn State lost a 24-7 decision to Syracuse, and Paterno decided it was time for a change at quarterback. Hufnagle was given the job and held on to it the rest of the way by leading Penn State to victories over Army, West Virginia, Maryland, Ohio, and Pitt.

Hufnagle at quarterback and Mitchell and Franco Harris at the running back positions collaborated to give the Nittany Lions a mighty potent offense the following season. With Mitchell breaking NCAA records for touchdowns in a season (29), for touchdowns rushing in one season (26), and for points (174), and rushing for a team record 1,567 yards, the Nittany Lions scored 454 points in 1971—the highest production in Penn State history. This powerful offense was responsible for an 11-1 record that year, including a victory over Texas in the Cotton Bowl.

"I can't believe there's a better all-around back in the country," said Paterno of Mitchell. "He runs well, he catches the ball excellently, he blocks for you. He's a leader, and lately he's been covering punts better than anyone on the squad.

"I really think Mitchell is the best short-yardage runner we've ever had up here. On third and short yardage he gets you that first down. He's a fierce competitor, and I mean FIERCE. I'd rather have him than anyone else."

In later years Paterno called Mitchell the greatest running back Penn State ever had.

"Probably Lenny Moore had the most talent," said Paterno, "but I think you would have to go with Mitchell based on what he did."

Franco Harris would have been the star on any Penn State team, but for Mitchell. He complemented the great Lydell with his gifted ability to run inside or out. In 1971 Harris rushed for 684 yards and with Mitchell gave the Nittany Lions perhaps their best 1-2 running combination in history.

"Harris was quick enough and had all the moves to be a halfback; Mitchell was strong and had the straight-ahead power to be a fullback," says Paterno. "The outstanding thing about them was their versatility. You could do so much with them because there was nothing they couldn't do."

Along with the two superb running backs, Paterno had what he considered the best all-around quarterback in Penn State history in Hufnagle.

"He could do everything awfully well, and he may not have done any one thing better than anybody" says Paterno. "But in every area of the game—running, the option, passing and leadership, he'd be either No. 1 or No. 2. A combination of all of that would make him the best."

Mitchell gave an indication of things to come in the first game of the season when he scored five touchdowns to lead a 56-3 rout of Navy. The service academy, whose fortunes had reached bottom, resorted to sideshow theatrics instead of good, sound football. A bikini-clad go-go girl made an appearance with "Go Navy" imprinted on her derriere. She raced onto the field for a pre-arranged meeting with Navy's version of "Superman," who had presumably been shot from a cannon. If it was meant to distract Penn State players, it did not.

In the second game of the season Penn State beat Iowa 44-14 as Mitchell carried for 211 yards and scored two touchdowns and Harris rushed for 145 yards and scored four times.

Except for a tense 16-14 triumph over Air Force, Penn State's games continued to be runaways in 1971. The Nittany Lions crushed Army 42-0, Syracuse 31-0, Texas Christian University 66-14, West Virginia 35-7, Maryland 63-27, North Carolina State 35-3, and Pitt 55-18. The TCU and Maryland games were notable for Albert Vitiello's kicking, as well as the running of Mitchell and Harris. Vitiello produced nine extra points in each for a Penn State record.

Looking forward to a Cotton Bowl game with Texas on New Year's Day, the Nittany Lions stubbed their toes in the last game of the season. A combination of Penn State mistakes and an opportunistic Tennessee defense helped the Volunteers upset the favored Nittany Lions 31-11 before a national TV audience. A 15-game winning streak was stopped in the process, and the loss revived old jibes about "weak" eastern football.

Penn State had something to prove in the Cotton Bowl. Paterno grimaced and promised that his team would try harder in Dallas.

"It was awfully important to us to beat Texas in the Cotton Bowl," says the coach. "I felt at the time we were trying to show people what we had done in previous years was not a fluke. There was so much that had been done that was ready to go down the drain if Texas had beaten us. We were in a part of the country where we had to show people we were a pretty good football team."

Texas, of course, was the team that had beaten Penn State out of the national championship two years before with presidential blessing. The Longhorns' Southwest Conference, also, was long reputed to be superior to the brand of football played

Veteran trainer Chuck Medlar tapes Charlie Zapiec for a game.

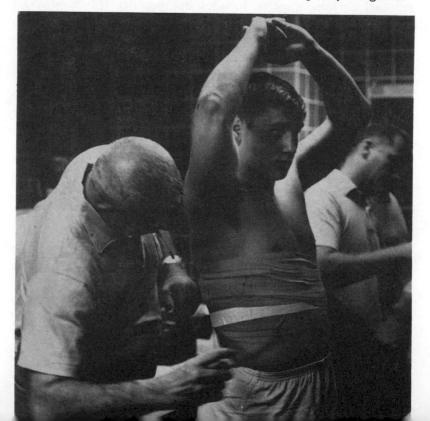

in the East. Detractors continually pointed out that Penn State fattened its record with "soft" opponents.

"I think we can play football with anybody in the country," said Mitchell, one of Penn State's all-America players along with Zapiec and offensive tackle Dave Joyner. "Very much has been

Lydell Mitchell plows through for some of his record-breaking yardage.

said this past year about the type of schedule Penn State plays. The schedule we play is no fault of ours. Schedules are made up a long time in advance. The Tennessee loss hurt, but this game against Texas can help us make up for it. We have a lot to prove. Our reputation as a major football power is in question."

While traveling deep into the heart of Texas, the Nittany Lions did find some friendly signs along the way. Messages were strung up all over town, obviously by Penn State men. They read, "Rattle the Cattle" and "Unhook The Horns." Of course the place was Texas-oriented, and numerous different signs were constructed by Longhorn adherents. "Kick The Hell Out Of Penn State," said one. "Go Cowboys, Hook 'Em Horns," said another. Then there was the traditional southern Hello: "Welcome Penn State Yawl."

The game was played on a rainy 50-degree afternoon before a crowd of 72,000, including former President Lyndon Johnson. Steve Valek's two field goals, including a Cotton Bowl record 40-yarder, gave Texas a 6-3 lead at the half. But the Longhorns found the lead hard to hold in the second half while constantly dropping the ball. Fumbles by Texas quarterback Eddie Phillips led to a touchdown run by Mitchell and a field goal by Vitiello in the third quarter. Hufnagle threw a 65-yard touchdown pass to Scott Skarzynski as Penn State scored 17 points in the period to break open the game.

"We finally showed people we could play major college football," said a satisfied Mitchell after the 30-6 Penn State success. "If we played Tennessee 10 more times, we'd beat 'em 10 times."

Mitchell chalked up 146 yards rushing, the ninth time he went over the 100-yard level in the last 12 games, and was chosen the game's most valuable offensive player.

"Mitchell's the best running back I've faced," said Texas defensive end Malcolm Minnick. "He's a lot like Oklahoma's Greg Pruitt, only he's bigger and tougher."

Penn State's obvious superiority was not only shown in its running game, but in a defense which held Texas without a touchdown. That was the first time that happened to the Longhorns in 80 games—or since 1964.

"I think they are stronger than we are physically, and although I hate to say it I think they wanted to win a little more," said Texas linebacker Tommy Woodard.

Paterno sought out Phillips, the Texas quarterback who made two costly fumbles, and attempted to console him. Then Paterno later told sports writers: "If they don't fumble the ball, it's a different game."

Paterno was obviously being gracious, but he knew what every college football fan in the nation knew, that Penn State was better than Texas that day.

"I don't think we have ever had a bigger win at a time when we needed it more," Paterno said.

There was no doubt about that.

"The Players Know
Who Won"

A telephone rang one quiet spring day in 1973 and touched off excitement on the Penn State campus.

"Did you hear the bombshell announcement?" asked an angular, young man. "Oklahoma has just forfeited the Sugar Bowl game!"

Upon learning that Oklahoma had forfeited its 1973 Sugar Bowl victory to Penn State because of recruiting irregularities, Nittany Lions' Coach Joe Paterno had a predictable reaction.

"Irrespective of the action Oklahoma or the Sugar Bowl would take in regard to the forfeit, our players and the Oklahoma players know who won the game," said Paterno, renown for his honest evaluations. "The Sugar Bowl was decided on the field of play, and regardless of this regrettable incident, the result of the game itself is unchanged."

Penn State had been beaten thoroughly. Though the score was only 14-0, it was a lopsided game. The Nittany Lions did not get across midfield until the final two minutes of the first half, and their deepest penetration was the Oklahoma 19 with six minutes left in the game.

"Keeping Penn State out of the end zone was a great accomplishment," said Oklahoma Coach Chuck Fairbanks.

It was at that. It was the first time that Penn State had not scored a point in 68 games. And the shutout had come on top of an excellent 10-1 season during which the Nittany Lions scored 358 points.

One of the reasons for Penn State's ineffectiveness in the

Sugar Bowl was the absence of star runner John Cappelletti. He was sidelined shortly before kickoff with a 102-degree fever. Cappelletti had become the third Penn State runner in history to go over 1,000 yards in a season. He had 1,117 in 1972.

"Losing Cappelletti definitely hurt us," said Paterno. "He's the kind of runner who can break two or three tackles. I don't want to take anything away from Oklahoma's win, however. They were just better than we were tonight."

There were not many teams better than Penn State that season, though. Quarterback John Hufnagle had an all-America year, completing almost 54 percent of his passes for 2,039 yards and a school record 15 touchdowns. Defensive end Bruce Bannon and linebacker John Skorupan were two others cited on all-America teams, and rightfully so. These standout players led the Nittany Lions to their 34th straight non-losing season, their ninth Lambert Trophy, and ranking in the wire service polls' Top Ten.

After an opening 28-21 loss to Tennessee, Penn State defeated Navy 21-10, Iowa 14-10, Illinois 35-17, Army 45-0, Syracuse 17-0, West Virginia 28-19, Maryland 46-16, North Carolina State 37-22, Boston College 45-26, and Pittsburgh 49-27.

The Nittany Lions not only looked good on the field but at the box office as well. They played before a record 320,122 people, including an all-time home high of 60,465 in the Syracuse game. The Penn State administration had prepared for such a happy event and steadily improved Beaver Stadium's seating capacity to 57,538 in 1972.

The situation was quite unique for a school whose athletic program was subservient to academics.

"The general feeling is that the Penn State program is a myth," said Dean Robert J. Scannell. "People say that if you dig into it, you'll find something rotten inside. But the thing you can't deny is when the athletes graduate at the end of four years."

If Penn State had been doing something illegal through the years, nobody discovered it. The Nittany Lions surfaced as a modern football power despite a heavy accent on scholastic achievement. Today Penn State has a reasonable ceiling on athletic scholarships, noticeably below many of the country's leading football schools.

Excellent prospects have been denied entry time and again because of sub-par academic records in high school. And all athletes at Penn State have been required to keep up with stiff scholastic standards.

"It breaks our hearts every year, from an athletic point of view, to see some of the players we could have if we only bend the rules a little," said Scannell.

The alliance of athletics and academics was dramatically reflected at Penn State's 1973 commencement exercises when Paterno was invited to be the main speaker. It was not often that a football coach was invited to be a university's commencement speaker, and Paterno accepted the assignment with "misgivings, trepidation, and humility."

The erudite Paterno then gave the graduating class of 4,650 a lot to think about in a speech that was sort of like a sophisticated halftime pep talk.

Paterno covered a wide range of topics, from society's ills to presidential pains.

"I'd like to know how could the president know so little about Watergate in 1973 and so much about college football in 1972," Paterno said.

It was an obvious shot at President Nixon for picking Texas to beat Penn State in the Cotton Bowl that season. The president made the wrong choice, for Penn State won.

Paterno painted American society as "fragmented and disillusioned...without consistent direction and without a common purpose.

"You may not make our society perfect, but you may make it better," he told the students.

Paterno ended on a personal note, explaining his reason for being a college football coach.

"I cannot adequately describe to you the love that permeates a good football team," he said. "But to be in a locker room before a big game and to gather a team around and to look at grown men with tears in their eyes, huddling close to each other...reaching out to be part of each other...to look into strong faces which say 'If we can only do it today'...to be with aggressive, ambitious people who have lost themselves in something bigger than they are-this is what living is all about.

"We have shared four years together, years we will never

The Nittany Lion mascot climbs the goal posts to signal one of Penn State's frequent victories before a typically big crowd at Beaver Stadium.

forget, and we hope this short journey has made us a little better."

Paterno wished the students "God speed," "good luck," and "peace" and stepped down from the speaker's platform amid cheers and applause.

Yet though he spoke to them of peace, they could not accept this word entirely from this tough coach with the soul of a poet. True, he had graciously visited Colorado players after they shut off Penn State's winning streak at 31. He had complimented them, causing one to say about him, "That's why they win, man. That's class." True, after his own team beat Kansas he was the one to say generously "There was enough glory in that game for both teams." But this also was the Paterno who had taken on the president of the United States.

So to no one's surprise, least of all Penn State's, Paterno was in the forefront of a new campaign within weeks after his "God speed" and "good luck" and "peace" commencement address. Recruiting abuses at some other schools in the NCAA, according to Paterno in the heat of 1973's summer, "are the worst I've seen in my 23 years of coaching." This was the first in a gridiron of salvos. No one expected it to be the last.

GAME BY GAME, 1887 through 1973

(No formal coaches until 1892)

1887—(2-0)

54	at Bucknell	0
24	Bucknell	0
78		**0**

1888—(0-2-1)

6	Dickinson	6
0	at Dickinson	16
0	Lehigh	30
6		**52**

1889—(2-2)

20	Swarthmore	6
0	at Lafayette	26
0	at Lehigh	106
12	Bucknell	0
32		**138**

1890—(2-2)

0	at Penn	20
0	at F & M	10
68	Altoona	0
23	at Bellefonte	0
91		**30**

1891—(6-2)

14	at Lafayette	4
2	at Lehigh	24
44	at Swarthmore	0
26	at F & M	6
18	at Gettysburg	0
10	at Bucknell	12
1	Dickinson (forfeit)	0
58	at Haverford	0
173		**46**

Coach G. W. Hoskins

1892—(5-1)

0	at Penn	20
44	Wyoming Seminary at Kingston	0
16	at Pittsburgh A. C.	0
18	Bucknell	0
18	Lafayette at Wilkes-Barre	0
16	Dickinson at Harrisburg	0
108		**20**

1893—(4-1)

6	at Virginia	0
6	at Penn	18
32	Pitt	0
36	at Bucknell	18
12	at Pittsburgh A. C.	0
92		**36**

1894—(6-0-1)

60	Gettysburg	0
72	Lafayette	0
6	at Navy	6
12	Bucknell at Williamsport	6
6	at W & J	0
9	at Oberlin	6
14	at Pittsburgh A. C.	0
179		**18**

1895—(2-2-3)

48	Gettysburg	0
0	at Cornell	0
16	Bucknell at Williamsport	0
4	at Penn	35
10	at Pittsburgh A. C.	11
6	at W & J	6
8	at Western Reserve	8
92		**60**

Coach Dr. S. B. Newton

1896—(3-4)

40	Gettysburg	0
10	Pitt	4
8	Dickinson	0
0	at Princeton	39
0	Bucknell at Williamsport	10
0	at Penn	27
5	Carlisle Indians at Harrisburg	48
63		**128**

1897—(3-6)

32	Gettysburg	0
0	at Lafayette	24
0	at Princeton	34
0	at Penn	24
0	at Navy	4
0	at Cornell	45
27	Bucknell at Williamsport	4
10	Bloomsburg Normal	0
0	Dickinson at Sunbury	6
69		**141**

1898—(6-4)

47	Gettysburg	0
0	at Penn	40
5	at Lafayette	0
45	Susquehanna	6
11	at Navy	16
0	at Princeton	5
5	D. C. & A. C. at Pittsburgh	18
16	Bucknell at Williamsport	0
11	at W & J	6
34	Dickinson at Williamsport	0
174		**91**

Coach Sam Boyle

1899—(4-6)

38	Mansfield	0
40	Gettysburg	0
6	at Army	0
0	at Princeton	12
0	at Navy	6
15	Dickinson	0
0	Bucknell at Williamsport	5
0	at Yale	42
0	at Penn	47
5	D. C. & A. C. at Pittsburgh	64
104		**176**

Coach W. N. Golden

1900—(4-6-1)

17	Susquehanna	0
12	Pitt at Bellefonte	0
0	at Army	0
0	at Princeton	26
5	at Penn	17

0	at Dickinson	18
0	D. C. & A. C. at Pittsburgh	29
6	Bucknell at Williamsport	0
0	at Navy	44
44	Gettysburg	0
0	Buffalo	10
84		**144**

1901—(5-3)

17	Susquehanna	0
27	Pitt at Bellefonte	0
6	at Penn	23
0	at Yale	22
11	at Navy	6
0	Homestead A. C. at Pittsburgh	39
39	Lehigh at Williamsport	0
12	Dickinson	0
112		**90**

1902—(7-3)

28	Dickinson Seminary	0
27	Pitt	0
0	at Penn	17
32	Villanova	0
0	at Yale	11
55	Susquehanna	0
6	at Navy	0
39	Gettysburg	0
28	at Dickinson	0
5	at Steelton Y.M.C.A.	6
219		**34**

Coach Dan Reed

1903—(5-3)

60	Dickinson Seminary	0
24	Allegheny	5
0	at Penn	39
0	at Yale	27
59	at Pitt	0
17	at Navy	0
0	Dickinson at Williamsport	6
22	W & J at Pittsburgh	0
182		**77**

Coach Tom Fennell

1904—(6-4)

0	at Penn	6
50	Allegheny	0
0	at Yale	24
34	West Virginia	0
12	W & J at Pittsburgh	0
30	Jersey Shore	0
9	at Navy	20
11	Dickinson at Williamsport	0
44	Geneva	0
5	at Pitt	22
195		**72**

1905—(8-3)

23	Lebanon Valley	0
29	Cal. State	0
0	Carlisle Indians at Harrisburg	11
18	Gettysburg	0
0	at Yale	12
29	Villanova	0
5	at Navy	11
73	Geneva	0
6	Dickinson at Williamsport	0
6	West Virginia	0
6	at Pitt	0
195		**34**

1906—(8-1-1)

24	Lebanon Valley	0
26	Allegheny	0
4	Carlisle Indians at Williamsport	0
0	Gettysburg	0
12	Bellefonte Academy	0
0	at Yale	10
5	at Navy	0
6	Dickinson at Williamsport	0
10	West Virginia	0
6	at Pitt	0
93		**10**

1907—(6-4)

27	Altoona A. A.	0
34	Geneva	0
5	Carlisle Indians at Williamsport	18
46	Grove City	0
8	at Cornell	6
75	Lebanon Valley	0
52	Dickinson at Williamsport	0
0	at Penn	28
4	at Navy	6
0	at Pitt	6
251		**64**

1908—(5-5)

5	Bellefonte Academy	6
31	Grove City	0
5	Carlisle Indians at Wilkes-Barre	12
0	at Penn	6
51	Geneva	0
12	West Virginia	0
4	at Cornell	10
33	Bucknell	6
0	at Navy	5
12	at Pitt	6
153		**51**

Coach Bill Hollenback

1909—(5-0-2)

31	Grove City	0
8	Carlisle Indians at Wilkes-Barre	8
46	Geneva	0
3	at Penn	3
33	at Bucknell	0
40	West Virginia	0
5	at Pitt	0
166		**11**

Coach Jack Hollenback

1910—(5-2-1)

58	Harrisburg A. C.	0
61	Carnegie Tech	0
45	Sterling A. C.	0
0	at Penn	10
0	Villanova	0
34	St. Bonaventure	0
45	Bucknell	3
0	at Pitt	11
243		**24**

Coach Bill Hollenback

1911—(8-0-1)

57	Geneva	0
31	Gettysburg	0
5	at Cornell	0
18	Villanova	0
22	at Penn	6
46	St. Bonaventure	0

17	Colgate	9
0	at Navy	0
3	at Pitt	0
199		**15**

1912—(8-0)

41	Carnegie Tech	0
30	W & J	0
29	at Cornell	6
25	Gettysburg	0
14	at Penn	0
71	Villanova	0
37	at Ohio State	0
38	at Pitt	0
285		**6**

1913—(2-6)

49	Carnegie Tech	0
16	Gettysburg	0
0	at W & J	17
0	at Harvard	29
0	at Penn	17
7	Notre Dame	14
0	at Navy	10
6	at Pitt	7
78		**94**

1914—(5-3-1)

13	Westminster	0
22	Muhlenberg	0
13	Gettysburg	0
30	Ursinus	0
13	at Harvard	13
17	at Lafayette	0
7	at Lehigh	20
3	Michigan State	6
3	at Pitt	13
121		**52**

Coach Dick Harlow

1915—(7-2)

26	Westminster	0
13	Lebanon Valley	0
13	at Penn	3
27	Gettysburg	12
28	West Virginia Wesleyan	0
0	at Harvard	13
7	Lehigh	0
33	at Lafayette	3
0	at Pitt	20
147		**51**

1916—(8-2)

27	Susquehanna	0
55	Westminster	0
50	Bucknell	7
39	West Virginia Wesleyan	0
0	at Penn	15
48	Gettysburg	2
79	Geneva	0
10	at Lehigh	7
40	Lafayette	0
0	at Pitt	31
348		**62**

1917—(5-4)

10	U.S. Army Amb. Cp. at Allentown	0
80	Gettysburg	0
99	St. Bonaventure	0
0	at W & J	7
8	West Virginia Wesleyan	7
7	at Dartmouth	10
0	Lehigh	9

57	Maryland	0
6	at Pitt	28
267		**61**

Coach Hugo Bezdek

1918—(1-2-1)

6	Wissahickon Barracks	6
3	Rutgers	26
7	at Lehigh	6
6	at Pitt	28
22		**66**

1919—(7-1)

33	Gettysburg	0
9	Bucknell	0
13	at Dartmouth	19
48	Ursinus	7
10	at Penn	0
20	Lehigh	7
20	at Cornell	0
20	at Pitt	0
173		**33**

1920—(7-0-2)

27	Muhlenberg	7
13	Gettysburg	0
14	Dartmouth	7
41	North Carolina State	0
109	Lebanon Valley	7
28	at Penn	7
20	Nebraska	0
7	at Lehigh	7
0	at Pitt	0
259		**35**

1921—(8-0-2)

53	Lebanon Valley	0
24	Gettysburg	0
35	North Carolina State	0
28	Lehigh	7
21	at Harvard	21
28	Georgia Tech at New York	7
28	Carnegie Tech	7
13	Navy at Philadelphia	7
0	at Pitt	0
21	at Washington	7
251		**56**

1922—(6-3-1)

54	St. Bonaventure	0
27	William and Mary	7
20	Gettysburg	0
32	Lebanon Valley	6
33	Middlebury	0
0	Syracuse at New York	0
0	Navy at Washington, D.C.	14
10	Carnegie Tech	0
6	at Penn	7
0	at Pitt	14
182		**48**

Rose Bowl

3	Southern California at Pasadena	14

1923—(6-2-1)

58	Lebanon Valley	0
16	North Carolina State	0
20	Gettysburg	0
21	Navy	3
13	West Virginia at New York	13
0	at Syracuse	10
7	Georgia Tech	0
21	at Penn	0
3	at Pitt	21
159		**47**

1924—(6-3-1)

47	Lebanon Valley	3
51	North Carolina State	6
26	Gettysburg	0
13	at Georgia Tech	15
6	Syracuse	10
6	at Navy	0
22	Carnegie Tech	7
0	at Penn	0
28	Marietta	0
3	at Pitt	24
202		**65**

1925—(4-4-1)

14	Lebanon Valley	0
13	Franklin and Marshall	0
7	Georgia Tech at New York	16
13	Marietta	0
13	Michigan State	6
0	at Syracuse	7
0	Notre Dame	0
0	at West Virginia	14
7	at Pitt	23
67		**66**

1926—(5-4)

82	Susquehanna	0
35	Lebanon Valley	0
48	Marietta	6
0	at Notre Dame	28
0	Syracuse	10
20	George Washington	12
0	at Penn	3
9	Bucknell	0
6	at Pitt	24
200		**83**

1927—(6-2-1)

27	Lebanon Valley	0
34	Gettysburg	13
7	Bucknell	13
20	at Penn	0
9	at Syracuse	6
40	Lafayette	6
13	George Washington	0
13	New York University	13
0	at Pitt	30
163		**81**

1928—(3-5-1)

25	Lebanon Valley	0
12	Gettysburg	0
0	Bucknell	6
0	at Penn	14
6	Syracuse	6
0	Notre Dame at Philadelphia	9
50	George Washington	0
0	at Lafayette	7
0	at Pitt	26
93		**68**

1929—(6-3)

16	Niagara	0
15	Lebanon Valley	0
26	Marshall	7
0	at New York U.	7
6	Lafayette	3
6	at Syracuse	4
19	at Penn	7
6	Bucknell	27
7	at Pitt	20
101		**75**

Coach Bob Higgins

1930—(3-4-2)

31	Niagara	14
27	Lebanon Valley	0
65	Marshall	0
0	at Lafayette	0
0	Colgate	40
7	at Bucknell	19
0	Syracuse	0
0	at Iowa	19
12	at Pitt	19
142		**111**

1931—(2-8)

0	Waynesburg	7
19	Lebanon Valley	6
0	at Temple	12
6	Dickinson	10
0	at Syracuse	7
6	Pitt	41
7	Colgate	32
0	at Lafayette	33
0	at West Virginia	19
31	Lehigh at Philadelphia	0
69		**167**

1932—(2-5)

27	Lebanon Valley	0
6	Waynesburg	7
13	at Harvard	46
6	Syracuse	12
0	at Colgate	31
18	Sewanee (U. of South)	6
12	at Temple	13
82		**115**

1933—(3-3-1)

32	Lebanon Valley	6
0	Muhlenberg	3
33	Lehigh	0
0	at Columbia	33
6	at Syracuse	12
40	Johns Hopkins	6
6	at Penn	6
117		**66**

1934—(4-4)

13	Lebanon Valley	0
32	Gettysburg	6
31	Lehigh	0
7	Columbia	14
0	Syracuse	16
0	Penn	3
25	Lafayette	6
7	Bucknell	13
115		**58**

1935—(4-4)

12	Lebanon Valley	6
2	Western Maryland	0
26	Lehigh	0
0	at Pitt	9
3	at Syracuse	7
27	Villanova	13
6	at Penn	33
0	at Bucknell	2
76		**70**

1936—(3-5)

45	Muhlenberg	0
0	Villanova	13
6	at Lehigh	7
7	at Cornell	13
18	Syracuse	34
7	at Pitt	19
12	at Penn	0
14	Bucknell	
109		**86**

1937—(5-3)

19	at Cornell	26
32	Gettysburg	6
20	Bucknell	14
14	Lehigh	7
13	at Syracuse	19
7	at Penn	0
21	Maryland	14
7	at Pitt	28
133		**114**

1938—(3-4-1)

33	Maryland	0
0	Bucknell	14
59	at Lehigh	6
6	at Cornell	21
33	Syracuse	6
0	Lafayette	7
7	at Penn	7
0	at Pitt	26
138		**87**

1939—(5-1-2)

13	Bucknell	3
49	Lehigh	7
0	at Cornell	47
6	at Syracuse	6
12	Maryland	0
10	at Penn	0
14	at Army	14
10	Pitt	0
114		**77**

1940—(6-1-1)

9	Bucknell	0
17	West Virginia	13
34	at Lehigh	0
18	at Temple	0
12	South Carolina	0
13	at Syracuse	13
25	New York U.	0
7	at Pitt	20
135		**46**

1941—(7-2)

0	Colgate at Buffalo, N.Y.	7
27	Bucknell	13
0	at Temple	14
40	Lehigh	6
42	at New York U.	0
34	Syracuse	19
7	West Virginia	0
31	at Pitt	7
19	at South Carolina	12
200		**78**

1942—(6-1-1)

14	Bucknell	7
19	at Lehigh	3
0	at Cornell	0
13	Colgate	10
0	at West Virginia	24
18	Syracuse	13

13	at Penn	7
14	Pitt	6
91		**70**

1943—(5-3-1)

14	Bucknell	0
0	at North Carolina	19
0	Colgate	0
6	at Navy	14
45	at Maryland	0
32	West Virginia	7
0	at Cornell	13
13	Temple	0
14	at Pitt	0
124		**53**

1944—(6-3)

58	Muhlenberg	13
14	at Navy	55
20	Bucknell	6
6	at Colgate	0
27	West Virginia	28
41	at Syracuse	0
7	at Temple	6
34	Maryland	19
0	at Pitt	14
207		**141**

1945—(5-3)

47	Muhlenberg	7
27	Colgate	7
0	at Navy	28
46	at Bucknell	7
26	Syracuse	0
27	Temple	0
0	at Michigan State	33
0	at Pitt	7
173		**89**

1946—(6-2)

48	Bucknell	6
9	at Syracuse	0
16	Michigan State	19
6	at Colgate	2
68	Fordham	0
26	Temple	0
12	at Navy	7
7	at Pitt	14
192		**48**

1947—(9-0)

27	Washington State at Hershey	6
54	Bucknell	0
75	at Fordham	0
40	Syracuse	0
21	West Virginia	14
46	Colgate	0
7	at Temple	0
20	Navy at Baltimore	7
29	at Pitt	0
319		**27**

Cotton Bowl

13	S.M.U. at Dallas, Texas	13

1948—(7-1-1)

35	Bucknell	0
34	at Syracuse	14
37	West Virginia	7
14	Michigan State	14
32	at Colgate	13
13	at Penn	0
47	Temple	0
0	at Pitt	7
7	Washington State	0
219		**55**

Coach Joe Bedenk

1949—(5-4)

6	Villanova	27
7	at Army	42
32	Boston College	14
22	Nebraska	7
0	at Michigan State	24
33	Syracuse	21
34	at West Virginia	14
28	at Temple	7
0	at Pitt	19
162		**175**

Coach Rip Engle

1950—(5-3-1)

34	Georgetown	14
7	at Army	41
7	at Syracuse	27
0	at Nebraska	19
7	Temple	7
20	at Boston College	13
27	West Virginia	0
18	Rutgers	14
21	at Pitt	20
141		**155**

1951—(5-4)

40	Boston University	34
14	Villanova at Allentown	20
15	at Nebraska	7
21	Michigan State	32
13	West Virginia	7
0	at Purdue	28
32	Syracuse	13
13	at Rutgers	7
7	at Pitt	13
155		**161**

1952—(7-2-1)

20	Temple	13
20	Purdue	20
35	William and Mary	23
35	at West Virginia	21
10	Nebraska	0
7	at Michigan State	34
14	at Penn	7
7	at Syracuse	25
7	Rutgers	6
17	at Pitt	0
172		**149**

1953—(6-3)

0	at Wisconsin	20
7	at Penn	13
35	at Boston University	13
20	Syracuse	14
27	Texas Christian	21
19	West Virginia	20
28	Fordham	21
54	at Rutgers	26
17	at Pitt	0
207		**148**

1954—(7-2)

14	at Illinois	12
13	at Syracuse	0
34	Virginia	7
14	West Virginia	19
7	at Texas Christian	20
35	at Penn	13
39	Holy Cross	7
37	Rutgers	14
13	at Pitt	0
206		**92**

1955—(5-4)

35	Boston University	0
6	at Army	35
26	Virginia at Richmond	7
14	Navy	34
7	at West Virginia	21
20	at Penn	0
21	Syracuse	20
34	at Rutgers	13
0	Pitt	20
163		**150**

1956—(6-2-1)

34	at Penn	0
7	at Army	14
43	Holy Cross	0
7	at Ohio State	6
16	West Virginia	6
9	at Syracuse	13
40	Boston University	7
14	North Carolina State	7
7	at Pitt	7
177		**60**

1957—(6-3)

19	at Penn	14
13	Army	27
21	William and Mary	13
20	Vanderbilt	32
20	at Syracuse	12
27	West Virginia	6
20	at Marquette	7
14	at Holy Cross	10
13	at Pitt	14
167		**135**

1958—(6-3-1)

7	at Nebraska	14
43	at Penn	0
0	at Army	26
40	Marquette	8
34	at Boston University	0
6	Syracuse	14
36	Furman	0
14	at West Virginia	14
32	Holy Cross	0
25	at Pitt	21
237		**97**

1959—(8-2)

19	at Missouri	8
21	V. M. I.	0
58	Colgate	20
17	at Army	11
21	Boston University	12
20	Illinois at Cleveland	9
28	at West Virginia	10
18	Syracuse	20
46	Holy Cross	0
7	at Pitt	22
255		**112**

Liberty Bowl

7	Alabama at Philadelphia	0

1960—(6-3)

20	Boston University	0
8	Missouri	21
27	at Army	16
15	at Syracuse	21
8	at Illinois	10
34	West Virginia	13
28	Maryland	9
33	at Holy Cross	8
14	at Pitt	3
187		**101**

Liberty Bowl

41 Oregon at Philadelphia ___ __ 12

1961—(7-3)

20	Navy	10
8	at Miami	25
32	at Boston University	0
6	Army	10
14	Syracuse	0
33	California	16
17	at Maryland	21
20	at West Virginia	6
34	Holy Cross	14
47	at Pitt	26
231		**128**

Gator Bowl

30 Georgia Tech at Jacksonville, Fla. 15

1962—(9-1)

41	Navy	7
20	Air Force	6
18	at Rice	7
6	at Army	9
20	Syracuse	19
23	at California	21
23	Maryland	7
34	West Virginia	6
48	at Holy Cross	20
16	at Pitt	0
249		**102**

Gator Bowl

7 Florida at Jacksonville, Fla. 17

1963—(7-3)

17	at Oregon	7
17	UCLA	14
28	Rice	7
7	Army	10
0	at Syracuse	9
20	West Virginia	9
17	at Maryland	15
10	at Ohio State	7
28	Holy Cross	14
21	at Pitt	22
165		**114**

1964—(6-4)

8	Navy	21
14	at UCLA	21
14	Oregon	22
6	at Army	2
14	Syracuse	21
37	at West Virginia	8
17	Maryland	9
27	at Ohio State	0
24	at Houston	7
28	Pitt	0
189		**111**

1965—(5-5)

0	Michigan State	23
22	UCLA	24
17	at Boston College	0
21	at Syracuse	28
44	West Virginia	6
17	at California	21
21	Kent State	6
14	Navy	6
27	at Pitt	30
19	at Maryland	7
202		**151**

Coach Joe Paterno

1966—(5-5)

15	Maryland	7
8	at Michigan State	42
0	at Army	11
30	Boston College	21
11	at UCLA	49
38	at West Virginia	6
33	California	15
10	Syracuse	12
0	at Georgia Tech	21
48	at Pitt	24
193		**208**

1967—(8-2)

22	at Navy	23
17	at Miami	8
15	UCLA	17
50	at Boston College	28
21	West Virginia	14
29	at Syracuse	20
38	at Maryland	3
13	North Carolina State	8
35	Ohio University	14
42	Pitt	6
282		**141**

Gator Bowl

17 Florida State at Jacksonville, Fla. 17

1968—(10-0)

31	Navy	6
25	Kansas State	9
31	at West Virginia	20
21	at UCLA	6
29	at Boston College	0
28	Army	24
22	Miami	7
57	at Maryland	13
65	at Pitt	9
30	Syracuse	12
339		**106**

Orange Bowl

15 Kansas at Miami, Fla. 14

1969—(10-0)

45	at Navy	22
27	Colorado	3
17	at Kansas State	14
20	West Virginia	0
15	at Syracuse	14
42	Ohio University	3
38	Boston College	16
48	Maryland	0
27	at Pitt	7
33	at North Carolina State	8
312		**87**

Orange Bowl

10 Missouri at Miami, Fla. 3

1970—(7-3)

55	Navy	7
13	at Colorado	41
16	at Wisconsin	29
28	at Boston College	3
7	Syracuse	24
38	at Army	14
42	West Virginia	8
34	at Maryland	0
32	Ohio University	22
35	Pitt	15
300		**163**

1971—(11-1)

56	at Navy _____	3
44	at Iowa _____	14
16	Air Force _____	14
42	Army _____	0
31	at Syracuse _____	0
66	Texas Christian _____	14
35	at West Virginia _____	7
63	Maryland _____	27
35	North Carolina State ____	3
55	at Pitt _____	18
11	at Tennessee _____	31
454		**131**

Cotton Bowl

30 Texas at Dallas, Texas _____ 6

1972—(10-2)

21	at Tennessee _____	28
21	Navy _____	10
14	Iowa _____	10
35	at Illinois _____	17
45	at Army _____	0
17	Syracuse _____	0
28	at West Virginia _____	19
46	Maryland _____	16
37	North Carolina State ____	22
45	at Boston College _____	26
49	Pittsburgh _____	27
358		**175**

Sugar Bowl

0 Oklahoma at New Orleans, La. 14

YEAR BY YEAR, 1887 through 1972

Year	Won	Lost	Tied	Points for	Points against	Coach	Captain
1887	2	0	0	78	0	None	G. H. Linsz
1888	0	2	1	6	52	None	G. H. Linsz
1889	2	2	0	32	138	None	J. C. Mock
1890	2	2	0	91	30	None	H. B. McLean
1891	6	2	0	173	46	None	C. E. Aull
1892	5	1	0	108	20	G. W. Hoskins	A. C. Reed
1893	4	1	0	92	36	G. W. Hoskins	E. J. Haley
1894	6	0	1	179	18	G. W. Hoskins	B. F. Fisher
1895	2	2	3	92	60	G. W. Hoskins	W. B. McCaskey
1896	3	4	0	63	128	Dr. S. B. Newton	J. A. Dunsmore
1897	3	6	0	69	141	Dr. S. B. Newton	J. M. Curtin
1898	6	4	0	174	91	Dr. S. B. Newton	L. F. Hayes
1899	4	6	0	104	176	Sam Boyle	C. A. Randolph
1900	4	6	1	84	144	W. N. Golden	L. R. Scholl
1901	5	3	0	112	90	W. N. Golden	E. E. Hewitt
1902	7	3	0	219	34	W. N. Golden	R. L. Cummings
1903	5	3	0	182	77	Dan Reed	E. A. Whitworth
1904	6	4	0	195	72	Tom Fennell	C. F. Forkum
1905	8	3	0	195	34	Tom Fennell	E. G. Yeckley
1906	8	1	1	93	10	Tom Fennell	W. T. Dunn
1907	6	4	0	251	64	Tom Fennell	H. M. Burns, Jr.
1908	5	5	0	153	51	Tom Fennell	E. McCleary
1909	5	0	2	166	11	Bill Hollenback	L. F. Vorhis
1910	5	2	1	243	24	Jack Hollenback	A. B. Gray
1911	8	0	1	199	15	Bill Hollenback	D. W. Very
1912	8	0	0	285	6	Bill Hollenback	J. L. Mauthe
1913	2	6	0	78	94	Bill Hollenback	E. E. Miller
1914	5	3	1	121	52	Bill Hollenback	E. W. Tobin
1915	7	2	0	147	51	Dick Harlow	W. W. Wood
1916	8	2	0	348	62	Dick Harlow	H. A. Clark
1917	5	4	0	267	61	Dick Harlow	R. A. Higgins, L. S. G. Conover
1918	1	2	1	22	66	Hugo Bezdek	E. J. B. Unger H. D. Robb

Year	W	L	T	PF	PA	Coach	Captain
1919	7	1	0	173	33	Hugo Bezdek	R. A. Higgins
1920	7	0	2	259	35	Hugo Bezdek	W. H. Hess
1921	8	0	2	251	56	Hugo Bezdek	G. A. Snell
1922	6	3	1	182	48	Hugo Bezdek	H. M. Bentz
1923	6	2	1	159	46	Hugo Bezdek	F. J. Bedenk
1924	6	3	1	202	65	Hugo Bezdek	B. G. Gray
1925	4	4	1	67	66	Hugo Bezdek	B. G. Gray
1926	5	4	0	200	83	Hugo Bezdek	K. R. Weston
1927	6	2	1	163	81	Hugo Bezdek	J. R. Roepke
1928	3	5	1	93	68	Hugo Bezdek	D. Greenshields, S. Hamas
1929	6	3	0	101	75	Hugo Bezdek	J. A. Martin
1930	3	4	2	142	111	Bob Higgins	Frank Deidrich
1931	2	8	0	69	166	Bob Higgins	G. T. Lasich
1932	2	5	0	82	115	Bob Higgins	George Collins
1933	3	3	1	117	66	Bob Higgins	T. A. Slusser
1934	4	4	0	115	58	Bob Higgins	M. B. Morrison
1935	4	4	0	76	70	Bob Higgins	R. E. Weber
1936	3	5	0	109	86	Bob Higgins	C. J. Cherundolo
1937	5	3	0	133	114	Bob Higgins	S. J. Donato
1938	3	4	1	138	87	Bob Higgins	D. H. Hanley
1939	5	1	2	114	77	Bob Higgins	S. S. Alter
1940	6	1	1	135	46	Bob Higgins	Leon Gajecki
1941	7	2	0	200	78	Bob Higgins	H. L. Krouse
1942	6	1	1	91	70	Bob Higgins	L. J. Palazzi
1943	5	3	1	124	53	Bob Higgins	John Jaffurs
1944	6	3	0	207	141	Bob Higgins	John Chuckran
1945	5	3	0	173	89	Bob Higgins	
1946	6	2	0	192	48	Bob Higgins	W. R. Moore
1947	9	0	0	319	27	Bob Higgins	J. A. Potsklan, J. J. Nolan
1948	7	1	1	219	55	Bob Higgins	J. J. Colone
1949	5	4	0	162	175	Joe Bedenk	N. Norton, R. Hicks
1950	5	3	1	141	155	Rip Engle	O. J. Dougherty
1951	5	4	0	155	161	Rip Engle	Art Betts, Len Shephard
1952	7	2	1	172	149	Rip Engle	Stewart Scheetz, Joe Gratson
1953	6	3	0	207	148	Rip Engle	Tony Rados, Don Malinak
1954	7	2	0	206	92	Rip Engle	Jim Garrity, Don Balthaser
1955	5	4	0	163	150	Rip Engle	Frank Reich, Otto Kneidinger
1956	6	2	1	177	60	Rip Engle	Sam Valentine
1957	6	3	0	167	135	Rip Engle	Joe Sabol
1958	6	3	1	237	97	Rip Engle	Steve Garban
1959	8	2	0	255	112	Rip Engle	Pat Botula
1960	6	3	0	187	101	Rip Engle	Hank Opperman
1961	7	3	0	231	128	Rip Engle	Jim Smith
1962	9	1	0	249	102	Rip Engle	Joe Galardi
1963	7	3	0	165	114	Rip Engle	Ralph Baker
1964	6	4	0	189	111	Rip Engle	Bill Bowes

1965	5	5	0	202	151	Rip Engle	Bob Andronici
1966	5	5	0	193	208	Joe Paterno	Mike Irwin, John Runnells
1967	8	2	0	282	141	Joe Paterno	Bill Lenkaitis Jim Litterelle
1968	10	0	0	339	106	Joe Paterno	John Kulka, Mike Reid, Steve Smear
1969	10	0	0	312	87	Joe Paterno	Mike Reid, Steve Smear, Tom Jackson
1970	7	3	0	300	163	Joe Paterno	Jack Ham, Warren Koegel
1971	10	1	0	454	131	Joe Paterno	Dave Joyner, Charlie Zapiec
1972	10	1	0	358	189	Joe Paterno	Gregg Ducatte, Jim Heller, John Hufnagel, Carl Schaukowitch

SUMMARY: Won 474 — Lost 232 — Tied 37

NOTE: Won-lost-tied records on these two pages are regular season records only and do **NOT** include bowl games.

ALL-TIME SERIES RECORDS

Opponent	Began	Penn State W	L	T	Opponent	Began	Penn State W	L	T
Air Force	1962	2	0	0	Furman	1958	1	0	0
Alabama	1959	*1	0	0	F. & M.	1890	2	1	0
Allegheny	1903	3	0	0	Geneva	1904	7	0	0
Altoona A.A.	1890	2	0	0	Georgetown	1950	1	0	0
Army	1899	8	10	2	George Wash.	1926	3	0	0
Army A.C.	1917	1	0	0	Georgia Tech.	1921	*3	3	0
Bellefonte Acad.	1890	2	1	0	Gettysburg	1891	27	0	1
Bloomsburg	1897	1	0	0	Grove City	1907	3	0	0
Boston College	1949	9	0	0	Harrisburg A.C.	1910	1	0	0
Boston U.	1951	8	0	0	Harvard	1913	0	3	2
Bucknell	1887	28	10	0	Haverford	1891	1	0	0
Buffalo	1900	0	1	0	Holy Cross	1954	9	0	0
California	1961	3	1	0	Homestead A.C.	1901	0	1	0
California State	1905	1	0	0	Houston	1964	1	0	0
Carlisle	1896	1	4	1	Illinois	1954	3	1	0
Carnegie Tech	1910	6	0	0	Iowa	1930	2	1	0
Colgate	1911	8	4	1	Jersey Shore	1904	1	0	0
Colorado	1969	1	1	0	Johns Hopkins	1933	1	0	0
Columbia	1933	0	2	0	Kansas	1969	*1	0	0
Cornell	1895	4	7	2	Kansas State	1968	2	0	0
Dartmouth	1917	1	2	0	Kent State	1965	1	0	0
D.C. & A.C.	1898	0	3	0	Lafayette	1889	10	5	1
Dickinson	1888	11	5	1	Lebanon Val.	1905	20	0	0
Dickinson Sem.	1902	2	0	0	Lehigh	1888	16	6	1
Florida	1962	0	*1	0	Mansfield	1899	1	0	0
Florida State	1967	0	0	*1	Marietta	1924	3	0	0
Fordham	1946	3	0	0	Marshall	1929	2	0	0

Marquette ____	1957	2	0	0		Steelton YMCA	1902	0	1	0
Maryland ____	1917	18	1	0		Sterling A.C. __	1910	1	0	0
Miami _____	1961	2	1	0		Susquehanna _	1898	6	0	0
Michigan St. __	1914	1	8	1		Swarthmore ___	1889	2	0	0
Middlebury ___	1922	1	0	0		Syracuse _____	1922	24	21	5
Missouri _____	1959	*2	1	0		Temple _____	1931	9	3	1
Muhlenberg __	1914	5	1	0		Tennessee ____	1971	0	2	0
Navy _____	1894	17	16	2		Texas _____	1972	*1	0	0
Nebraska _____	1920	4	2	0		Tex. Christian _	1953	2	1	0
New York U. __	1927	2	1	1		UCLA _____	1963	2	4	0
Niagara _____	1929	2	0	0		Ursinus _____	1914	2	0	0
N. Carolina St.	1920	9	0	0		Vanderbilt _____	1957	0	1	0
North Carolina	1943	0	1	0		Villanova _____	1902	5	3	1
Notre Dame __	1913	0	3	1		Virginia _____	1893	3	0	0
Oberlin _____	1894	1	0	0		V. M. I. _____	1959	1	0	0
Ohio State ____	1912	4	0	0		Washington ___	1921	1	0	0
Ohio University	1967	3	0	0		Wash.-Jeff. ____	1894	5	2	1
Oklahoma ____	1972	0	*1	0		Washington St._	1947	2	0	0
Oregon _____	1960	*2	1	0		Waynesburg __	1931	0	2	0
P. A. C. _____	1892	1	0	0		W. Maryland __	1935	1	0	0
Penn _____	1890	18	25	4		W. Reserve ___	1895	0	0	1
Pitt _____	1893	34	35	3		Westminster __	1914	3	0	0
Pittsburgh A.C.	1893	2	1	0		West Virginia _	1904	30	7	2
Princeton _____	1896	0	5	0		W.Va. Wes. ___	1915	3	0	0
Purdue _____	1951	0	1	1		Wm. and Mary	1922	3	0	0
Rice _____	1962	2	0	0		Wisconsin ____	1953	0	2	0
Rutgers _____	1918	6	1	0		Wissahicken B'k	1918	0	0	1
St. Bonaventure	1910	4	0	0		Wyoming Sem._	1892	1	0	0
Sewanee _____	1932	1	0	0		Yale _____	1899	0	7	0
South Carolina_	1940	2	0	0						
S. California __	1923	0	*1	0						
S. Methodist __	1947	0	0	*1						

* Includes bowl game

LIONS' BOWL APPEARANCES

JANUARY 1, 1923, Rose Bowl: Southern California 14, Penn State 3.
    (Coach Hugo Bezdek)
JANUARY 1, 1948, Cotton Bowl: S.M.U. 13, Penn State 13.
    (Coach Bob Higgins)
DECEMBER 19, 1959, Liberty Bowl: Penn State 7, Alabama 0.
    (Coach Rip Engle)
DECEMBER 17, 1960, Liberty Bowl: Penn State 41, Oregon 12.
    (Coach Rip Engle)
DECEMBER 30, 1961, Gator Bowl: Penn State 30, Georgia Tech 15.
    (Coach Rip Engle)
DECEMBER 29, 1962, Gator Bowl: Florida 17, Penn State 7.
    (Coach Rip Engle)
DECEMBER 30, 1967, Gator Bowl: Penn State 17, Florida State 17.
    (Coach Joe Paterno)
JANUARY 1, 1969, Orange Bowl: Penn State 15, Kansas 14
    (Coach Joe Paterno)
JANUARY 1, 1970, Orange Bowl: Penn State 10, Missouri 3
    (Coach Joe Paterno)

JANUARY 1, 1972, Cotton Bowl: Penn State 30, Texas 6
(Coach Joe Paterno)
DECEMBER 31, 1972, Sugar Bowl: Oklahoma 14, Penn State 0.
(Coach Joe Paterno)

ALL-AMERICANS
(First Team Selections Only)

W. T. (Mother) Dunn, center, 1906, selected by Walter Camp. He died November 19, 1962, in Hawaii, where he was a physician for many years.

Bob Higgins, end, 1919, selected by Walter Camp. Coach at his alma mater from 1930 through 1948. He lived in State College, Pa., following his retirement until his death on June 6, 1969.

Charley Way, halfback, 1920, selected by Walter Camp. He lives in Thorndale, Pa.

Glenn Killinger, halfback, 1921, selected by Walter Camp. Former Dean at West Chester State College, West Chester, Pa., where he was a successful football and baseball coach and athletic director for many years. Now retired.

Joe Bedenk, guard, 1923, selected by Walter Camp. Baseball coach at his alma mater from 1931 through 1962, head football coach in 1949. Retired, he lives in State College, Pa.

Harry E. (Light Horse) Wilson, halfback, 1923, selected by 500 Coaches, Percy Haughton and second team Walter Camp. Later played at U.S. Military Academy, where he made the first teams of Rockne, Tad Jones and Pop Warner All-American teams in 1926. A retired Air Force colonel, now living in New Smyrna Beach, Fla.

Leon Gajecki, center, 1940, selected by NEA Service, Inc. With Humble Oil & Refinery, he lives in Pitman, N.J.

Steve Suhey, guard, 1947, selected by Collier's. Jewelry and yearbook salesman, he lives in State College, Pa., and is married to Bob Higgins' daughter Virginia.

Sam Tamburo, end, 1948, selected by Collier's. Living and working in New Kensington, Pa.

Sam Valentine, guard, 1956, selected by Football Writers Association of America (LOOK magazine). With Youngstown Sheet & Tube Co.

Richie Lucas, quarterback, 1959, selected to first team by United Press-International, U. S. Coaches Association, American Football Writers Association (LOOK magazine), NCAA Football Guide, Central Press Association, St. Louis Sporting News, News Enterprise Association, Detroit Football News, Movietone News, Hearst Syndicate. He was named to the Associated Press second team. With the Buffalo Bills of the American Football league for two years, he now is Penn State athletic business manager.

Bob Mitinger, end, 1961, selected by U. S. Coaches Association. Now practicing law in State College.

Dave Robinson, end, 1962, selected to first team Associated Press, American Football Writers Association (LOOK Magazine), News Enterprise Association, TIME magazine. He was named to second team United Press International and St. Louis Sporting News. Now with the Washington Redskins.

310

Roger Kochman, halfback, 1962, selected to first team U. S. Coaches Association. He was named to second team St. Louis Sporting News and United Press International. With Buffalo Bills until 1963 injury ended his playing career, he now is with Bell Telephone in Pittsburgh, Pa.

Glenn Ressler, middle guard and center, 1964, selected to first team U. S. Coaches Association, News Enterprise Association, American Football Writers Association (LOOK), St. Louis Sporting News, TIME magazine, NBC-TV, CBS-TV, N. Y. Daily News, Helms Hall of Fame, Detroit Football News. He was named to the AP and UPI second teams. Now with Baltimore Colts.

Ted Kwalick, tight end, 1967, 1968 — first team selection in 1968 to Associated Press, United Press International, Football Writers (LOOK), Newspaper Enterprise Association (NEA), U.S. Football Coaches, Sporting News, Central Press Association, Detroit Football News, New York Daily News, ABC-TV, TIME Magazine. In 1967 he was first team U.S. Football Coaches and NEA and second team AP and UPI. First two-time All-American in Penn State history. Now with San Francisco '49ers.

Dennis Onkotz, linebacker, 1968, 1969 — first team selection in 1969 to Associated Press, United Press International, Football Writers (LOOK) and Football News; selected to same first teams in 1968 plus Central Press Association and New York Daily News. Now attending Penn State graduate school.

Mike Reid, defensive tackle, 1969, selected first team on EVERY All-America team selected in 1969. Now with Cincinnati Bengals.

Charlie Pittman, offensive halfback, 1969, 1st team U.S. Football Coaches, 2nd team United Press International. Now working in real estate in Baltimore, Md.

Neal Smith, safety, 1969, first team, United Press International, News Enterprise Association (NEA), New York Daily News; third team Associated Press. A civil engineer, now living in Port Trevorton, Pa.

Jack Ham, linebacker, 1970, selected to EVERY All-America team. Now with the Pittsburgh Steelers.

Dave Joyner, offensive tackle, 1971, first team United Press International, Football News, Gridiron, Walter Camp, American Football Coaches Association (Kodak) and American Football Writers Association; second team Associated Press and NEA. He is attending Milton S. Hershey Medical School.

Lydell Mitchell, offensive halfback, 1971, first team Associated Press, Football News, Gridiron; second team United Press International and American Football Writers Association. Now with the Baltimore Colts.

Charlie Zapiec, linebacker, 1971, first team Newspaper Enterprise Association.

Bruce Bannon, defensive end, 1972, first team American Football Coaches Association, Newspaper Enterprise Association, (NEA), United Press International, Gridiron, Football News and Walter Camp Football Foundation. Drafted by New York Jets.

John Hufnagel, quarterback, 1972, first team Associated Press and Walter Camp Football Foundation. Drafted by the Denver Broncos.

John Skorupan, linebacker, 1972, first team Associated Press, Football Writers Association and Newspaper Enterprise Association. Drafted by the Buffalo Bills.

311

ALL-TIME PENN STATE LETTERMEN

Abbey, Don, 1967, 68, 69
Adams, Charlie, 1969
Addie, Walt, 1972
Adessa, J. P., 1936, 37
Ahrenhold, Frank,
  1969, 70. 71
Alberigi, R. A., 1955, 56
Alexander, Dave, 1959, 60
Allen, Bruce, 1944
Allen, Doug, 1970, 72
Allen, George, 1968
Allen, R. G., 1955
Allen, W. W., 1925
Alter, S. S., 1937, 38, 39
Amprim, L. R., 1949
Anders, P. L., 1950, 51
Anderson, C. W.,
  1931, 32, 33
Anderson, Dick,
  1961, 62, 63
Andrews, F. J., 1935
Andrews, Ken, 1971, 72
Andronici, Robert L.,
  1964, 65
Angevine, Leon,
  1966, 67, 68
Arbuthnot, J. H.,
  1901, 02, 03
Arnelle, Jesse,
  1951, 52, 53, 54
Arnst. J. W., 1956
Artelt, T. W.,
  1922, 23, 24
Atherton, C. M.,
  1890, 91, 92, 93, 94
Aull, C. E., 1889, 90, 91
Aumiller, Jack, 1971
Avery, G. F., 1950
Baer, R. B., 1920. 21
Bailey, D. P., 1952, 53, 54
Baiorunos, Jack, 1972
Baker, Ralph, 1961, 62
Baldinger, Shelton, 1943
Bannon, Bruce, 1970,
  71, 72
Baran, Stan, 1969
Barney, D. L., 1952
Bathaser, D. E.,
  1952, 53, 54
Ballou, V., 1908
Banbury, J. R., 1941, 42

Barantovich, A. J.,
  1936, 37, 38
Barber, S. C., 1958, 59, 60
Barclay, W. L., 1887
Barber, W. B., 1950
Barnett, W. D., 1907
Barney, D. L., 1950, 51
Barr, A. A., 1904, 05
Barr, J. F., 1949, 50, 51
Barrett, F. J., 1910
Barrett, Richard A., 1965
Barron, A. M., 1910, 13, 14
Barron, D. M., 1947
Bartek, L. J., 1950, 51
Barth, L. R., 1934, 35, 36
Barry, P. A., 1911
Batdorf, J. W., 1930
Beatty, C. F., 1947, 48, 49
Bebout, J. D., 1911, 12, 13
Beck, C. R., 1916, 20
Beckwith, Dan, 1971
Bedenk, F. J., 1921, 22, 23
Bedick, Tom, 1962, 63
Bedoski, A. J.,
  1931, 32, 33
Bell, C. F., 1945, 46, 47
Bellas, Albert, 1944, 45
Bellas, Joseph J., 1964, 65
Bennett, R. L., 1900, 01
Bentz, H. N., 1920, 21, 22
Berfield, W. F., 1958, 60
Bergman, C. R., 1924, 26
Berry, N. P., 1931, 32, 33
Berryman, R. N.,
  1911, 12, 13, 15
Betts, A. H., 1950, 51
Biesecker, A. S., 1901
Black, J., 1917
Blair, R. W., 1905
Blair, W. A., 1898
Bland, Dave, 1971, 72
Blasenstein, Joe,
  1960, 61, 62
Blockson, C. L.,
  1953, 54, 55
Bohart, J. L., 1957, 58
Bohn, W. W., 1889, 90
Bonham, J. H., 1941
Booth, John, 1971
Botts, Mike, 1969, 71

Botula, Patrick, 1957,
  58, 59
Bowden, A. T., 1952
Bower, James, 1964
Bowes, Bill, 1962, 63, 64
Bozick, John, 1958, 59, 60
Bradley, Dave,
  1966, 67, 68
Bresecker, A. S.,
  1901, 02, 03
Brewster, J. H., 1931, 32
Brezna, Steve, 1968
Briggs, B. E., 1937
Brosky, W. B., 1941
Brown, Conrad, 1950
Brown, E. F., 1940, 42, 43
Brown, E. L., 1895
Brown, G. W.,
  1918, 19, 20
Brown, I. W., 1918
Brown, J. A., 1951
Brown, Rick, 1971, 72
Brown, S. H., 1891, 92
Bruhn, Earl, 1944
Bruno, J. C., 1956
Buchan, Sandy,
  1962, 63, 64
Bulvin, Jerry, 1970
Bunn, K. B., 1949, 50
Burkhart, Charlie,
  1968, 69
Burns, H. M., 1906. 07
Burns, P. M., 1944, 45
Burns, W. B., 1899
Butterfield, Dick, 1960
Buzin, Rich, 1966, 67
Calderone, J. J., 1955, 56
Caldwell, J. W., 1955
Campbell, C. H., 1905, 06
Campbell, Bob,
  1966, 67, 68
Cappelletti, John, 1971,
  72
Caprara, E. J., 1956, 57
Capretto, Bob, 1966, 67
Carter, Gary, 1968, 69, 70
Cartwright, C. R.,
  1890, 91
Caskey, Howard, 1944, 45
Castignola, J., 1943
Caum, Don, 1961, 62, 63

313

Jackson, J. P. 1887
Jackson, Tom,
   1967, 68, 69
Jacob, G. A., 1950
Jaffurs, J. J., 1941, 42, 43
James, D. R., 1914
Janerette, Charles,
   1958, 59
Joachim, Steve, 1971
Joe, Larry, 1942, 47, 48
Johnson, Barry, 1971
Johnson, C. H.,
   1949, 50, 51
Johnson, F. H., 1909, 10
Johnson, G. R., 1888
Johnson, H. C., 1899
Johnson, Paul,
   1967, 68, 69
Johnson, Pete,
   1967, 68, 69
Johnson, R. B., 1923
Jonas, Don, 1958, 60, 61
Jones, B. C., 1916
Jones, R. C., 1952, 53
Joyner, Dave, 1969, 70, 71
Junk, J. L., 1901, 02
Kane, E. E., 1931
Kane, Robert T., 1964, 65
Kane, W. P., 1955, 56
Kaplan, M. L.,
   1928, 29, 30
Kasperian, David,
   1957, 58
Kates, Jim, 1967, 68, 69
Kelly, P. F., 1947, 48, 49
Kerns, J. M. L.,
   1940, 41, 42
Kerr, Jim, 1959, 60
Kerr, W. G., 1912
Kessler, C. M., 1887
Killinger, W. G.,
   1918, 20, 21
Kemmerer, T. R., 1952
King, F. X., 1911
Kinsey, W. J., 1935
Kirk, K. B., 1918
Kleist, E. R., 1955
Kline, Bob, 1961
Klingensmith, Gary,
   1963, 64
Klossner, Gary, 1971
Kmit, Ed, 1964
Knabb, A. H., 1918, 21

Knapp, R. E.,
   1933, 34, 35
Knechtel, Bob, 1970, 71
Kneidinger, O. I.,
   1953, 54, 55
Kniaz, W. M.,
   1938, 39, 40
Knittle, A. P., 1891
Kochman, Roger,
   1959, 61, 62
Koegel, Warren,
   1968, 69, 70
Koerber, J. R., 1950
Kohlhaas, E. E.,
   1957, 58, 59
Koiwai, Mark, 1970
Kollar, James C., 1965, 66
Kominic, W. E., 1934
Koniszewski, Jack, 1972
Kopach, S. J., 1940
Korbini, F. R., 1958, 59
Kosanovich, Bronco,
   1944, 45, 46
Kraft, R. G., 1917
Krall, J. W., 1926, 27
Kratt, G. E., 1914
Kratzke, Theodore, H.,
   1941, 45
Kreizman, Louis, 1932, 33
Krenicky, Doug, 1968
Krouse, H. L.,
   1939, 40, 41
Krupa, J. H., 1934, 36
Krushank, A., 1916
Kuba, Dave, 1962
Kulka, George, 1968, 69
Kulka, John, 1966, 67, 68
Kunit, Don C., 1964, 65
Kunkle, B. D.,
   1905, 06, 07
Kwalick, Ted, 1966, 67, 68
Kwalik, L. S., 1955
Kyle, W. J., 1946, 47
Lafferty, E. D., 1923, 24
LaFleur, Wm., J., 1943, 47
Lagler, Regis, 1972
Lamb, L. L., 1912, 13, 14
Landis, George,
   1968, 69, 70
Lang, A. B., 1936
Lang, Floyd, 1945
Lang, Jon, 1960
LaPorta, Phil, 1971, 72

Lasich, G. T.,
   1929, 30, 31
Laslavic, Jim, 1970, 71, 72
Latorre, Harry, 1934, 35
Law, T. C., 1955, 56
Lenda, Edwin R.,
   1965, 66
Lenkaitis, William E.,
   1965, 66, 67
Leonard, W. H.,
   1950, 51, 52
Lesh, F. T., 1909
Lesko, A. J., 1926, 27
Levinson, J. C., 1949
Leyden, H. R., 1887, 88
Light, C. H., 1923, 24
Lightner, J. K., 1920, 21
Lindenmuth, W. E., 1937
Lins, G. H.,
   1887, 88, 89
Linski, Frank, 1967
Lippincott, Lincoln, 1968
Liske, Peter, 1961, 62, 63
Litterelle, Jim, 1966, 67
Levezey, J. P., 1929, 30
Livziey, J. F., 1956
Lockerman, J. L., 1956
Logue, L. H., 1918, 22
Lohr, W. P., 1932
Longacre, R. E., 1923
Lord, C. A., 1914
Loyd, N. M., 1890
Lucas, R. J., 1957, 58, 59
Lucyk, Dan, 1966, 67
Ludwig, Larry, 1971, 72
Lundberg, A. H., 1915
Lungren, J. G.,
   1925, 26, 27
Luther, William,
   1947, 48, 49
Lyle, Craig, 1970, 71, 72
MacKensie, H. T., 1918
Maddigan, Dan, 1959
Madera, C. R., 1921
Mahoney, R. S.,
   1925, 26, 27
Malinak, Donald,
   1951, 52, 53
Malley, C. E., 1932
Marchi, M., 1943, 45
Markiewicz, R. D.,
   1956, 57
Markovich, Mark, 1971, 72

315

Schaukowitch, Carl,
1970, 71, 72
Scheetz, S. C., 1950, 51, 52
Scherer, W. B., 1948
Schleicher, M. J.,
1956, 57, 58
Schoderbek, P. P.,
1951, 52, 53
Scholl, L. R.,
1896, 97, 98, 99, 1900,
01
Schoonover, K. D.,
1941, 42
Schreckengaust, Steven S.,
1964, 65
Schiazza, G. D., 1951
Schroyer, John, 1942
Schuster, R. L., 1920, 23
Schuyler, R. L.,
1934, 35, 36
Schwab, Jim, 1961
Scott, C. E., 1894, 95
Scott, Jim, 1971, 72
Scrabis, R. D., 1958
Sebastianelli, Ted, 1968
Seitz, Ellery R.,
1963, 64, 65
Shank, D. W., 1951, 52
Shattuck, F. W., 1950, 51
Shattuck, Paul, 1953
Shawley, C. W.,
1928, 29, 30
Shephard, L. T.
1949, 50, 51
Sherman, Thomas J.,
1965, 66, 67
Sherry, J. E., 1952, 53, 54
Shields, J. F., 1891
Shields, R. K., 1931
Shoemaker, Tom, 1971, 72
Shopa, Peter, 1951, 52,
57
Shumaker, Earl,
1953, 54, 55
Shumock, J. J., 1950, 51
Sieminski, Charles,
1960, 61, 62
Sigel, H. N., 1932, 33, 34
Sills, F. D., 1937
Silick, A. R., 1950, 51
Silvano, T. J., 1934, 35, 36
Simko, John, 1962, 63, 64
Simon, David, 1951, 52

Simon, John, 1944, 45,
47, 48
Sincek, Frank, 1962
Sink, Robert, 1964
Sisler, C., 1943
Skarzynski, Scott, 1970,
71, 72
Skemp, J. D., 1937
Skemp, L. N., 1932
Skorupan, John, 1970,
71, 72
Sladki, John J., 1965, 66
Slamp, K. R., 1925
Slobodnjak, M., 1943
Slusser, T. A.,
1931, 32, 33
Smaltz, W. R.,
1939, 40, 41
Smart, J. E., 1926
Smear, Steve, 1967, 68, 69
Smidansky, J. W.,
1948, 49, 50
Smith, A. L., 1901
Smith, C. R., 1904
Smith, James, 1960, 61
Smith, J. F., 1934, 35, 36
Smith, Mike, 1968, 69, 70
Smith, Neal, 1967, 68, 69
Smith, R. A., 1951, 52
Smith, R. McC.,
1907, 08, 09
Smith, R. H., 1904
Smith, T. M., 1948
Smith, W. B., 1955, 57, 58
Smozinsky, E., 1921
Smyth, W., 1943
Snell, G. A., 1919, 20, 21
Snyder, R. G., 1930, 31
Sobczak, W. L.,
1958, 59, 60
Sowers, Charles, 1954
Spaziani, Frank,
1966, 67, 68
Speers, Fred, 1971
Spence, G. K., 1894
Spencer, Larry, 1944
Spires, Mike, 1972
St. Clair, C. M., 1942
Stahley, J. N., 1928, 29
Stofko, Ed, 1967, 68, 69
Stark, K. K., 1920
Steinbacher, Donald E.,
1965

Stellatella, Sam,
1957, 58, 59
Stellfox, L. M., 1957
Stempeck, S. C., 1930, 31
Stewart, Edward W.,
1963, 64, 65
Stilley, Steve, 1971, 72
Stoken, John, 1944
Straub, Bill, 1953, 54, 55
Stravinski, C., 1938, 39, 40
Struchor, J. J., 1950
Stuart, Tom, 1966
Stuart, W. A., 1893
Stuckrath, Ed, 1962, 63, 64
Stump, Terry, 1968, 69, 70
Sturges, C. R., 1948
Surma, Vic, 1968, 69, 70
Stynchula, A. R.,
1957, 58, 59
Suhey, Stephen,
1942, 46, 47
Sunday, L. Mc., 1936
Susko, John, 1972
Suter, H. M., 1894
Swain, W., 1916
Sweet, L. D., 1901
Szajna, R. G., 1951, 52
Taccalozzi, Dino, 1944, 45
Tamburo, S. J.,
1945, 46, 47, 48
Tavener, O. H., 1917
Taylor, C. F., 1899
Taylor, H. S., 1891, 92
Tepsic, Joseph, 1945
Tesner, Buddy, 1972
Thomas, C., 1895
Thomas, W. C., 1914, 15
Thompson, B. F., 1952
Thompson, C. M., 1895
Thompson, I. P., 1903
Thompson, S. M., 1906
Tietjens, Ron, 1961, 62
Tobin, E. W., 1912, 13, 14
Tomlinson, K. S., 1951
Toretti, S. J., 1936, 37, 38
Torris, Buddy,
1960, 61, 62
Trent, Jim, 1971
Trautmann, A. R., 1950
Triplett, Wallace,
1946, 47, 48
Truitt, Dave, 1960
Trumbull, R., 1943
Turinski, Bill, 1962

Twaddle, J. P., 1951
Urbanik, Tom, 1963, 64
Ulinski, R. V., 1947
Unger, E. J. B., 1918
Urban, Jack, 1959
Urion, R. M., 1948
Valentine, S. J.,
  1954, 55, 56
VanAnden, F., 1939
VanLenten, Wilbur,
  1941, 42
VanSickle, D. P., 1952
Vargo, Joe, 1963, 64
Vargo, T. E., 1938, 39, 40
Vendor, J., 1943
Ventresco, Ralph, 1945
Ventresco, R. F., 1941
Very, D. W.,
  1909, 10, 11, 12
Vesling, Keith, 1951, 52, 53
Vierzbicki, Joseph J.,
  1965
Vitiello, Alberto, 1971, 72
Vogel, O. J., 1913
Voll, Edwin, 1944
Vorhis, L. F.,
  1906, 07, 08, 09
Vukmer, Bob, 1966
Wagner, Marshall, 1970
Wahl, J. B., 1931
Walker, S., 1895
Walters, L. K.,
  1955, 56, 57
Walters, R. L., 1942, 46
Wantshouse, H. M., 1932
Warehime, A. R., 1934
Waresak, Frank, 1962
Washabaugh, G. C.,
  1937, 38, 39
Watson, J. A., 1915
Watson, J. E., 1909, 10
Watson, R. S., 1924

Waugaman, C. E.,
  1936, 37
Way, C. A., 1917, 19, 20
Wayne, Tony, 1961
Weaver, H. A.,
  1907, 08, 09, 10
Weaver, Jim, 1966
Weaver, P. L., 1941, 46
Weber, R. E., 1933, 34, 35
Wear, R. F., 1941
Wear, W. W., 1935, 36, 37
Wehmer, W. C.,
  1956, 57, 58
Weitzel, R. D.,
  1942, 46, 47
Weller, J. S., 1887
Welsh, F. S., 1907
Welty, D. E., 1912, 13, 14
Wentz, B. W., 1922
Weston, H. B., 1913
Weston, K. R.,
  1924, 25, 26
White, Ed, 1959
White, J. B., 1892, 93
White, Jack R., 1965, 66
White, L. C., 1938, 39, 40
White, L. R., 1903, 04
Whitney, Robert, 1912
Whitworth, E. A.,
  1901, 02, 03
Wible, T. E., 1937
Williams, B. F., 1956, 57
Williams, Frank, 1972
Williams, Jim, 1962
Williams, R. K., 1918, 20
Williams, R. J., 1946, 47
Williams, Robert,
  1942, 43
Williamson, 1892
Wille, C. B., 1932
Wilson, A. S., 1911, 12
Wilson, Charlie,
  1968, 69, 70
Wilson, C. C., 1950, 51

Wilson, Dick, 1959, 60, 61
Wilson, H. E.,
  1921, 22, 23
Wilson, T. C., 1925
Wismer, F. K.,
  1933, 34, 35
Wolfe, Steve, 1964
Wolff, A. B., 1927, 28
Wolfkeil, Wayne, 1953
Wolosky, John, 1947
Wood, E. K., 1899
Wood, W. W.,
  1913, 14, 15
Woodward, C. V.,
  1903, 04
Woodward, James, 1940
Woolbert, R. E., 1932, 33
Woolridge, H. R., 1933
Wray, W., 1904, 05, 06
Wright, N. R., 1907
Wydman, Gary, 1961, 64
Yanosich, Matt, 1951, 52
Yarabinetz, Thomas M.,
  1965
Yeafer, F., 1915
Yeckley, E. G.,
  1902, 03, 04, 05
Yeckley, G. W., 1938
Yerger, H. C., 1915
Yett, D. A., 1934, 36
Yocum, J. H., 1890
Yost, Bud, 1962, 63, 64
Younker, Ron, 1953, 54
Yowell, Bob, 1967
Yukica, J. M., 1951, 52
Zapiec, Charlie,
  1968, 69, 71
Zawacki, S. L., 1931, 32
Zelinsky, Joe, 1967
Zern, E. N., 1901
Zink, H. A., 1907
Zorella, John, 1928, 29, 30
Zubaty, Ed, 1967
Zufall, Donald M., 1965

EDITOR'S NOTE:

The list of all-time Penn State football lettermen includes every varsity letter-winner since the sport was officially started at Penn State in 1887.

The Nittany Lions have had 31 players earn four football letters, five men win five letters and one player achieve the unusual distinction of being a six-time letterman. The longevity award goes to L. R. Scholl, who won his varsity S in 1896, 1897, 1898, 1899, 1900 and 1901.

The list of five-time lettermen includes Charles M. Atherton (1890-94), H. P. Dowler (1889-93), R. A. "Bob" Higgins (1914-19), C. C. Hildebrand (1887-91) and J. S. Rumble (1896-1900).

PATERNO NATION'S 'WINNINGEST' COACH

Joe Paterno has retained his position as the nation's "winningest" major college football coach.

Statistics released by National Collegiate Sports Services give Paterno the top winning percentage among active coaches with at least five years as head coach at a major college. Paterno has led the list all three years he has been eligible.

In seven years as Penn State's head coach, Paterno has compiled a record of 63 wins, 13 losses and a tie for a winning percentage of .825. Arizona's Frank Kush is second with a .784 percentage in 15 seasons.

Paterno has built Penn State's program into one of the nation's finest. The Nittany Lions have been ranked in the top ten and gone to a major bowl game five of the last six years. They were 10-2 last year.

The nation's winningest coaches (ties count as half won, half lost):

	Yrs.	Won	Lost	Tied	Pct.
Joe Paterno, Penn State	7	63	13	1	.825
Frank Kush, Arizona State	15	121	33	1	.784
Bo Schembechler, Michigan	10	78	23	3	.76444
Darrell Royal, Texas	19	153	46	4	.76435
Paul Bryant, Alabama	28	220	69	16	.748
Woody Hayes, Ohio State	27	182	60	7	.745
Charles McClendon, LSU	11	88	29	5	.742
John McKay, Southern Cal	13	100	33	6	.741
Frank Broyles, Arkansas	16	123	46	3	.724
Ara Parseghian, Notre Dame	22	149	56	6	.720

JOE PATERNO'S PENN STATE RECORD AT A GLANCE

	Won	Lost	Tied
1966	5	5	0
1967	8	2	0

Tied by Florida State, 17-17, in Gator Bowl

1968	10	0	0

Defeated Kansas, 15-14, in Orange Bowl

1969	10	0	0

Defeated Missouri, 10-3, in Orange Bowl

1970	7	3	0
1971	10	1	0

Defeated Texas, 30-6, in Cotton Bowl

1972	10	1	0

Lost to Oklahoma, 14-0, in Sugar Bowl

Totals: Won 63, Lost 13, Tied 1

LEGEND OF THE NITTANY LION

Penn State's athletic symbol, chosen by the student body in 1906, is a mountain lion once said to have roamed the central-Pennsylvania mountains. Because Penn State is located in the Nittany Valley at the foot of Mt. Nittany, the lion was designated as a Nittany Lion. Nittany evolved from the word Nita-Nee, which was the favorite cognomen for Indian maidens.

Legend tells us that one Nita-Nee, the daughter of Chief O-Ko-Cho who lived near the mouth of Penn's Cave, fell in love with a trader named Malachi Boyer. For this Boyer was imprisoned and forced to die in Penn's Cave. The tearful maiden and her lost lover became legend and her name now graces the stately mountain and the athletic teams of Penn State.